# Love, Dad

## How My Father Died...
## Then Told Me He Didn't

# Mike Anthony

ALSO BY MIKE ANTHONY

*Life At Hamilton*

ISBN-13: 978-1-951805-66-1 print edition
ISBN-13: 978-1-951805-67-8 ebook edition

Waterside Productions
2055 Oxford Ave
Cardiff, CA 92007
www.waterside.com

*To Dad.*

*Thanks for calling when you got there.*

# Contents

# Introduction

"The most exciting phrase to hear in science, the one that heralds the most discoveries, is not 'Eureka!' but 'That's funny.'"

ISAAC ASIMOV

In the popular television show *The Good Place*, four people find themselves in the afterlife. While attempting to communicate to an immortal being what it's like to be human, the show's main character, Eleanor Shellstrop, tells him, "All humans are aware of death. So . . . we're all a little bit sad. All the time. That's just the deal . . . but we don't get offered any other ones."

It is the great conundrum in which we find ourselves. Around the time we begin to form solid memories and start to truly appreciate the joy it is to be alive, we learn that this aliveness ends. As our goldfish goes "home," and our dog crosses the "rainbow bridge," and our grandfather goes to be "in the sky," we learn that we die. Always. One-hundred percent of the time. Underneath all of our great joys, our first loves and stunning sunsets, our graduations, achievements and living, there is the nagging knowledge, no matter how deeply we try to bury it, that . . . We. Will. Die. So indeed, we are all a little bit sad. All the time.

But, what if there was information available that might mitigate this sadness? What if there were things that have happened and been rigorously documented, thoroughly researched by some of the greatest minds to ever walk the planet, which indicate that the demise of the physical body might not be the end of us? How much more joyful would our joys be if we weren't constantly reminded that they are temporary, that they exist in a fleeting bubble of awareness, only to pop and disappear as though they had never existed at all? I can give you, from my perspective at least, the answer: a lot.

When my dad died in September of 2011, to say I was devastated would not express clearly enough the psychological situation I found myself in. I'd heard the term "existential crisis" before, and I had some idea of what it meant. However, like trying to imagine how it felt for Armstrong to bounce around on the moon, you might grasp the concept, but simply can't truly "get it" until you are there. And I was there. When I got the phone call, I was suddenly, shockingly, and fully there.

The story you are about to read is true. Everything in it happened as written. No one was more surprised by that than me. Though I've always wondered, since I was a child, about what we are and how and why we're here, and what happens to us when we die, I did not imagine I'd ever have such direct evidence to suggest that something, *something* "other worldly" does, indeed, happen to us. I could never have guessed that my dad's death, by far the most traumatizing personal event in my life, would lead me to realize that the science I've always been drawn to and fascinated by and loved is incorrect on such a major front, and that when the heart stops beating and the brain is no longer registering activity, somehow, a part of us continues, and is able, in some cases, to make that known to the physical world.

When the first unexplainable (at least within our current materialist scientific paradigm) event occurred, I was stunned. It seemed to me that what had happened would need to be, absent a "paranormal" explanation, a coincidence of monumental proportions. But still, my skeptical leanings prompted further investigation. And when these things began to happen under controlled situations in which I was certain a "paranormal" explanation was the only one that could hold water, my mind reeled. How could it be that something of such significance had escaped the notice and following scrutiny of science? Science, after all, was entirely about figuring out how our universe works. To have such a gaping hole in that survey of things was shocking to me. It could not possibly be that I was the first person to notice such anomalies, such occurrences that did not match what our science would predict. After my dad passed, they were so prevalent, yet so difficult, if not impossible, to explain by "normal means," that I wondered how it could be that no scientist ever had one of these things happen to them—one of these "anomalies" that are so blatant they simply cannot be ignored. If I'd continued on with my high school and early college ambitions to become a science teacher or scientist instead of becoming an actor, and just *one* of these events had occurred, it would have been enough for me to start writing research proposals. To me, it was akin to Galileo noticing shadows moving on Jupiter's moons, leading him to believe that something about the current theory of how things work was wrong. "Anomalies" are events that happen that aren't "supposed" to. They are events that our current theories and equations do not predict or even allow for. But if one happens, to me, that is where science must step in. It is not science's job to say, "We don't understand how this could happen, so it couldn't have." It is science's job to observe whatever it is and then rework the theories and equations to encompass the "anomaly." Just because something may happen only once, shouldn't mean it deserves to be disregarded. In my opinion, those anomalies may be the most important events, events that point to a larger reality awaiting our discovery. After my dad passed, I didn't experience just one anomaly. There were many. And I didn't have to work all that hard to find them.

Since I was so easily able to set up situations where, for instance, a person claiming to be a "medium" somehow gave accurate, specific information that there is no apparent "rational" way they could have known, it seemed to me a phenomenon ripe for scientific study. This wasn't like Ben Franklin with a key and a kite waiting outside in a storm—I found these circumstances could be set up at will with certain people. And since I was just an actor who had stumbled upon this, it was dumbfounding to think that someone much, much smarter and better equipped hadn't already stumbled upon it . . . which is when I started to do some research, and was staggered to learn that they had.

The more I read of the research that has been carried out by not only reputable scientists, but in some cases institutions and people held in the highest academic esteem—a Nobel Prize Winner, Harvard University, the University of Arizona, the University of Virginia (UVA) and Princeton University, Cornell, Duke and on and on—the more surprised I was that I had to go looking for this information rather than having seen it splashed across every headline. If the Journal of the American Medical Association concludes that saturated fat isn't the cardiovascular culprit we thought it was, it's on the nightly news. But when the JAMA Book Review Editor concluded, based on the rigorous, meticulous research carried out for fifty years by UVA, that reincarnation might be a real thing—that it seems to *actually happen*—no one heard about it—not even within the vast majority of the academic community.

Given all of this and how strong some of the evidence is—which is there for anyone who is so inclined to peruse it—I began to suspect something else was going on. It is not that I was the first person to stumble upon the idea that my departed dad was trying to communicate with me—far from it. It was, rather, that our scientific institutions at the highest levels have been actively ignoring the evidence. To accept these things would mean, essentially, that we'd be starting over in a lot of foundational ways. To accept that consciousness is not an emergent property of trillions of physical protons, neutrons and electrons that make up a brain, but rather another fundamental part of the universe, means we are wrong about . . . like, almost everything. To upend and throw out that many years of research is, obviously, not only a big deal, but it now seems to me, it's being actively avoided, and the evidence that might do the upending, routinely dismissed. As renowned theoretical physicist Dr. Amit Goswami said to me, "The scientists twist themselves into knots to try to explain the double slit experiment, when simply accepting that consciousness is not created by the brain would solve all of their problems. But they resist and resist."

The famed double slit experiment shows that sometimes light and matter behave as a spread-out wave, existing in a "superposition," which theoretically means *everywhere*, and sometimes as discrete, localized particles, and what seems to be the determining factor is whether or not a person is looking at the light or matter. Somehow, it seems like consciousness is involved in the equation and is the factor that causes a "wave of probability" to snap into existence as a definite thing in place and time. Until a human observer looks at a photon or electron or atom (which is what makes up everything we know of), that photon or electron or atom isn't there. It's everywhere. It is our looking at the atom—not touching or interacting with it in any way, just *looking* at it—that seems to cause the atom's probability wave to collapse, and for it to snap into physical existence in a definite place. And this notion makes (most of) science rather queasy—so much so that to avoid it, ever more complex theories have been offered to try and explain the double slit results—the "knots" created by the resistance to the evidence Dr. Goswami referred to.

Why they resist and how cognitive dissonance allows them to ignore the evidence is the subject for another book. But it at least helped explain to me why I was not taught in high school that the evidence for reincarnation is so strong that it is difficult to explain in any other way, the same way I was taught that there is a link between smoking and disease. The evidence, friends, is just as significant, and you can discover that for yourselves.

In this book, I'd like to take you along on my personal journey, a journey that began with my dad's unexpected passing and led to my participation in a Netflix series called *Surviving Death* that just happened to be exploring the same topics at the same time that I was. I know that could easily have been a coincidence, but given the way it all happened, it sure doesn't feel like it.

When I took my seat in front of the cameras, it was a bit hard to focus. The steps that had led me to that moment filled my mind, and I couldn't help but be overwhelmed by what I believed my dad had done to make it all happen. The dominos that needed to fall in order to be in that chair, where someone was putting makeup on my face to reduce my sheen, were all systematically toppled over, a chain reaction triggered by my father, it seemed. Given his love for me and his family, it's not at all surprising that he went through the enormous effort that I believe he did. What is surprising, though, is that if he in fact did it, he did it all without a body.

# CHAPTER ONE

# The Call

"Everything is going to be okay. Everything is going to be okay. Everything is going to be okay." I just kept repeating it over and over, unable, it seemed, to say anything else. I can't know, sitting here today, if I believed that at all. It's more likely I didn't when I try and go back to that moment and be there again in the feeling of it.

My sister's screams howled from the phone that shook in my trembling hands. *Wails* is the more apt way to put it. She was wailing, and it was only then that I'd understood the word that I'd read in ancient Greek plays. And my mom, off in the distance, was screaming too. I imagined she must be running from somewhere, because her cries became louder and louder, soon mixing in with my sister's, until my phone vibrated with intermittent sobbing and the sucking in of breath as more screams were prepared. These sounds were the second-worst I'd ever heard, and they threw me deeper into what I would later come to understand was a panic attack. The panic attack began, I realize now, the moment I heard the first-worst sounds I'd ever encountered, which came in the package of words barely shaped, hanging in the air with a terrible lack of articulation, malformed by angst, almost unintelligible, the deficit of definition making them all the more piercing: "He's gone. He's gone. Oh my God, he's gone."

I was at work when I received the heart-wrenching call. My dad had been found dead on the floor in his house by the police. The last time I saw him was the last time I was going to see him. My mind raced. *Had I said anything I would regret for the rest of my life? Had I said, as I always did every time I left him, "I love you?"* A quick rifling through a brain that I now know was breaking, relieved me when the search came back with a definite *"Yes." Okay, what else? What else happened in our last moments together? Did I hug him hard enough? Hard enough to know I wasn't just saying the words "I love you," but that I actually loved him? Oh no . . . we'd had a debate, as we often did. But now we'd had a debate during the last time we'd ever have together. Was it done in the spirit of fun and love that it always was? Did we actually enjoy it, as we usually did, me coming from the liberal side of the spectrum, and he from the fiscally conservative?* And my breaking brain put me momentarily at ease again, as I assured myself he knew I enjoyed the debates, even if I may have gotten more heated than I would have had I known that would be our last. For the next hours, I rode a train home, interestingly beside two strangers who'd started a friendly political tussle with each other not unlike the one I'd just had with my dad. I noted it (enough to remember it clearly nine years later), but made little of it, and returned to the retracing of steps between my dad and I during our last evening together, which had been twenty-four hours before.

The previous day, Monday, September 26th, 2011, my dad and I were at my mom's house after a long, sun-drenched day with the family. It was a perfect day, really. I was living in New York City at that time and got home to Connecticut maybe every other week to visit. Though I'd not planned on going that particular week, my dad called and said he really wanted to see me. In what is now one of the great reliefs of my life, I adjusted my schedule and made the trip. My mom happened to have the day off as well, so we made plans to all be together. Though divorced for decades, my parents remained close, having known each other since they were twelve years old. My mother had been unfaithful when they were still a very young couple

2

and soon married the man she'd been unfaithful with, but my dad, being the uncommonly good person he was, eventually befriended my step-father, so we could all remain as close as possible. So, that Monday, I spent the entire uncommonly warm September day with my dad, my sister and her kids and husband, and my mom and step-father.

In the evening, after everyone else had retired to bed, my dad and I watched football together and sparred over healthcare reform. He then told me why he'd wanted to see me that day: he'd decided it was time to start putting the money he'd saved and worked so hard for, often at minimum wage, into my and my sister's names. His mom, we now know, was in the early stages of Alzheimer's disease at that point, and her money was being spent on her care. He didn't want that to happen to him. I said, "Dad, you're not going anywhere for a long time, and I don't want your money. Someday, *many* years from now, when you pass, it would only make me sad to get money that you made and didn't spend. You've been working your whole life. I want you to start having fun." To which he said, "You guys *are* my fun." We finished watching the game and called a truce on solving America's medical system woes, and at around midnight he got up to leave. I walked him down the stairs to the front door, gave him a hug and said, "I love you." And he said the same. And then he left. I called out to him when he was halfway across the lawn on the way to his car, saying that I'd come back the following week too, so we could go see a movie together that had just come out, and he smiled at me one last time over his shoulder. And a thunderous clap of terrible clarity struck me right then in my train seat and roiled my stomach: that would be the last time I'd see my dad's face. The thought made me nearly wretch, and I wondered if my seat mate would be more forgiving after being vomited on if I told him it was because I was never going to see my dad again, and not because I'd had too much to drink. I guessed he'd be rather annoyed either way (we have only so much capacity for kindness when partially digested pizza is on our pants). I

3

concentrated on breathing, and again thought about that smiling face. I needed to remember it. I would have given anything for a device that could see and record the pictures in my mind. I zoomed in on that face. I tried to bring back every detail of that smile, intent on emblazoning it forever in my memory, etching it so deeply into my neural pathways that no amount of time or added memories would ever swallow it. I thought about the shirt he was wearing, the exact tilt of his head when he looked back at me, and the sparkle in those amazing green eyes that my mom had instantly fallen in love with upon seeing them for the first time when she and my dad were in seventh grade. I resolved to redraw the scene on my hippocampus and memorize all of it. Forever. But, right then on the train, no matter how hard I tried, I couldn't remember if I'd hugged him hard enough. It was certainly not long enough. And a sick feeling grabbed my everything when I realized I'd not have him in my arms like that again. I should have hugged him harder, and I became angry with my day-ago self for not realizing it when he had the chance.

The day following his last smile and my not hard-enough hug, Tuesday, I was back at work managing the bar at the Brooks-Atkinson Theatre in New York City. A few days before, I'd been chided by Woody Allen (who was directing the play) for being too loud. That has absolutely no relevance to anything at all, but I like that story. The show was a series of three one-act plays, and the evening had two intermissions. Just before the first intermission, I got a worried call from my sister asking if my dad had come back to New York with me. I instantly knew something was wrong. I answered, "No, why?" She had gotten a call from someone he worked with—he didn't show up that day. My dad never missed a day of work, *ever*. I mean, he may have *actually* never called in sick. So, to not only not go to work, but also to not let anyone know why he wasn't there—impossible.

The first act came down and as intermission started, I began serving drinks. My brother-in-law was back in Connecticut at that moment, driving frantically to my dad's house. When he arrived, the police were there on the front lawn blocking the door. They wouldn't let him in. "What happened???" he was shouting, having to be restrained from entering. "That's my father-in-law. What happened?" The police had to make sure there had been no funny business, no foul play. They had to be certain it was simply a desperately loved man whose heart had stopped. My brother-in-law drove back to his house wondering how to tell my sister. It was, by far, the longest five-minute drive of his life.

My phone rang behind the bar. The second intermission was about two minutes away. My heart pounded as I answered. It was my sister. She was screaming. I was able to make out, "He's gone." The screaming continued. Applause could be heard. The second intermission was happening. Suddenly, I was making people rum-and-cokes. "My dad died," I said to my bar-partner, as the crush of people descended on the bar. "What?!?" he said. "My dad." And I continued to make drinks, asking people how they were liking the show. I later realized that I was in what psychiatrists call "shock."

After intermission ended, I called my sister back. She was in her driveway wailing. My mom had gone over to her house. I was worried that I was going to lose more people over this, so great was the shock and searing pain of losing my dad. "Everything is going to be okay, everything is going to be okay," I kept repeating, trying to calm her. I finished out the paperwork, counted the money and paid the bartenders. Then, I walked to Grand Central Station, still in the throws of my first ever (but not last) panic attack.

The commotion of Grand Central whirled around me, people laughing and hugging goodbye and zigging and zagging this way and that, being "normal" in a way I wondered if I'd ever be again. I looked up at the old-fashioned, flappy train station schedule board, making a quick mental note that this was the very same sign my dad's eyes saw the first time he entered Grand Central. I knew in an instant that this would be a new part of my life—the distinction between the things my dad knew about and the things that would happen henceforth that he wouldn't. A part of me somehow found a fleeting moment to worry about the inevitable time someone somewhere would decide that the Grand Central information sign would need to be upgraded and replaced with a new one, one my dad would not know about, pushing him a step further from my world.

I found my track number and as I had a million times before, but never before, made my way to my train. Normally, I walk all the way up to the front car where the ridership is less dense and find an open window seat, preferring to use my train time to keep to myself while listening to a podcast, working on my computer, or gazing out the window listening to music. On this night, however, I simply sat in the first empty seat I came upon. A man already sitting in the next seat moved his bag and I let myself fall into the aisle seat beside him. For the first time since hearing the moaned words, "He's gone," I stopped moving. The movement I'd maintained in my body, I realized, had been a way to reroute movement from my mind. On the quiet train, though, still for the first time, my mind reeled and struggled to place the current situation into some sort of realistic context. But it couldn't. My dad being gone was something so removed from anything I considered possible that it was like trying to envision what it might have been like to have been born in France in 1712, or having a super power that allowed me to see through walls. No matter how hard I tried to wrangle the thought that I would never see my dad again, I just couldn't do it. A wall of some kind prohibited me from feeling the truth of the matter. So, I didn't cry. Rather, it became something of an intellectual exercise trying to grasp the nuts and bolts of what my dad being dead meant. While my brain tried to process my new reality, my shocking and unexpected new reality, one in which my dad wouldn't ever answer the phone again when I called, I became aware that the person across the aisle from me was having a debate with the man in the seat in front of him. The man in front had been reading a newspaper and there was an article involving Barack Obama. The person beside me noticed that and eventually leaned into the aisle and said something to the man with the paper. As it turned out, the man with the paper was a Democrat and, like me, a big fan of Obama, and the man to my left was a Republican. Once they began to respectfully, though spiritedly, deliberate, they did not stop for the rest of the two-hour trip. The situation soon struck me as oddly coincidental. The debate these two men were having was exactly the one my dad and I had, over and over again since Obama's election, and that we'd revived the night before. For the entire trip to Connecticut, our previous night's engagement was echoed by these men, and with the same friendly vigor. So lively was their good-natured tete-a-tete, in fact, that it commandeered my thoughts and kept me focused on it, rather than on the loss I was struggling to comprehend. *How odd and sort of lucky*, I thought, *that I happened to sit in the seat I did*, as I wasn't certain how I would have fared if I'd been left alone inside my brain for those two hours. Instead, I took the same side I had in the debate the night before, and the man beside me, in notably similar terms, spoke for my dad.

# CHAPTER TWO

# The Best Man

To properly convey the series of events comprising the bulk of this book and how meaningful they were, I've got to make it clear how close my dad and I were, and how, to my family, he was a pillar holding up an otherwise shaky construction. Like many families, mine wasn't simple. But no matter how unclear things got, the one constant was my father and his sort of superhuman goodness and love.

One of my earliest memories is the sound of something breaking downstairs in our house. I crawled out of bed and quietly padded my three-year-old feet down the hallway of our raised ranch. I went maybe a third of the way down the upper stairway and sat on a step, which afforded a view across the lower staircase and into the downstairs living room. There, my mom and dad stood in their robes across the room from each other. My mom was picking things up from a shelf that lined the wall on her side and throwing them at my dad. The crash I'd heard, I now saw, was a lamp that had smashed against the wall behind him. She was screaming things I can't remember, but I do recall that it was frightening. I eventually learned that problems had been brewing for some time, but that was the first I became aware of them, as far as I can remember. They never saw me, and I eventually crawled back up the steps and went down the hall to my room, trying to take in this new part of my reality. And that, of course, was just the beginning of the new things my world view was about to expand to incorporate.

Not long after witnessing that fight, my dad, very late one night, came into the bedroom that my little sister and I were asleep in, lifted us up, and carried us one by one to the car, which was already on and warmed up for us in the driveway. As he put the seatbelts around us in the backseat, I remember being entirely confused. Nothing like this had ever happened before. My sister and I quickly fell back to sleep and the next thing I remembered was waking up parked in front of someone's house—and my dad was in the front seat crying. Another new thing to add to my universe. I'd never heard my dad cry before, and though I didn't know why he was doing it, I knew I didn't like seeing it. When he saw that I was awake, he bravely caressed my hair and said, "It's okay, we're just taking a ride. Go back to sleep."

I don't remember arriving home. The next thing I recalled was waking up in the morning, the events of the night before feeling like a dream. *Dad didn't wake us up in the middle of the night and take us for a ride somewhere, did he?* He had, though. He would keep the secret of why we took the trip that night to himself for years, and he wouldn't tell me what it was all about until I pried it from him when I was in my late teens. My mom, sometime after, during or around the fight I saw, had been behaving oddly, and my dad began to suspect she might be having an affair. On the night he cried silently in the front seat, my mom had told him she had to go to her best friend's house, because she was having trouble of some kind. Thinking this might be a lie, once the hour had gotten very late and she still wasn't home, he gathered us up out of our deep sleeps and put us in the car so he could drive to her friend's house. When I woke up to see my dad's face wet with tears, it was because my mom's car was not in the driveway he was staring at—the driveway of her friend's house, where at 2am it should have been had she been telling the truth. What I woke up to see was my dad's heart breaking. Though he'd known something was amiss, that empty driveway made it concrete.

As I said, he would not tell me this story for many, many years, and even then, it took much work to slowly coax the telling. He felt bad that I remembered the night at all. See, even after the crushing blow of losing the love of his life, his middle school sweetheart that he'd met at twelve years old, married right after high school, and quickly had two children with, he loved her still. So good a man was my dad, that no matter what anger he must have held towards her, there was simply no way he was going to taint how his adoring children who loved him like crazy felt about their mom, whom they loved just as much. So, somehow he kept it all in, kept all of that pain to himself, and let us go on thinking that "Sometimes things just don't work out, even when people love each other."

We would later learn that my mom, still a kid herself, having never had any other boyfriend, having never even kissed anyone other than my dad, went through postpartum depression when I was born and began to feel like she'd made a mistake, like she'd married her best friend, but a person with whom the passion that had been there in their teens was now gone. And when she got a new job as a bank teller, she quickly fell head over heels in love with her married boss. That man was the one she was with that night when she'd said she was at her friend's house, and he also fell head over heels in love with her, so they began an affair. Eventually, he divorced his wife and my mom divorced my dad, and shortly thereafter, they married each other. And to this day, 38 years later, they remain married.

I tell you this story not to simply share difficult memories or to make anyone feel bad. I share it to show how special of a man my dad was. Such was his love for his children that he eventually somehow swallowed his crushing pain and his pride, and shook the hand of the man who'd helped to upend his fairy tale life, so he could remain as close to us as possible. My sister and I carry no resentment about any of this. It was clear my mom and dad were not meant to be, and given the life she built with my stepfather, it's clear they were meant to be. But my dad never got over losing my mom. He'd eventually remarry about fifteen years later, but it didn't take. As it turned out, my mom was the only one for him. Sometimes, your soulmate loves someone else. And all you can do is love them from afar. So, he lived alone and spent all of his time and energy worrying about his children and grandchildren (who were 4 and 9 when he passed, and loved him beyond measure). Sometimes, the universe seems to leave only the option to just sit with the unrequited feelings and focus on giving out your copious love in all the ways you *can*. And my, did he find ways.

Don't get me wrong, though; the "soulmate stuff" didn't only go in one direction. My mom also felt like they had a connection that went deeper than most, one that might even transcend lives, were such a thing possible, but, for whatever reason, they "didn't work" as a unit this time around. Given the connection and love that remained between them, once the initial upheaval had passed and my dad's heart was able to heal as much as it could or ever would, they once again became friends. When my dad remarried, my mom wept with joy that he'd again found happiness. So, you know . . . like all families, complicated stuff. On many occasions my mom would say to my sister and me when speaking of the divorce all those very many years ago, "I will take the guilt to my grave. It will be the last thing I think of, the pain I caused that good man. The best man." And when my dad unexpectedly collapsed on his floor and died, my mom sat for hours by his body, unwilling to let go of his hand. Though they were not "meant to be," he was, nonetheless, "her person." And so deep was her grief and my sister's, that I worried I might lose them, too.

When I got off the train in New Haven at about 2am, my stepfather was there waiting for me. I hugged him harder than I have in my whole life, and for the first time since getting the news, I cried in his arms right in front of the station. And he cried, too. Perhaps oddly, this is my favorite moment in my life between my stepdad and I. And then we drove to my sister's house where my entire family had gathered. I walked up the stairs and looked into the faces of the people my dad had so suddenly left behind and saw how lost every single one of them was. How were we going to do this? How could there be a world without "Dad, Robert, Poppy Bob" in it? If there were ever a time we'd need my dad, ever a moment when his comforting eyes and gentle way and "It's going to be okay" attitude and all-consuming love were needed, it was now. It was gone, though. Science says it disappeared when his heart stopped beating. Suddenly, the science I'd always loved and once thought I'd spend my life teaching, was a harbinger of pain and crisis. I didn't know then that the same science I suddenly loathed, would, as it had when I was a kid, once again excite my interest and quell my fears. Science, it turned out, was what I needed. Faith wouldn't do—I needed evidence to tell me that all that my dad was didn't simply cease to exist.

# CHAPTER THREE

# 21 Grams

The morning after my dad passed, I went to his house. When I pulled into the driveway, the sight of his car sitting there punched me in the gut. My dad's cars were a thing for me. Never wanting to spend money on anything but his kids, he wouldn't ever buy a new car, instead spending his life finding "deals." I walked up to his last deal sitting in his driveway exactly as he'd left it two nights before when he got out of it for the last time. I put my arms on the roof and peered into the window. Inside, his driving glasses sat in their case, placed lovingly there by those tough, gentle hands. Everything my dad touched, he touched with care. He made the most out of everything, because "waste not, want not." Whatever he could make last beyond its intended shelf life equaled more pennies he could save to help me and my sister. So, as I stared at the glasses that no longer worked as well as they should have, sitting in a case so old that it no longer stayed closed, I wept. For the first time since learning that he was dead, I sobbed in uncontrolled fits. My mom came over and put her arms around me and we sobbed together, there on his car, trying to soak in whatever of him might have made its way into the frame of the Ford.

My sister soon arrived, and together she and I began the impossible task of going through my dad's physically recorded life. We found boxes containing every drawing we'd ever made him, every school award we'd ever gotten, every Christmas card we'd ever given him, no matter how generic or how little time we might have spent picking it out—to him, clearly, it had been worth saving. Closet after closet was filled with keepsakes. Though he wasn't a man who often verbalized his copious emotional capacity, his love was of a sort uncommon, a depth seldom found. A "blue collar" working man on the outside, he was sentimental and soft on the inside, which led to him saving everything. And it also led to a particular way of communicating what was of the utmost importance to him with his children. Coming from a family where emotions were not always openly expressed, he found ways to more easily share with us how he was feeling. One day, for instance, when my sister and I were in high school, he asked if we would take a ride with him. As we set off down a scenic road, he put a tape in the "new" tape deck that his latest "deal" had. As the Carol King song, "Child of Mine" began to play, he said to us, "This is how I feel about you." And then we all quietly listened, hanging onto every word, and we cried. My dad would do this a lot – use music to communicate with us how he was feeling or what he found of value that he wanted to pass along. So, when we found a torn off piece of paper on his desk with the scrawled words, "Believe, a country song," we thought he must have made the note regarding a song he'd heard on the radio that he liked and wanted to remember. Having a "filing system" all his own, which consisted mostly of handwritten entries on pieces of notebook paper, it took some time to sift through his desk. After saving for years at his FedEx job, he'd tried his hand at the stock market. He set up an office in his home as his base of operations where he'd spend his day off from work, and it was here that the mountains of scribbled records of daily stock prices were piled. From the looks of it, you might think he owned stock in thousands of different companies worth millions of dollars. But we would soon learn that for all of those records he kept, he'd owned just a few, and had risked quite little in them. Like everything else in his life, though, he gave those few, no matter how small the investment might look to the average person, great attention. Notebooks worth of attention.

Eventually, we found another scrawled note amidst the pile of indecipherable numbers and stock exchange symbols, this one also on a piece of paper that was maybe two inches by an inch that had been torn off from a larger sheet. On this one he'd written "Believe, tell Jen." Jen is my sister, and we quickly put the two notes together, thinking he must have, on two separate occasions, heard a country song called "Believe," and had wanted to share it with Jen. Alas, he'd either forgotten or died before having the chance to tell her, because he'd never mentioned it to either of us, and neither of us had ever heard the song or knew what it was or who it might be by. And it just absolutely broke our hearts to think of my dad taking the time to twice write down separate notes about this song and no longer being here to tell us why. The thought was a debilitating blow. And it wouldn't be the last.

On the morning of the wake, Jen, Mom and I sat in my mom's living room looking at photo albums and pulling out pictures we'd place on a poster board to have at the funeral home. My mom decided she wanted there to be music playing throughout the night, so we set about putting a playlist together of wake-appropriate songs, whatever those might be. As we did so, I recalled the two pieces of scrap paper we'd found within the piles of notebooks on my dad's desk the day before. "Go to iTunes and look for "Believe" in country music," I said. The first song that came up was "Believe" by Brooks and Dunn. I wasn't a country music fan, and though I'd heard of Brooks and Dunn, I had no idea what sort of music they made, and while my mom and sister did casually listen to country music from time to time, and both knew a portion of Brooks and Dunn's repertoire, neither of them were familiar with "Believe." So, we quickly purchased the song, and then the three of us sat together on the couch as we listened to it for the first time. The song, as it turns out, is about a man who'd just passed. Before doing so, though, he spoke to his neighbor's young son. He tells the boy how, many years before, he'd lost his wife and baby. That was obviously unimaginably awful, and the boy wonders how he survived such a devastating loss. The man responds by telling the boy that he knows he will see them again. When the boy asks what he means, he says he's come to believe that there is much more to life than "just what we can see," and that this "can't be all there is." And by the time the song comes to the conclusion that, "You can't tell me that it all ends in a slow ride in a hearse," we were soaked in tears.

What a remarkable coincidence, we thought, that my dad, who so often used music as a way to share with us his deepest feelings, should have twice written down this song, probably about seven years earlier when it was first released and playing on the radio, only to forget to "Tell Jen," and have it resurface all this time later when we happened to find the two scraps of paper among his piles and piles of notebooks. *How many songs*, we wondered, *in the vast sea of songs, are about the idea of life after death?* Needless to say, the track made the playlist for the wake.

When we arrived at the funeral home, seeing "my dad" in the casket was the strangest sight of my life. Though it looked exactly like him, lying there in the Red Sox shirt he so often wore, it simply wasn't. I wondered what it could be, scientifically speaking, that made this body so unrecognizable from the last time I saw it a few days before. *How can just the beating of a heart make this vast a difference? How can just the flow of blood turn an entity so vibrantly packed with love and ideas and passion and joy and regrets and hopes and everything that made my dad my dad, into the collection of carbon molecules that I was now looking at?* It was just . . . wrong. It just felt wrong. That simply wasn't my father in that coffin, and I couldn't wrap my mind around it. If I took every bit of your body, divided it down to its smallest parts, and spread them out on the ground alongside the bits of a table divided down to its smallest parts, the two sets of stuff would be indistinguishable. Looking through our most powerful microscope, your body and a table are exactly the same. So, why is a table a table, and you . . . you? There are no other parts—there's just the stuff that makes up atoms. And yet, you and a table are remarkably, infinitely different. Why? What do you have that a table doesn't? My dad's body in the casket was still the exact same stuff, and would be the exact same stuff under a strong enough microscope. So, why was he so not the same? What was the thing that had given those atoms in my dad their distinct "Dadness," and where did it go? It brought to mind the experiment published in 1907 by Duncan MacDougall, who attempted to precisely weigh a person's body just before and just after death, deducing that any difference he found would therefore equal the weight of the soul. After going through this process with six people, he determined the weight of the soul to be 21 grams. Of course, the experiment was widely criticized for its flawed methods and summarily rejected by the scientific community. Nonetheless, looking at my dad's body, I understood why one might think a soul was a real thing, and perhaps the reason my dad's body did not, to me, resemble my dad.

The following morning, as we took that slow ride in a hearse, "Believe" played over and over again in my head as I desperately wished it was true. I wished that the science I'd learned in college might be wrong or at least incomplete, and that the world I saw out of the limousine's window while my dad's body rolled along ahead of us might not be "all there is." Even though MacDougall's experimental set-up had some disqualifying cracks, I hoped that someone else, at some point, had come along with a better experiment, and that science had indeed confirmed there is more to a person than the blood and bones that make them up. Alas though, science, in the intervening years, had only hardened in its stance that the end is the end—as far as I knew, anyway. As we pulled into the cemetery, the gaping hole in the earth ready to swallow making me feel sick, I made a mental note to check into that.

We had the funeral and did all the things you do. We got through it, as people do. I'd decided to stay for the rest of the week at my mom's house before returning to work. That night, I pulled from my bag a sweatshirt of my dad's that I'd taken from his house. It was a sweatshirt I'd given him when I got into grad school after purchasing it from our campus store. It read on the front, "Wayne State Dad," and he wore it all the time. So, as I lay there trying to contemplate what kind of world a world without him in it was, I again began to cry. I nestled my head into the sweatshirt and took a deep breath, and this then thirty-four-year-old man fell asleep cradling it. For the next month, I'd sleep with that shirt.

A few days after the funeral, I got into my car and began the drive back to New York from Connecticut. It had been seven days since my dad passed, and it was the first time I'd been alone since—and the aloneness was crushing. My mind had been so occupied with the sudden need to make plans for his services and kept busy with visits and well-wishes from family and friends, that the full enormity of what my dad's passing meant hadn't fully hit me. From the moment I'd gotten the news that he was gone, while continuing to make drinks for customers and asking them how they were enjoying the show—up until this moment, I now realized, I'd been numb. And quite suddenly, the novocaine of shock and then activity wore off, and the pain hit me with a mighty force. As I drove down the highway, I cried harder than I had since I was a kid when my Transformer's head broke off. The weight of my dad's absence was too much, and needing to hear his voice, I dialed his number to listen to his voicemail greeting, but that only hurt more. And as I wept with even greater abandon, my vision of the highway blurred by tears, the radio that had quietly been on in the background the entire time somehow made its way into my awareness. I instantly became quiet, though I was afraid to actually listen. If I'd heard what I thought I had, well, it would almost be too much to take. But if I didn't, that outcome was worse. So, I gingerly turned the volume knob, slowly at first, and then all the way up, when these words blasted through my radio: "You can't tell me that it all ends in a slow ride in a hearse."

*How? How could this be?* My tears turned instantly from those borne of sorrow to those of joy as my rational brain struggled to make sense of what was happening. I had never heard this song before a few days ago. The song was rather obscure, seven years old and simply not played very often on the radio—so I was later told. Ever since the advent of iPods and then iPhones, I almost never listened to the radio, preferring instead to play my own music. On this day, though, I simply didn't have the energy to plug my phone in, which was why the radio had been on instead in the background, tuned to whatever station happened to be playing that song. No matter how unequivocally science considers this a coincidence, in that moment, I found myself filled with elation, absolutely certain my dad had somehow figured out a way to influence the sequence of events leading to this particular song being played on this particular station at this particular moment. The feeling is impossible to describe, but it was as though I was touching, for a brief moment, the mystical. I screamed to myself in the car "Oh my God! Oh my God! Dad? Dad? Is this you, somehow?" I then quickly dialed my sister's number, and when she answered I shouted, "Listen to this! Listen to this!" before holding the phone to the speaker. She was likewise amazed, and as a more frequent radio listener, one who listens to Connecticut's country station, she reminded me again that she had never heard the song on the radio before.

Eventually, my rational mind asserted its authority and the mystical feeling subsided (though, to this day, recalling that moment brings it back). I eventually slid back down the hill the song had built and put me on top of, only to fall deeper into the abyss as a full-on existential crisis took hold. I was feeling so bad, in fact, just hours after feeling the bliss "Believe" had brought, that I started to wonder if I would be able to work that evening. Being a bartender for Broadway requires a certain amount of focus and friendliness, and I now worried I was ready for neither. Though my boss had kindly offered me as much time off as I needed, I'd decided to come right back to work, thinking it would keep my busy brain in check. But now, as I walked toward the subway, I wasn't sure.

I lived in Queens at the time and took the elevated 7 train to get into Manhattan. Upon reaching the top of the steps and slowly heading to the far end of the platform, I looked down at my feet. With every step I took, I felt myself closer to reaching for my phone and making the call to say I wouldn't be coming in. But then the thought of sitting at home alone surfaced, and it frightened me. With my hand on my phone, I wondered which would be harder, working through the angst, or sitting alone with it in my apartment, when suddenly, a flutter down in the tracks caught my attention. A large, bright orange butterfly was passing by my feet. Upon my seeing it, the flight path it had been taking abruptly shifted, and up in front of my face it flitted, nearly touching me before flying off into the sky. I combed through my brain trying to recall the last time I'd seen a big butterfly like this up on the elevated subway platform in Queens. I used the thought to keep my mind occupied as my train descended below ground— along with my temporarily buoyed spirit.

Getting through that shift at work was one of the hardest things I'd ever done. The anguish of not being able to call my dad was now overwhelming me. The fear of his finality was creeping in. *How long would it be,* I wondered, *before I could no longer clearly hear his voice or see his face?* I dialed his number to listen to his voicemail greeting again. This, too, would soon be gone when the phone company terminated his account for lack of payment. I quickly found an app that would allow me to record my voicemail messages. Luckily, I had saved a number of them from my dad, and during a break, I did so. My dad had a precious way of ending his voice messages as though he were signing off a letter, softly saying, "Love, Dad." I replayed it and replayed it. And with each replaying the quiet and gentle "Love, Dad" that had always swelled my heart, now tore it further asunder, each echo breaking it into pieces smaller and more numerous, until I was sure I'd never be able to collect them or recall how they fit. It occurred to me that I recently took photos of my father, which I now needed to see. I left work, and alone again on my walk to the train, tried to keep the panic at bay. I walked faster and faster, picking up speed the closer I got to my apartment. Some part of my psyche was fighting his dissolution into the ether, using at first, the recorded sound of his voice—and maybe with the digitally preserved look of his face, I'd be able to manage this psychological crisis. I couldn't wait to get to my computer and open the file containing the pixels in the form of that face—a file that came within three weeks of not existing.

Less than a month before my dad passed, my mom had decided to have a "just because" family gathering in her backyard. This, I thought, would be the perfect time to roll out my brand new camera. Though not a photographer, I've always told myself I'd be good at it if I just had the right equipment. So, I'd finally gotten it (and soon proved myself wrong about that). It was a full frame camera (whatever that means) with lots of "ISO and F stop" stuff (whatever that means) with multiple lenses. Luckily it had an "automatic" mode, which meant that even with my lack of skill, properly exposed photographs would be possible. So, as we ate and laughed around picnic tables on that perfect August afternoon, I got to work doing what I'd come to do—I'd taken the new camera with me that day specifically to take pictures of my family, and especially of my dad—and I don't know why. My dad, as far as we knew, was in great health. He had an active job as a FedEx delivery person and was always the first to jump in if someone needed physical help with something. Seeing him help me move into my latest apartment, carrying couches and tables and everything else up flights of stairs, no matter how many times I said, "Dad! Please leave that. I'll get it! You just watch the car," it was hard to believe my sixty-year-old father had taken that many trips around the sun, or that he didn't have many, many more left to go. So, I don't know why I had this urge to get photographs of him that day. And not just photographs: my fancy new camera also took high definition video, I discovered. I'd been sitting at a table with my dad, sister, niece, and brother-in-law, with my dad directly across from me. Under the guise of wanting to get everyone on camera saying a piece of wisdom they'd gathered, I turned to my sister and said, "Jen, what have you learned thus far in life?" I went around the table, having everyone respond, saving my dad for last. In reality, for whatever reason, it was his answer that I'd wanted to get on film. See, my dad was not a picture person. For him, everything was always about you. He wanted the focus always on others. His entire life, in fact, had been dedicated almost exclusively to helping my sister and me, often at his own expense. He drove cars always on the verge of breaking down, his roof leaked and his clothes hadn't been updated since the seventies. He saved his hard-earned money like no one else I have ever known. And yet, when it came to my sister and me, he spent it as though it was nothing. Because of his lack of ego and the primacy of those in his orbit, it was tough to get him on camera, as the experience of having his picture taken made him somehow feel uncomfortable— which is why, that day, I took so many photos of him. The zoom lens on my new camera afforded me the ability to take candid shots of him from a distance. When I look back at the photos from that day, it's striking what percentage spotlight his visage. I don't know if I somehow sensed, in a way science doesn't currently understand, that something wasn't right with him, or if I'd subconsciously picked up on cues that he wasn't feeling well. All I can say for certain is that the urge to get good photos of my father was strong. When I turned the camera toward him for the last time that day and the last time in his life, as it would turn out, I said, "Okay, Dad. What's the most important thing you've learned?"

"Have patience. Good things will come," he said.

That evening, after the party, I uploaded the photo and video files to my computer. I looked briefly through them on the big screen, happy to find that the automatic mode of the camera worked well. I finally had some good, in-focus pictures of my dad and a nice video of him, too. I turned the computer off and would not give those photos a good look again until now.

Arriving home, now sweating a bit from the accelerated pace, I hastily unlocked the door, took off my shoes, dropped my bag, and immediately turned on the computer. I clicked on the file and up they popped for the first time since the night I'd uploaded them. I realized in that moment that these were now my most treasured possessions. I made duplicate after duplicate of the photos, wishing I'd been born in a time when science had figured out how to make duplicate after duplicate of those I love. I added the pictures to iPhoto, sent them to my phone, then texted them to my family. The more places I could spread them, the safer it felt. Scrolling through to find the best shots of my dad, I stopped on one with a big, yellow butterfly. I'd nearly forgotten about that part of the day.

My mom's best friends were at the party. She and my dad had known Nancy and Mike since they were preteens. Though they remained lifelong friends, since my parents' divorce, it was rare that the four of them were together like this. When they were, though, it was like no time had passed. And that day, as they shared stories of "The good ole days," a large yellow butterfly came by. That's not unusual, of course—butterflies are around in Connecticut in August. What made this butterfly stand out was the fact that it stayed for quite a long time. And it didn't stay off in the yard somewhere: it was flying between all of us, going from one table to another. It came so close that it touched a few people, to the humorous alarm of Grandma Titi, my brother-in-law's grandmother who feared insects, even of the non-stinging and with pretty wings variety. As this butterfly (which we later learned was a Swallowtail) zigged this way and that, I took photos of it. When it landed, I got some close ups. "Oh look," I said, showing my mom on the camera's screen the photo I'd just taken, "it looks like it has little heart shapes at the ends of its wings." It behaved in what we considered to be such an odd manner, hovering around us the way a puppy might, that my mom eventually said, "Maybe it's a sign from grandma." Her mother had passed about ten years earlier, and she thought that this would have been a time my grandmother would want to be around, with the whole family and these lifelong friends together in this now much less-frequent way (times that my grandmother absolutely lived for). When my mom said it, I don't know how much she actually believed it. I, personally, found it rather unlikely that a dead person could somehow control the flight path of a butterfly and direct it into our yard for a while. But, of course, I wasn't going to say that to my mom. Instead, we all lightheartedly agreed that, "Yes, maybe it is!" After an unusual ten-minute visit, the butterfly took off into the sky.

Looking through the photos, one in particular caught my attention. While I was trying to capture a photo of the Swallowtail in flight, I'd taken one unintentionally framed by my dad on one side and my mom on the other. The butterfly is just over Mom's shoulder. Upon coming across it now, I sent the photo to my mom. She called me immediately and said, "I'm going to think of this as your dad saying he'll be watching over me." Again, I was certain the butterfly was just coincidence and my desire to take photos that day was chance. The idea of my dad somehow still being able to watch over us was beautiful, but stinging, because I didn't have hard evidence suggesting that could be true, no matter how much we wanted it to be. However, having the butterfly appear at my feet earlier that evening on the subway platform, then flying up to almost touch my face, and then rediscovering these photos upon coming home that same night, it was impossible to not think, even for the briefest of non-scientifically guided moments, *Dad?* And even though my skepticism eventually dulled any mystical attributes I might have initially felt regarding these events, they gave me the lift I needed to get through that first week without him.

Though I so desperately wanted to believe the song playing on the radio and the butterfly crossing my path might be "signs" from my disembodied dad, my brain just wouldn't let me have it. That butterfly would be the first among many others I and my family would begin to see at seemingly meaningful times, but the scientifically-oriented side of me would always retort, "You aren't suddenly seeing more butterflies. You are suddenly ascribing a meaning to them that wasn't there before and isn't there now." I know about patternicity and pareidolia and how the brain loves to fill in information that might not actually be there, based on experience and expectation. I'd had the "mystery" of the rainbow unweaved by Richard Dawkins and other brilliant scientists, and I knew what they'd have to say about me even remotely considering the possibility that what we perceive as the "self" is anything more than an emergent property created by evolution and the functioning of the brain, let alone actually entertaining the notion as one worthy of further cognitive energy.

It was going to take much more than some songs and Swallowtails to really make me wonder if it might be possible that some part of my dad had survived the death of his body.

And much more was about to come.

# CHAPTER FOUR

# Call Me
# When You Get There

The first week back at work was extraordinarily difficult as the reality of my dad no longer being alive sank harrowingly in and then subsumed me. I was sent into a dark place. A place I didn't know existed, and would never wish anyone else to discover. Depression is not the word. It was something else, and it was worse. It was utter hopelessness. More than just the depthless sadness brought on by the loss of a person I deeply loved, my dad's passing caused in me a full-blown existential crisis. I'd been brought up as a Catholic, but we weren't a very religious family. I'd been baptized and gone to Catechism when I was a kid, and made my first communion and got confirmed, most of which, I felt, was my mom sort of "covering the bases"—sort of a, "Well, even if baptism isn't the only way into heaven, might as well not take a chance," kind of thing. So, we went to church on the big holidays like Christmas and Easter, but once I was in middle school, even that faded away. And when I finally read the Bible, it mostly brought confusion. I couldn't believe that some of the stuff contained therein could have been inspired by the same God I imagined made the cosmos. The stunning pictures made possible by Hubble and human ingenuity depicted a universe, in my opinion, far too immense and grand to have been created by the same god who said, "Make sure you don't wear a shirt made with two kinds of fabric." And by the time I asked a priest what in the world dinosaurs were and why the Bible had nothing to say about them, and he told me that their fossils were placed there to test my faith, I had serious doubts. One way or the other, those fossils had done the trick.

So, I began to look to other religious texts, such as the Bhagavad Gita, for answers. And though I found some things that sounded nice in almost all of the sacred scriptures of the various major religions, ultimately, none of them fully resonated with me. When meeting a new person, for instance, whenever the conversation turned to religion, after years of saying, "Well, I was raised Catholic, but . . ." I instead began to simply offer, "I'm spiritual, but not religious." What that really meant was, "I have no idea." As far as I could see, to be devoutly religious was the same thing as being obstinately atheistic, since the tenets of neither of those positions could be proven. Even given how scientifically oriented I was (especially once I'd gotten to high school and then college), and though I knew most of the scientists I was reading books about did not believe in a god, I left the possibility open that there are forces in the universe we haven't yet discovered. And in my mind, the word "god" and the words "strong nuclear force" could be the same thing.

All of this is to say that upon my dad's death, I did not have a strong faith to fall back on. Unlike others who I knew for whom their religion and beliefs about heaven were a balm, I had no such relief from my darkest thought. And that thought was this: what if the energy I knew as "my dad" was simply the end result of trillions and trillions of random events, of atoms knocking into each other in such a way that, eventually, they made my dad's body and his brain, which in turn made the perception he had of himself and generated all of "his" thoughts and dreams and desires and even his "love"? What if all "he" ever thought and felt, including "his" "feelings" about "me" and "my sister," were just the result of chemicals bouncing around "his" brain, and once that brain no longer received oxygen and powered down and died, so too did everything "he" ever "was"? What if "my dad" truly was just a collection of atoms that existed in a certain way for a short time, a way that "I"—just another collection of atoms existing in a certain way for a short time—recognized as "dad," that, upon "his" death, entered a new phase of their quantum journey, never to be seen again in the way "I" knew them? Well, that thought consumed me. Scientist Richard Dawkins (a strict "materialist" who, like the vast majority of scientists, believes absolutely that there is nothing but "material" in the universe, and that "you" are an illusion to "yourself" created by the brain), in his book, *Unweaving the Rainbow*, discusses how lucky we are to be "alive." He asks us to consider the odds against us being alive, given the fact that the universe is made of trillions of atoms and has been here for billions of years, with billions of years left to go. The chances, he says, that the exact events that needed to happen for your father's specific sperm (out of the hundreds of millions) to reach your mother's egg are astronomically, incalculably small. For all of the atoms that make up your brain to end up in your brain and give you the unimaginably brief sense of "you" is like winning the lottery billions of times. He takes great comfort in this thought. To him, we are fortunate beyond calculable odds that the "spotlight" of awareness falls on us for the eighty years that it does, out of an infinite amount of years when we will not be in the spotlight. But this suddenly didn't feel lucky to me! It would have been easier to never "know" anything, to have remained unaware in the sea of time and atoms, it felt, than to be ever so briefly aware, spending that awareness with the knowledge of the pending unawareness to come. Where Dawkins felt gratitude, I was feeling despair. Or, I guess, "my" atoms were feeling despair. Somehow.

To think that all my dad had ever done and dreamed, that all of his joy and desire, his every hope that ever bloomed, his millions of ideas, his cosmic compassion—if everything that was my dad could suddenly disappear as though they had never been, completely wiped from existence . . . well, then what was the point of anything? Why do anything at all if the ultimate result is permanent erasure? That was the unsettling and terrible and only thought that played on a loop for the week after my dad's services, and indeed, was the thought tumbling on a ceaseless spin cycle in the atoms of "my" brain when my mom called me one evening and said something that would be the beginning of a new chapter in my life.

At work while the first act of the play was going on, I sat behind the same bar I was behind when I'd gotten the life-altering call two weeks earlier when my sister screamed the words, "He's gone." I'd been reading a book, doing whatever I possibly could to try and keep my mind from the angst-ridden place it now defaulted to whenever I didn't fight with enormous effort to keep it focused elsewhere. I realize now that I had a form of PTSD, I think, and being back in the same physical place where I'd answered that phone was particularly trying. So, I read my books, attempting with all my might to understand them, to focus my mind on them, and for that time, at least, create a different reality where my world hadn't crumbled. There I was, distracting myself, when the phone rang and it was my mom. A instantaneous wave of panic cascaded through my system. This was something that lasted for a while—another symptom, I imagine, of the post traumatic stress of receiving the terrible news via phone. I quickly answered it with a worried "Hello," to which my mom responded in a tone of voice I hadn't heard since before Dad died. She had been in such a grief-stricken state, that she was nearly always crying. Phone conversations were quiet and difficult as she struggled to speak. Her voice had been low and trembling, and betrayed the awesome effort it had been taking her to just get out of bed. So, when she started speaking on this night, I knew something very different was going on. A great deal of her brightness had returned. Without any preamble she said, "I think I just got a message from Dad."

"What?"

"I think I just got a message from your father."

"What do you mean?"

"Do you remember your cousin Chris?"

"Chris? No, I don't think so?"

"Yes, you do . . . Chris. We were at his wedding. He married your cousin Tracy."

"I remember a Tracy."

"Of course you remember Tracy. Anyway, Chris just called me."

Chris is a second cousin (I think—the whole tiered cousin thing has always been more perplexing to me than Sudoku) who I almost never saw. The last time, in fact, that my immediate family had been in a room with Chris had been a decade or so earlier when he married into our family. I couldn't place him until I was shown a photo of him later. Chris had never called my mom's house before. She hadn't spoken to him in years. Thinking about it now, it must have taken some amount of courage for Chris to pick up the phone and make the call. He knew about my dad's passing through the family grapevine, but was not at all close with my father—in fact, I don't know if they'd ever even met. When the house phone rang (this was during the time of a far away place when some people still had "land lines" with no caller ID), Mom picked it up only in case it might be my sister or me. She had little desire to speak with anyone else. When it wasn't one of us, she immediately regretted answering, not sure she had the energy for a conversation.

"Liz?" The voice asked.

"Yes?"

"This is Chris." When my mom didn't immediately respond he added, "Chris Cox, your cousin."

"Oh, yes. Hi Chris." My mom is an extremely friendly person, and she perked up when she realized who it was, assuming he was calling, though somewhat surprisingly as they weren't close, to offer his condolences. But instead he said, "Liz, this is going to sound weird, but do you know what I do?"

"Um . . . No?"

"Okay. Well, ugh this is weird, but I have a hobby."

"Okay," she said, now totally perplexed as to what this call could possibly be about, especially in this time of incredible grief.

"I'm part of a ghost hunting team."

"Okay." Now she was truly thrown.

"Yeah. So, we investigate places that people think might be haunted. We use technical equipment and electronic devices that pick up on things like electromagnetic fields and stuff like that. I know this sounds crazy."

"No!" She said, fully wondering if Chris was crazy.

"So, one of the other things we do, one of the other ways we try to figure out if a place might be haunted by a spirit is we have a medium on our team."

"A medium?"

"Yes, she's a medium. Do you know what that is?"

"I've heard about them, yes. We actually saw one once."

"Oh great! So yeah, our medium, Christina Treger, is able to pick up on spirits. She gets visions and sometimes hears sounds and words and names, and gets strong feelings."

"Yes. Okay."

"So, I know this is going to sound completely bizarre, and I really hesitated to make this call, because I know how nuts some people might think it is, and I don't know what your beliefs are about this stuff . . ."

"I'm open," she interrupted. Which is true. My mom, like me, isn't a religious person. She has also always loved science and has spent her life in the medical field, first as an OR nurse, then moving to labor and delivery, and finally pediatrics. But she also suspects that, "something bigger than us" might be going on and she had left open the possibility that we do not entirely end at death. After reassuring Chris that she was interested in what he had to say, he continued.

"So, last week, my wife Tracy's sister started to have the smell of fish in her house. It was intensely strong and they just could not figure out what was causing it. It got so overwhelming with absolutely no explanation for it that they called me knowing I was into the paranormal, and they asked if I'd ever heard of anything like that happening. I told them that yes, sometimes smells can be associated with paranormal activity."

"I see," my mom said, having no idea where this might be going or how in the world she might be involved.

"So, my team went to the house, including our medium, Christina. Christina said the fish smell was a message intended to point us in the direction of someone who just passed—very recently passed. We had no idea who the person was or who they might be connected to, as no one in our family has recently died. Then Christina said, 'There's a connection to a fish restaurant with this man's family. He *desperately* needs to get a message to them that he is okay. I'm hearing the name Robert.' Then I remembered that your daughter owns a fish restaurant, and I suddenly put it together that this must be your Robert."

And my mom was silent for a while trying to process this unexpected turn of events. As they spoke more, my mom realized how difficult it must have been for Chris to make that phone call. But given the way it all transpired, he thoroughly believed the fish smell was a message from my dad. Christina, who did not know my dad or my family, and certainly had no idea that he'd passed, got the distinct sense that this man was not going to give up until the message had been delivered. And this thought eventually gave Chris the needed courage to pick up the phone and call a grieving woman just a week after burying her ex-husband, without having any idea how well or poorly she might take a call like this. The only reason he went through with it was because, to him, the evidence suggested my dad had woken up on "the other side," took a quick look around, and found a way to get to the nearest medium even remotely connected to our family.

My mom told me the odd story, and as intermission was about to begin, we hung up. A new feeling was inside me. Though I needed *much* more information on this whole event, I clung to the hope, no matter how vague, that my dad, or some part of him, had survived death and wanted us to know. I knew right away that I'd be calling Chris and his medium friend Christina, as well. The latent scientist in me needed to gather as many facts as I could. I was leery, however. Though I wanted desperately to believe something like this might be possible, this was not the first I'd heard of "mediumship."

# CHAPTER FIVE

# A Big A** Butterfly

When I was a kid, I was utterly fascinated by magnets. What in the world was the invisible process going on that caused one object to be pushed away from another without touching it? I was similarly transfixed by airplanes. We lived not far from an airport, and my dad would take my sister and me to watch planes take off. The parked airliners were massive! I couldn't believe how big they were, and could only imagine how heavy they might be. To watch them thunder down the runway and lift into the air was spellbinding. It was difficult to fathom what force kept such an enormous and heavy object aloft. Boats had the same hold on my imagination. Why did a rock sink, but these much larger objects stay bobbing on the surface? But it was seeing Halley's Comet when I was nine that really required I find some answers. This new thing in the sky was absolutely fascinating to me. Where did it come from? How did we know it would be back, and know exactly when that would be? The thing that really got me, though, was that it looked stationary. When I learned it was traveling at 2,000 mph, my mind absolutely spun. How in the world could something moving *so fast* look like it was frozen in place?

For all of these reasons, science quickly became my favorite subject in school. And when my curiosity was brought into contact with the best teacher I'd ever have, like hydrogen mixing with oxygen, something new was made, and my lifelong interest coalesced.

Mr. Sawyer was the teacher everyone wanted. He was known far and wide for his enthusiasm and humor, and his love for science was extremely contagious, making his classes by far the most sought after. When you received your schedule at the beginning of the year and Mr. Sawyer was on it, that was cause for much celebration. Mr. Sawyer was mesmerizing. The amount he knew and his singular way of sharing it was something to behold. Each time I walked into class, I could barely contain my excitement, wondering what new facet of how reality works would be revealed that day. What Mr. Sawyer conveyed most was wonder. He marveled at the universe and made us marvel, too. Learning about light and its unfathomable speed was extraordinary. Then, discovering how long it took that light to go from the sun to the earth, and the years it took to reach the nearest galaxy was exhilarating. My classmates and I left his class every day with our minds blown. Learning from Mr. Sawyer that planes stay aloft because of Bernouli's Principle felt like the unlocking of a deep mystery, and I was so thankful that someone had gone to all the great trouble to find the key. Every day in seventh period, a new question was answered, and the universe came more and more into focus. Finding out about what the human brain had accomplished, the mysteries it has decoded, astounded me. One day, we learned how Eratosthenes, using just a stick and a shadow in 240 B.C., calculated how many miles around the Earth is. That fact alone made me fall in love with the human capacity to figure things out, and become completely enamored of the process by which we do it: Science.

I'd first had Mr. Sawyer in eighth grade, and then to my very great luck, when I graduated to high school he was assigned there as well, giving me four more years of his singular tutelage. I had been a very shy kid and being the teacher he was, he recognized that immediately, as well as my love for science. He slowly drew me out of my shell, and beyond being my teacher, I began to see him as a friend. So perfectly taken was I by what I watched Mr. Sawyer do every day, kindling imaginations and curiosities, I decided that was how I wanted to spend my life as well, and went off to college intending to become a science teacher.

What continued to absorb me in my undergraduate years were the unanswered questions, the areas of study that continued to defy our intellectual penetration. Given that we were a species that had been able to compute the circumference of the planet with a stick two thousand years ago, the fact that anything remained unsolved was a surprise to me. But to find out just how much remained uncovered, was an absolute jolt, and was actually one of the reasons I ended up leaving the science degree track I was on after three years of undergrad, to follow my other passion of theater instead.

One day in a physics class when I was a freshman in college, we were studying gravity. We learned about all the reasons we know it's there, and what it does and how it mathematically works and fits into our equations. At the end of the lecture, the professor asked, "Does anyone have any questions?" I raised my hand to say, "But, what is it?"

"What do you mean?"

"What actually is gravity?"

"It's a force!"

"I know it's a 'force,' but what is it *exactly*?"

"It is one of the four fundamental forces of nature, it is the one that causes objects with mass to be attracted to each other."

He seemed a bit annoyed by this point, as though I was being intentionally abstruse. But I pressed ahead. "Yes, I get that. But what exactly is happening? What makes the 'force'? What is physically going on between the sun and the planets that causes the 'attraction'?" And after further back and forth involving mathematics I no longer recall, I was stunned, absolutely stunned to find that his ultimate answer was, essentially, "We don't know."

Wait. *What?* We don't know? We don't know? How can that be? How can it be that we don't know what one of the four "fundamental" forces of the universe is? Yes, we know the results of it, but we don't know the process by which it works. This was utterly shocking to me. But that would not be the last of the surprising gaps in our knowledge that I would come across.

We build our entire understanding of physics on the concept of "charge." We say that certain particles have a "positive" charge, and others have a "negative." But what exactly does that mean? And the short answer is, again, we don't know. We don't know what gives particles their "charge." We just know that the universe seems to work that way. And the same lack of understanding we have of the very small interactions between things extends to the very large.

In 1997, scientists were befuddled to find that the universe appeared to not be slowing its rate of expansion, as all our "laws" of physics would predict, but to actually be accelerating. This was completely against our every theoretic and mathematical prediction. But no matter how elegant our equations are, and how beautifully they answer so many questions, they could not account for this new observation, and we were left dumbfounded. So, we had to make something up to explain it. That thing we call "dark energy." And here's the kicker: not only does this stuff that no one has ever seen or detected have to exist in order to make our current understanding of physics the full one, this stuff has to make up 68% of the universe. Again: if our current "laws" are correct, this "dark" (so called because it has never been identified) energy must make up the majority of the universe.

That was unsettling for me in college, the idea of spending so much time learning about things that might be absolutely wrong. Certainly, we need to blaze those paths, and go all the way down them, sometimes, before we realize we've taken a wrong turn way back there, but I wasn't sure I was cut out for such a journey, or if I might want to spend my life on Earth in a different way. And then I learned about "dark matter." Just like the unexplainable expansion rate of the universe, it turned out the "law" of "gravity" wasn't holding up so well, either. It still worked great when it came to predicting how fast a feather and a bowling ball fall in a vacuum, but when we started to come up with instrumentation that allowed us to peer ever further into the cosmos, we discovered that the cosmos wasn't working the way our law of gravity said it should. So, we made up more stuff. This stuff, again called "dark" because not a bit of it has ever been detected, needs to make up an astounding 95% of the universe if our mathematical understanding of gravity is correct. 95%. And of the 5% of matter that we do "see" in the universe, well, there's quite a bit we don't understand there, either. For a long time we thought atoms were the smallest bits of the universe. Now we're down to things like quarks. If you want to know what makes up a quark, we're going to need to get into theories. One of the main ones is "string theory," which theorizes that the most fundamental pieces of matter, such as quarks, are made up of vibrating "strings" of energy. And at this point, it gets wildly complicated, and is well beyond the scope of this book. But the bottom line is this: I found out that asking what made a quark a quark, or what made the "string" that makes the quark vibrate, was similar to the conversation with my professor that day about what gravity actually is, in physical terms. Because, once you get past the theoretical math of bewilderingly complicated varieties that takes many years, and some amount of genius, in my opinion, to truly grasp, what we are left with is this: we don't know what makes up a quark, and if it is a vibrating string, we have absolutely no idea what makes the string vibrate.

So, though I loved science, and how it answered all of the questions it did, and is used in all the marvelous ways we use it, I was intrigued even further by the questions it raised. This all left me with an open mind. Though I was skeptical by nature, when I one day watched a video of the "Phoenix Lights," an event in 1997 of an object or objects that thousands of observers saw in Arizona (including the governor of Arizona, he would later admit), and many at what appeared to be a close range, and it was generally treated with national ridicule, I thought, *Well, who knows?* The mainstream scientists weighed in on the impossibility of any form of life reaching us from another star, given the incomprehensible distances it would need to travel. And I understood that argument, but at the same time thought, *But, we don't even know what gravity is. Who is to say what some other intelligence, with, say, a few hundred or thousand or even a million-year head start on us (and given the age of the universe, a million years is inconsequential) could have figured out about travel? And how do we know they travel the way we think of travel? Maybe they figured out how to use the 68% of "dark energy" in some way we can't even fathom.*

Science, to me, was an amazing tool, and I stood (and stand) in awe of how the human intellect has used it. But I also see its limits—or, perhaps *our* limits, is a better way to put it. And that position allowed the door to stay open enough for me to question whether or not the mainstream view that there is nothing outside of the material world is ultimately the truth. After all, the "truth" has shifted many, many times. Science is always at a new precipice of understanding. For me, it was not outside the realm of possibility that we might one day discover new "fundamental forces." Could, perhaps, the consciousness that mainstream science says is simply an emergent property of a material system, actually, instead, be one of those forces? It seemed to me the question remained open. And this was one of the reasons Mr. Sawyer had such an impact on his students: his curiosity was as much ensnared by what we'd figured out, as what we hadn't. He loved to talk about things like the possibilities of "Big Foot" or the "Loch Ness Monster" or ghosts. Once a week, he allowed some time for his class to discuss these "out there" things, and so popular were those chats, that a friend and I eventually approached Mr. Sawyer with a proposition: what about forming an after-school club focused on these weird topics? After all, if there could be a chess club, and Spanish and math clubs, why not a "Phenomenology Club?"

I'm not sure how he got it approved, but he did. So, once a week after school on Wednesdays (which instantly became my favorite day of the week), the Phenomenology Club met to tackle the unknown—UFOs, out of body experiences, spirit photography, "cryptids," you name it. And one week, we took a look at seances and Ouija boards and the various ways people have tried to "contact the dead." Mr. Sawyer brought in an old book which had pictures of people bound to chairs with what looked like cotton coming out of their mouths and ears. Upon inspecting the photographs, one word came to mind: fake. As open as I was to the idea that we are far from having the universe entirely unraveled, these photos were a step too far for me, looking entirely fabricated, and I wondered how uncomfortable it must have been for these "mediums" to keep the cotton in their mouths like this. They called the cotton "ectoplasm," but even with that fancy word (a word I knew from *Ghostbusters*), I concluded, after my short perusal of the photographs, that there was not much worth studying there. The year before our club started, the film *Ghost* had popularized the idea of mediumship. In it, a woman defrauding people by pretending she can communicate with their deceased loved ones, gets the shock of her life when, suddenly, she actually does see a dead person. I loved the film and the idea of surviving beyond death, and being able to come back and help a loved one still on earth was a lovely thought to me. But it seemed that stuff like that happened only in movies—and in old black and white photos that I found extremely suspect:

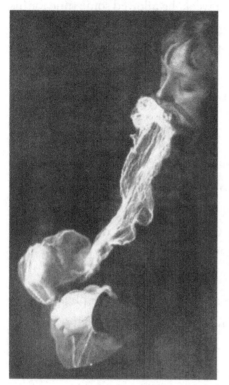 

**ABOVE RIGHT/OPPOSITE PAGE:** Photo(s) from *Jack Webber Physical Medium: The Back Story*, courtesy of Denzil Fairbairn and Saturday Night Press Publications

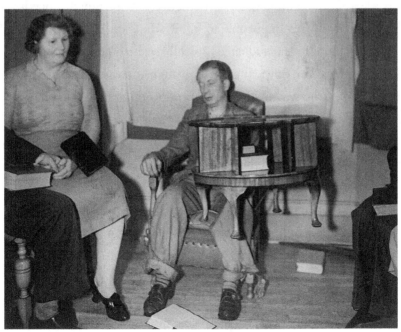

I'd soon find out, though, that it wasn't all just a Hollywood conceit. Mediumship, I'd discover, was a phenomenon that many people claimed was real.

A few years after graduating from high school and leaving the Phenomenology Club behind, a new show premiered on television called *Crossing Over* with John Edward. In it, Edward, a man claiming the ability to receive messages from people on "the other side" in the form of visions, sounds, feelings and smells (much like Whoopi Goldberg's Oda Mae Brown in *Ghost*), gave what he called "readings" to apparently random people sitting in the studio audience. He'd often start by saying something like, "I'm being pulled in this direction," as though some physical force was tugging at him, leading him to a specific area of the audience. Then, he would many times focus his attention on someone, saying, for instance, "I think I'm with you. Do you have a husband who passed?" Usually, the person would say, "Yes," and often tears would almost immediately begin to flow. It was always quite emotional, but though I was intrigued, since it was a television show, it was impossible to know what was really going on. The responses of those in the audience typically seemed genuine and heartfelt, and the information Edward gave was often quite specific, nevertheless, there was simply no way to know how produced the show was. It may have been that they were recording for hours each day, then putting only the highlights into the half-hour episode. I assumed, also, that the producers knew the names of those in the attendance, which I'd guessed they received during the ticketing process. Even though this was before the time of Facebook and social media, it was still possible to learn a lot about a person once you had their billing information, depending upon how much effort you put in. I assumed a television show had enormous resources and could find ways of gathering information about the audience before the show was taped. Still, the often visceral response people had to some of the things Edward said was enough to keep me watching—and keep me wondering.

Eventually, I'd have a chance to put mediumship to the test myself, when after my grandmother's passing, my family set up a sitting with someone who claimed the same ability as John Edward.

My sister, my mom, my aunt and cousin and I met at a woman's office in a small office complex in Connecticut. I'd expected something of the fanfare depicted in *Ghost*—being led to a dim back room where we'd all sit around a table with a crystal ball in the middle, perhaps with Gregorian chants setting the mood. But to my surprise, we entered a room with a drop ceiling and florescent lights and sat around a regular old table, not a crystal or tarot card deck to be found. When the "medium" entered the room, none of the pageantry of Oda Mae accompanied her, as a very nice woman in very average casual clothing sat down. As she spoke, she seemed so "normal." If this woman had said she were a kindergarten teacher, I'd have thought, *Of course she is.* She was kind and intelligent. I'm not entirely sure what I was expecting, but this wasn't it. Who could have guessed Hollywood would have led me astray? When she started to do her medium thing, another blow to my preconceptions was dealt: unlike with the very specific and meaningful messages I'd watched John Edward so often deliver, nothing she was saying made much sense, or if it did, it was something that would have applied to almost anyone. She began by asking generally of the six of us something like, "Does anyone have a female they've lost? It could be a mother or grandmother figure? Or possibly an aunt, or someone who might feel like an aunt?" Of course, all six of us were able to answer "Yes" to that question. At another point, she asked about another female, and when we didn't know who she was talking about, she said, "Or it could be a male that I misinterpreted as a female." At which point I thought, *I think I could be a medium.* She kept looking up and to the side saying, "Yes, thank you . . . I see, thank you," as though she was talking to a person we couldn't see who was apparently providing her with the (incorrect) information. I thought about suggesting she find a better invisible informant, because this dude seemed to be having a rough day. Had there been cameras filming this from multiple angles, as in the *Crossing Over* studio, no amount of editing, it seemed, could have made this session appear very compelling. The final blow for any chance in my mind that this could be a real phenomenon came when my aunt asked her a question about me. The woman claimed not only to be a medium, but also psychic with the ability to perceive future events. At the time, I was making a living as an actor. I wasn't an actor of note, by any means, but I was a member of Actors' Equity Association, the professional actors' union, and doing okay, having just recently moved to New York after graduating from college. My aunt asked, "Do you see anything around theater for Michael?" She looked at me for a moment to "tune in," before saying, "I don't. I don't see like acting or anything like that, or being on stage. I see something like heating and air conditioning . . . like being an air conditioning technician." I enjoy air conditioning in the summer, but that is absolutely all I know about it . . . or have ever thought about it. I said, "Oh, interesting," and then left the session a bit early while my family finished up—I had to drive back to New York as I was due on stage for a play I was in that night.

So, though it was intriguing, to say the least, to get the call from my mom saying that my dad had tried to get a message to us, I couldn't simply accept it at face value. I called Chris and asked him tell me in detail, step by step, what had happened. He spent a long time on the phone with me, explaining the course of events. As I suspected, he said the call to my mom was difficult for him to make, not only because he had no idea how she might react to such a call, but because he was still "in the paranormal closet." He held a job as a hospital administrator, and thought it prudent that those in his professional sphere not know what he did with his weekends. After he finished repeating the same basic story that my mom had, I asked if I could speak with his medium friend who had gotten the message. "Of course!" he said.

As I dialed her number, I tried to formulate what to say. Something like, "I know you told my cousin you 'heard' a message from my father, but after previous experience with people saying they 'hear' stuff like that, I trust you very little" didn't seem like the right thing. Instead, I went with, "Hi, I'm Mike, Chris' cousin." Secretly, what I was trying to ascertain first was this person's mental well-being. At this point, I felt there could be multiple explanations for "mediumship." According to mainstream science and Occam's Razor, the most parsimonious explanation is that people who claim this ability are lying. They may be lying for a multitude of reasons, the main one, as I saw it, being financial gain. John Edward had made quite a nice career out of doing whatever it was he was doing, and the woman who saw my destiny as an air-conditioner repair person charged a few hundred dollars to give me that information. In the case of the woman with whom I was now speaking, however, no money had been exchanged, and there seemed no possibility of it heading in that direction, as Christina practiced her "ability" out of simple interest. The ghost-hunting team she was part of was not a business. "Ghost hunting" was a hobby and they made no money for their efforts. Christina did not give "readings" to people other than friends, and even then, no money was ever exchanged. So, the financial reason for lying seemed to be out—in this case. Another reason someone might lie, beyond using it unscrupulously to profit, I imagined, would be because they felt it was helping people. I could see situations in which people who might truly believe in life after death, or perhaps even not, feel as though what they offer is comfort—how they do that being a secondary consideration. I could understand a person rationalizing their own lying and making money doing so as morally sound, in the sense that they are, indeed, offering a service. People, when faced with grief, are often desperate for consolation, and I could envision a "medium" discovering this "gift" of being able to pick up on subtle cues and developing that ability, then using it to bring comfort to people wanting to believe that their loved ones are still around and capable of delivering messages to them. "What harm," a person might ponder, "in lying about where the 'information' is coming from, so long as the 'information' helps someone feel better? If they get to the end of life and that truly is the end, well then, no one will know the difference, and I would have brought some peace to them while they lived. If life does go on and they discover I'd lied about 'knowing' it does, and 'communicating' with their dead dad, well, they'll be so excited that life actually does go on, they'll surely quickly forget my fib." Christina, I felt, could potentially fall into this category. No, she didn't use what she claimed as an ability to make money, but offering comfort in this way, I could imagine, might feel quite good and even become addicting. A third explanation for mediumship, in my mind, was some form of psychosis. A "medium" might absolutely believe they are hearing voices, and perhaps they are, albeit voices generated in a different way than they believe. Most of us are aware, of course, of the condition known as schizophrenia, which at times, includes the "hearing" of voices. So far as we can tell, and certainly what mainstream science believes is the case, these "voices" are generated by the person's own brain, which, in some way has malfunctioned and turned against them. These voices sometimes suggest terrible things be done, such as harming themselves or others. Evolutionarily speaking, it's difficult to see why this condition would not have been stamped out, since not only is it dangerous to the person suffering from the condition, I imagine it makes it less likely a person struggling in this way finds partners to reproduce with, thereby keeping the genetic instructions passing from generation to generation. Regardless, mainstream science has no doubt that these voices come from nowhere but inside the person's brain. If that is so, why would it not be possible to also "hear" benevolent voices, or voices claiming to be dead people? Christina didn't know it when we spoke the first time, but mainly what I wondered was, *Is this person crazy?*

Moments into the conversation, that option seemed to be out, at least to me. Having had one semester of psychology in college, I am certainly not qualified to make such a determination, but Christina sounded quite "stable," or whatever the correct medical word for "not lacking sanity" is. She seemed intelligent, kind, and compassionate. She talked about how hard it is to lose someone, even when, as she says she does, one believes completely that they have not forever disappeared. She discussed the trauma that can be left by the physical loss. She also seemed uncomfortable with the designation "medium," saying, "I'm not a medium. I just have always gotten very strong feelings." I asked her more about that and how the information comes to her. She told me that she's had these senses for as long as she can remember. She sees pictures in her mind that feel to her as though they were placed there rather than generated by her, and she gets very strong feelings that she perceives as not being her own. After talking for some time about how the experience of mediumship works for her, I asked her to tell me in granular detail what happened when this entity she now believed is my dad (she didn't know who this man was when she first sensed "him") made itself known to her. As she was describing the intense desire this entity had to let his family know he was okay, and how she had been given the image of a fish restaurant and then the name 'Robert,' she said something new: "I keep seeing a big ass, yellow, beautiful butterfly. Like a big, yellow, Monarch. I think this is connected to your mom. He wants to take me to the backyard where this butterfly is, maybe where you or your mom saw this butterfly, and tell you to remember what the feeling of that time in the yard was like. Does that mean anything to you?"

Hmm. Again, I'm guessing that if you're pretending to be a medium, asking about a butterfly might be one of the safer bets. Who hasn't seen a butterfly? Even a "big ass" butterfly—a turn of phrase I found quite charming in my new medium friend. Among the many who have, I bet a large number might be able to suddenly ascribe a meaning to a sighting if given the opportunity. Nonetheless, I felt my heart begin to race. Just a day or so earlier, I'd been going through the pictures I'd taken in the backyard during the "just because" party a few weeks before my dad passed. I'd paused on the photos of the large yellow butterfly that had visited for what seemed like an inordinately long time, and my mom had found great comfort in an accidental picture I'd taken framed by my dad on one side, her on the other, and the butterfly appearing as though it was by her shoulder. And a week before this phone call I was now on, the butterfly had flown down in the subway track and then up by my face, for some reason giving me the nudge to go to work. Though the butterfly in my mom's yard was a Swallowtail and not a Monarch as Christina said (the one in the subway track was a Monarch), her mention of "a big, yellow butterfly" and "remembering the feeling of that time in the yard" was tantalizing, all the same.

As the conversation with Christina continued, she gave generic impressions she'd gotten "from my dad," the main one being, as you might expect, that he loves us and needed us to know he was okay. Obviously, statements like that are not evidential. But her mention of the butterfly was, in that moment, quite striking to me. I knew that the statement would be useless to science, and considered evidence of nothing and no more than a coincidence, but even so, the other part of my brain was quite surprised and couldn't help but wonder, especially when combined with the name 'Robert' she claimed to have heard, and the connection she felt this Robert's family had to a fish restaurant.

After hanging up the phone with Christina, there were two things I'd concluded: this woman wasn't insane, and she wasn't trying to get anything from me. It seemed that she was a kind person who completely believed what she was saying, and though it was somewhat uncomfortable for her, she felt that a stranger without a body was speaking to her and was not going to stop trying to communicate until his message had been delivered.

She was relieved by the time we ended the phone call, since she realized this sort of thing is not for everyone and that some might actually find it upsetting. She had no way of knowing our religious beliefs, either, so she'd been worried about that, as well, as some religions might consider "talking with the dead" less than desirable. That was my overall impression of Christina—she seemed like someone who had found herself in a position that she had no hand in creating. After all, she was called in by my cousin to help with a fish smell so strong they thought it might be "paranormal," and she ended up having this dead guy desperately asking her to deliver a message to a family she didn't know at all. It felt as though Christina went through with the call to me simply because she sensed "my dad" needed her to. I thought about the faces of those people sitting in the audience at *Crossing Over* with John Edward, overcome with emotion at the belief he was communicating with their loved ones. When Christina said, "He's showing me a big yellow butterfly," I had my very first sense of what those people were feeling. The difference was that they'd gone to great lengths to put themselves in a position to get those messages from Edward. If I were to believe Christina, my dad had been the one to go through all of the effort to get the message to us from "the other side." If there were any chance at all that it could be true, even just the tiniest glimmer of a possibility, it seemed it was only fair that next time, I try to meet him halfway. And that next time was about to fall into my lap.

# CHAPTER SIX

# Is There a Manual for This?

In a deep depression and existential crisis of her own, my sister, Jen, drove to work one morning barely able to function. Her radio was tuned to 95.7, a pop station in Connecticut, when she heard, "And now we're back with psychic medium Angelina Diana!" and her breath caught with excitement. In the few months prior to my dad's passing, Jen would occasionally catch this periodically recurring segment that the radio station had on certain Friday mornings with a woman claiming to have mediumistic and psychic abilities. Listeners would call into the show giving only their first names in the hopes of hearing from deceased loved ones, or to ask how likely it is they would find the love of their life, or whether or not they should take the new job they've been offered. This seemed a bit unwise to me, making major life decisions based on what a person who claims to hear voices and predict the future says, but my sister found the "connecting to the other side" portion of the show fascinating and was always glad when she happened to tune in on the ride to work. But on this morning, when the deejay said, "Angelina Diana," my sister sat up. It had been a while since she'd heard the segment, and just a day or two before, we'd gotten the phone call from Chris about his medium friend claiming my dad was desperate to get a message to us. After talking to Christina, I told my sister how nice she was and what she'd said about the "big (ass), yellow butterfly," and that "He wants you to remember that day in the yard," and Jen was intrigued. Hearing this woman now on the radio, just a day or so after I'd spoken with Christina, Jen immediately decided that she would get in touch with Angelina Diana to set up a "private reading." As soon as she got to her office, she found Angelina's website and booked the earliest available date, which was two weeks away.

My sister excitedly called me after she'd made the appointment. This was the first I'd ever heard of Angelina Diana. Jen told me about happening upon her on the radio a few months before our dad passed, and how she found it an attention-grabbing coincidence to have just caught her segment again so soon after we'd gotten the call from our cousin. From everything Jen said, what happened on the radio when Angelina claimed a connection with "the other side" was nothing whatsoever like the experience my family had the only time we'd met with a person claiming to be a medium (the one who foresaw my future in air conditioning). But I had my doubts. I knew now how ferociously people want, and even need, to believe death is not the end. This, after all, is what the "professional skeptics" say is the prime way these "charlatans" make a living—preying on the addled minds of the recently bereaved. Having now lost my own father, I completely understood how that would be possible. However, given the experience we'd just had, where out of the blue, a family member had contacted us with what he believed was a message from a medium, and the follow-up experience I had on the phone with that person when she mentioned the "big yellow butterfly," I was intrigued when my sister called to say she'd booked an appointment with Angelina Diana.

Angelina lived outside of Hartford, CT., and we lived in Guilford, CT., which is about a forty-five-minute drive. Jen discovered on Angelina's website that she does house calls for people living within the state. *Ah ha!* I thought. *Of course, she does! What better way to get information about people? Not only does she have your phone number, but now she has your address, too! With Google, who knows what she could uncover about us with those pieces of information?* Indeed, my sleuthing mind went into overdrive over this detail. And beyond Google, Facebook had become mainstream by that point, as well. It seemed to me that there was an endless amount of information someone could gather if they had your name, phone number, address and the internet. Not to mention private detectives with surveillance equipment—who knew to what lengths these people would go to put on a good show. At the time, I easily swept aside the fact that Angelina also did readings at her house, as well as on the radio once a month where she read for perfect strangers that randomly called in (I'd later investigate this further, spending time at the radio station while Angelina did this, and I learned that they truly were random callers giving just a first name). My mind focused, instead, on the potential avenues for deceit. I'd decided, therefore, that I would need to come up with a way to test Angelina—a way that no amount of internet sleuthing could help with. And a simple solution came to mind: I would choose a code word or phrase, something that I'd ask my dad to get Angelina to say. I would share this code with no one. It would be between my dad and me. I figured if he had somehow been able to produce a fish smell at a second cousin's house so they would call their brother-in-law who was a ghost hunter . . . so he would call his medium friend . . . so she would get him to call my mom . . . which would get me to call him . . . and I'd get him to get her to call me, then surely he could get a medium to repeat a word or phrase that I had suggested. That, I thought, should be easy compared to whatever he had to do the first time around, if any of this is real.

In the meantime, while I tried to figure out what my code would be, my sister was filled with both excitement and great anxiety. The idea of hearing from my dead father was overwhelming to her, but the idea of not hearing from him was far worse. She began to play the various scenarios out in her mind. If this session went the same way our previous meeting with a medium had, the woman who kept thanking her invisible assistant, and who I personally had trouble believing was doing anything "paranormal," Jen would be devastated. The phone call from Chris had offered a reprieve from the crushing grief, as even the slightest opening of the door of possibility that my dad might still be around in some form science can't yet detect was enough to let a bit of light in—a bit of hope. Jen is a highly intelligent, rational person, however, and therefore, she would require adequate proof in order to truly accept the possibility of my dad's continued existence. The "message" delivered by our cousin and his medium friend was certainly intriguing, but we knew that as the days accumulated, the analytical part of our brains would certainly need much more to go on than one mention of a butterfly in the backyard. If that, "much more," did not come through in this meeting with Angelina Diana, this woman supposedly so good at doing what she does that she has a recurring segment on one of Connecticut's most popular radio stations, Jen knew great doubt about my father's continued presence would be ushered in. That thought was enough to cause panic to rise within her. But the other possibility made her just as anxious. If Angelina began to communicate messages she claimed were from my father, and my sister believed they were evidential of his presence, if she believed Angelina was saying things there was no way she could know by any "normal" means, well, my sister feared she might completely lose control of her emotions. An anxious person by nature, this thought made her positively schvitz. So, she was relieved when, the next day, she heard an advertisement on that same radio station for a large event Angelina was holding at a two-hundred seat theater, and some tickets were still available. "Perfect!" my sister thought. She decided to get tickets for her, her husband and our mom. It was open seating, so Jen figured they would go and sit in the back just so she could get a sense of how Angelina works. She thought that if she knew what to expect, it would lessen her anxiety when Angelina came to my mom's house the following week. Since so many people would be at this event, she felt they could easily fade into anonymity and observe the proceedings from afar.

In a "group show," Angelina works in a theater or other large room such as a banquet hall in a hotel, for instance. There can be anywhere from fifty to hundreds of people at these, so the chances of getting a reading are often quite small. People, of course, typically are hoping beyond hope that the medium will turn towards them at some point in the proceedings, praying each time the medium finishes up with one person or family, that they will turn now to them and say, "I'm being pulled over here," as I'd seen so many times on *Crossing Over.* In those large events, however, it often isn't to be. This is especially true in Angelina's case, as she usually spends a good amount of time with each person with whom she interacts, continuing to deliver messages until the "spirit person" stops offering them. So Jen, with a private reading already booked for the following week, had no expectation of getting a reading that evening and, in fact, was counting on nothing happening. Given the level of anxiety she was feeling, the anonymity of the large group brought her the comfort she needed while she investigated Angelina's mode of operation.

When the doors opened, my brother-in-law, Toma, Jen, and our mom filed into the theater waiting for people to choose seats so that they could sit in the back row. As mentioned, most wanted to be as close to the stage as possible, believing that would increase their chances of Angelina coming to them. When they thought the majority of attendees had arrived, my family finally sat down about eight rows back in the two-hundred seat theater. Before Angelina came on stage, more people showed up, meaning that my family was no longer in the last row, with two more rows having filled in behind them. However, Jen felt far enough back and in the middle of a large enough group of people that she was safe from having to do anything other than watch the proceedings and get a feel for what they were like—which made what happened next a moment that would change my sister's life forever.

The morning of the event with Angelina, though Jen had no expectation of getting a reading, and in fact, was hoping to remain quiet and unnoticed in the large crowd, she thought she'd better prepare an experiment, just in case. Given my sister's rationality and intellect, she knew this "medium business" would only be meaningful for her if she could prove to herself, beyond a reasonable doubt, that something out of the ordinary was going on. No simple message of "he loves you" or "he misses you" would do. Jen would need specifics to be provided—specifics that she felt certain no one could be aware of and that were not available anywhere on Facebook or provided in a published obituary, for instance. Even though, in light of the fact that there would be two-hundred people in this theater choosing their own seats, it seemed highly unlikely Angelina could have taken the names on the ticket list, learned all about them via the internet or private detectives or whatever other methods an unscrupulous person might use, memorized all that information and then matched it with the faces she saw in the sea of randomly placed attendees, Jen still wanted further assurances in the unlikely event Angelina should speak to her. So, she devised a simple test. She decided to speak to my dad while alone in her house that morning and ask him to deliver a specific message. She told him that the only way she could be sure it was really him would be if he somehow referenced what she was now going to say. Like me, she decided to come up with a secret message she wanted to hear.

In the immediate days after my dad's passing, I had given my sister a book. This book had been given to me when I was fifteen years old by Mr. Sawyer, the science teacher who'd led the Phenomenology Club. Knowing how desperate I was for answers that science wasn't yet able to provide, one day after school he said, "Here, let me know what you think about this." It was called *Emmanuel's Book: A Manual for Living Comfortably in the Cosmos,* and I read it from cover to cover that night." Among all the books I have ever read, it is the one that has stuck most with me. It was written by a woman named Pat Rodegast, along with her "guide" Emmanuel, whom she "channeled." I had never heard of channeling before, not even among the varied paranormal topics we considered in Phenomenology Club. When someone claims to "channel," I learned, they say they are allowing some other entity to use their body and vocal cords to speak directly to this world from wherever they are. According to Pat, Emmanuel came to her over many years of meditation, at first appearing as a light somewhere off to the side of her line of vision within her closed eyes and gradually coming more center over the years, until finally "he" was right in front of her closed eyes, seen as a glowing light and speaking clearly to her. From there, she first repeated what he said, eventually granting him permission to speak for himself through her.

Obviously, mainstream science would call all of this some form of psychosis. Personally, it sounded strange to me as well, but I trusted Mr. Sawyer's judgement on this sort of thing. I cracked the book open when I got home and didn't stop reading until I'd finished it. Whether this woman was actually "channeling" some "higher" entity, or it was some part of her own brain, the book was beautiful. It was full of humor and what I perceived as wisdom. "Emmanuel" spoke of what human beings are, why we are here, where we came from, and where we're headed. He answered all the big questions each of us have asked, and he did so with a gentleness and joy that was difficult for me to ignore. I came away from the book thinking, *Whether or not this is true, I hope it is.* There was no way to prove any of it, of course, but I found great comfort in the book nonetheless. Since my brain works the way it does, though, I couldn't just leave it at that. I came to learn that the author lived in Connecticut. So one day, a friend and I went to her house to meet her. She was in her sixties, and extremely warm and kind to these two sixteen-year-old strangers who had shown up at her door. She'd probably remind a lot of people of their grandmothers. After inviting us into her living room, she spoke for a while about how she came to "know" Emmanuel and what it was like having him "around." Though she was obviously intelligent, her words didn't quite match the poetry I'd read in Emmanuel's Book. Then, at one point she said, "I'm going to close my eyes for a few moments, and the next voice you hear will be Emmanuel's." When he began speaking, suddenly the poetry was there. We were allowed to ask questions, whatever we might be curious to ask, and he answered on the spot in the same beautiful way he sounded in my head when reading the book. I still didn't know what to make of "channeling," or what part of the brain it might come from, or if, just maybe, it didn't come from the brain, as Pat believed, but was indeed some entity not in a human body. Irrespective of their origin, the messages "Emmanuel" or Pat or whomever spoke that day stayed with me and provided me peace. The main message was that human beings are capable of perceiving only a very small part of a much larger reality. In the same way that magnifying glasses can make clear what our eyes cannot, and microscopes can see what magnifying glasses cannot, the human brain is capable of perceiving only to a certain point. If there were no such things as microscopes and telescopes, we might forever go on thinking and believing that the world was exactly what our eyes said it was. But these new instruments gave us new views. According to Emmanuel, all of human experience is rather like living in a world without microscopes and telescopes, leading us to believe completely that the level of reality we perceive with our senses is the only level of reality there is. Though I had no way of knowing whether anything Emmanuel said through this nice woman was true, the idea that there was more to existence than we currently understood resonated with me. After all, even our science, time and again, has been proven incomplete, and more layers of the onion of physics have been peeled back as our instrumentation gets ever more refined and sensitive. Given that, it was not hard for me to believe it possible that consciousness might be something that exists beyond the borders of our skulls and may have attributes that allow it to be transferred to or registered by other brains. Whether or not any of that was true was obviously well beyond proving and certainly considered absurd by the mainstream science I had learned. In any case, the words in *Emmanuel's Book*, no matter what birthed them, had brought me comfort.

And now, having lost my dad, *Emmanuel's Book* was providing an even greater solace. The gist of the book is that human beings live many lives and often do so in "soul groups" that come back again and again together. The body, he said, is a physical vessel through which we, who are non-physical "spiritual" entities, experience a very focused portion of existence through the lens of the human brain. The brain basically behaves as a filter, allowing only a very small portion of the whole to penetrate. We experience the portion that does get through as being human. "Death," Emmanuel said, is no more than "taking off a tight shoe at the end of a long day," or "walking out of a stuffy room into a perfect spring afternoon." It is the release of the hold of the human brain on our awareness and waking up again to the "greater truth." To think of it another way, when light passes through a prism, it gets divided into its constituent wavelengths as each frequency of light is diverted by the prism at a slightly different angle. Emmanuel might say the human brain acts as a prism which extracts only a part of the whole, allowing it to be separately perceived. "Death" is the dissolution of the prism as the full perception is restored.

Knowing how hard of a time my sister was having, now questioning everything about life and what it could possibly be for, and—like me—wondering if living was worth it if we all simply disappear, I gave *Emmanuel's Book* to her. Unbeknownst to Jen, we were both wrestling with the very same questions. No matter how much *Emmanuel's Book* had soothed me in the past, being confronted directly with these questions with the passing of my dad, it was doing little to assuage my fears. But not knowing how else to help my sister, I gave it to her anyway. Though I didn't know it at the time, she read it and clung to what it had to say. However, she needed more than faith or a feeling in order to believe any of it was actually true. So, on the morning of Angelina's group reading at the theater, Jen said to my father, "Dad, if you are able to get a message to me through Angelina tonight, I need you to tell me that what I am reading in this book, in *Emmanuel's Book*, is true. If I know that this stuff is true and that life goes on and that I will see you again, I will be able to move forward. But you have to tell me that I'm on the right track with this book. That's how I will know it is you, if you somehow get her to reference this book." And with that, her experiment was set. Just in case.

Even with the comfort the large number of people gathered in the theater brought her, still, Jen was on edge. So much of her happiness and well-being, and ability to simply continue on with life, was riding on the idea that death was not the end of life. And in this moment, this woman that she'd been listening to for the last few months on the radio was the greatest chance my sister saw to open that idea up to her as a real possibility. As they sat there waiting for Angelina Diana to come on stage, Jen looked around the audience pondering what these peoples' stories were. She wondered who in that room might be as desperate as she, who, right now in this moment, might be entirely reeling, absolutely thrown perhaps irrevocably off-course by the death of someone they loved without limit, worried that the pattern of energy they knew as their dad or mom or aunt or grandfather or son or daughter was now forever gone. She hoped that lives might be changed that evening. Being the person Jen is, she wanted to see people leave this night with a renewed hope. She wanted to see the tears she could hear forming in the eyes of those she'd heard on the radio clearly visible in that room, as people were given proof that those they loved still loved them back. And then the lights dimmed and it was time.

Angelina walked out on the stage looking as though she was meant for television. Had you seen her coming down the street with her perfectly styled blonde hair, painstakingly applied makeup and piercing green eyes, you might be more apt to think she was an actress rather than a self-professed communicator with the dead. To Jen's relief, when Angelina began to speak, she seemed warm and with a sense of humor. For about twenty minutes, Angelina described what the process of mediumship is like for her. She said that the "spirit world" uses her as a microphone. They are always there, according to her, and always ready to communicate, but to get the signal from "their side" to ours can take great effort, and it's often helpful to get it amplified. "That's where I come in," Angelina announced to the expectant audience. For whatever reason, Angelina says she is able to pick up on the subtle communiques in the form of sounds, strong feelings, visions, smells, and tastes. It's not, however, like simply relaying a message, she explained. She isn't able to hear the departed speak in full sentences. When she does catch sounds, she said it's as though someone is speaking underwater to her. She often gets the beginning sound of a name, for instance. So, if someone's name is Mary, she might hear the "M" and maybe the "r," and simply say, "I'm hearing an M sounding name, like Martha or Maria or Mary." When she sees the images she says the spirit folks share with her, she has to try to interpret what they mean. So, if someone liked to garden, for instance, and wanted to identify themselves in that way, they might show her a hoe. As you can imagine, this process lends itself to miscommunication, and things get lost in translation. (Of course, for a scientist, red flags are currently going up all over the place, as they should). The process of interpretation is not a science, Angelina would say, but an art. She says she has learned to work with the spirit world to use certain symbols that always mean the same thing to her, such as, for instance, if she is shown a carnation, that might always mean someone's birthday is coming up, but most of the time she is trying to figure out on the fly what the images and sounds and feelings she's experiencing are intended to convey. One of the issues here, the skeptics will rightly highlight, is that most people who see a medium desperately want what the medium says to mean something. They want the medium to be right and might quickly start to stretch things to fit in some way that, in reality, they may not—an example of confirmation bias in the extreme. Also, there have been many cases of "mediums" being caught cheating, and one of the ways they are able to do it is that we help them. We might offer up information that the "medium" then uses in some way, perhaps later on after you've forgotten you said it. They might "fish" until we say something that they then drill down on. Going into this situation with Angelina Diana, these things were vaguely on my sister's mind, and she was curious to see if she could detect anything that smacked of fraud. While my sister turned that thought over in her mind, Angelina said, "Okay, I'm ready to begin." Then, she promptly walked from the far side of the stage she was on, over to the side of the theater my sister was on, and pointed right at Jen and said, "I'm with you."

To say my sister was shocked is certainly a colossal understatement. Feeling disguised in the large crowd, having gone there only to get a sense of how Angelina operates, Jen wasn't expecting to get a reading at any point in the evening, let alone right off the bat. Without warning, Angelina was communicating with the other side, and Jen was handed a microphone. Angelina said, sans any preamble, "There is a man standing behind you. Did you lose your dad?" Unable to speak, Jen simply nodded "Yes," then began to rock back and forth in her seat, filled now with extreme anxiety at what was happening. But Angelina didn't pause, saying immediately next, "He's wearing a Red Sox shirt." Now my sister's rocking went to full on convulsions as her husband rubbed her back. Whatever was going on here, it certainly wasn't fishing. Jen had yet to say a word. If Angelina was guessing, the first one she got right was maybe a 1 out of 10. There are maybe ten close relationships a medium who is faking it might guess as the most likely relationships one might be compelled to seek out a medium to contact. You've got son, daughter, sister, brother, husband, wife, mom, dad, grandmother, grandfather. There are also, obviously, aunts and cousins and friends, etc., but these are probably the highest percentage guesses. Taking into account the person's age, a guessing medium might narrow that down. My sister was in her early thirties at the time, so any of those relationships were in the realm of possibility, but were I pretending to be a medium, I might first guess grandparent as the most odds-on chance for a "hit." But Angelina immediately said, "Father." Okay, though still certainly within the realm of possibility of a lucky guess. But what she said next floored my family. "He's wearing a Red Sox shirt." My dad was a Red Sox fan. But not only that, we buried him in a Red Sox shirt. In fact, we buried him in the Red Sox shirt he was wearing on the day of that picnic, the day of the butterfly, and it is what he has on in all of the pictures we'd just been looking at. The odds that guessing "He's wearing a Red Sox shirt" might be meaningful to someone are significantly more difficult to estimate, obviously. He lived in Connecticut, which is a mix of Red Sox and Yankee fans, so I suppose you might hazard that if the guy liked baseball, there'd be a fifty-fifty chance he liked one of those teams. On top of that, in my dad's obituary we mentioned that, "He enjoyed rooting for the Red Sox." I can see a scenario where a person who does this fraudulently for a living might investigate the names of the people who have purchased tickets. It's not unreasonable to think that with some digging, Angelina might have found my sister on Facebook and then tracked down my father's obituary after learning his name somewhere on my sister's page. I find it unlikely that this is the case given the sheer number of people in the audience, but it obviously can't be entirely ruled out. Maybe she had a whole team working on this stuff? Still, to hear, "Did you lose your dad?" followed immediately by, "He's standing behind you in a Red Sox shirt," was stunning in that moment. If those two things were the only two things she said that resonated with us, that would still have been enough to keep me wondering whether or not this could be real and thinking further investigation is warranted. But Angelina wasn't done. She continued, "He tells me he passed very quickly. He says, 'here and gone.' Like he didn't even know it was happening. It's almost like he felt a little dizzy and laid down, like 'I'm just going to rest my eyes for a minute,' and then he was gone, without any pain at all." This piece of information was not in the obituary, nor anywhere online. When my mom and sister found my dad, he was lying on the ground near the doorway of a back room, as though he was on his way to leave the room and go out to the kitchen. His knees were bent up and his hand was up by his head, making it look as though he perhaps felt something was off, then laid down right where he was with his knees up and his hand behind his head. Whatever happened, it appeared as though it had been peaceful and very, very fast. Given the gentle way his legs were positioned and the placement of his hand by his head, no sign of struggle could be discerned. Indeed, they thought, *It looks like he was taking a nap on the floor.* The notion was an important one for us, and in fact, one we clung to unable to cope with the alternate scenario that he might have felt pain and been afraid and was unable to get to the phone. The way it looked to my family, as though he had laid gently down, brought a modicum of deeply needed comfort. So, when Angelina said this, it was very impactful. And the odds that this might be a guess seemed quite small. At this point, as my sister told me the story over the phone immediately following the event on her drive back, I started to think, *Hmm. Now I am truly curious.* But, there was one more piece to the message Angelina claimed was coming from our dad. She said to Jen, "He shows me that you are sort of lost and trying to figure things out. He shows me you reading something. Something like . . . a manual."

A manual. Which sounded a great deal to my sister like, "Emmanuel." And the odds of that . . . well, you tell me.

I'd been at work, which is why I hadn't attended the event, and when my sister called me, I had to lower the volume on my phone. She was screaming—an altogether different scream than the one I'd heard just two weeks earlier. "OH MY GOD. OH MY GOD. YOU ARE NOT GOING TO BELIEVE THIS!!!" she shouted before I could even finish saying, "Hello." After privately asking my dad that morning to let her know that what she was reading in this book, *Emmanuel's Book*, is the way of things, and then hearing Angelina say that afternoon, "He shows me you reading something like . . . a manual," Jen was completely convinced that Angelina was the "real deal." (And recall the book's subtitle actually includes Angelina's words, as its *A Manual for Living Comfortable in the Cosmos*). She would later write to me and say, "In that moment I knew that not only does life go on, but that he is still with me, still nurturing a relationship with me, and that it isn't over for us." In a single moment, a part of her brain filter fell away, her perception of reality widened, and a new hope was born.

Jen had gotten her evidence. And now it was my turn.

# CHAPTER SEVEN

# You Can't Forer Me

When Jen called me, her elation was contagious. For hours afterwards, I felt as though I was floating. These moments, when the border of what we know appears to be breached, offering a keyhole view of a heretofore hidden frontier, can be exhilarating. Suddenly, a universe of possibilities and new questions arise. It feels as though you have been let in on a secret, granted a perspective that the majority of the world is not privy to. I imagined that this must be how Magellan felt when "new" lands came into view and a fresh world, at least to him, was uncovered. Over and over, I replayed what my sister had said. Again and again, I considered what the chances of all of it being luck could be. My first thought was to hire a statistician, but I couldn't find one on Craigslist. And even if I could, I wondered how the conversation explaining what I was looking for would go and how long it would be before they said, "I'm sorry, I have another call."

With or without professional mathematic help, the experience my sister had was enough for me to know I needed to investigate further. The "a manual" moment was the one I zeroed in on. The others, as unlikely as it seemed, could have been the result of luck, or more likely, some sort of cheating. After a bit of quick research, I learned that skeptics who believe there is absolutely no such thing as anything "paranormal," including any form of ESP or telepathy or consciousness existing or having any influence whatsoever outside the confines of the skull, therefore conclude (often before any research is done or even considered) that anyone professing to be a medium must be cheating. To do this, there are two basic methods: "cold reading" and "hot reading." In the cold reading case, which would be considered the more common, the "medium" uses various cues to quickly ascertain information about a "sitter" ("sitter" is the term used for the person the medium is reading—and of course, the term "reading" lends itself to the interpretation that the medium is looking for clues, "reading" the book that is the person. If mediums had agents and I was one, I'd advise my clients to change this word). The "medium" will use any visual cues they can gather, such as age, clothing, jewelry, accessories, body language, etc, as well as things like, for instance, accent or use of language and manner of speaking. The medium, who again, a skeptic believes *must* be lying, since that is in their view the *only* possibility, might be someone who is more adept than the average human (and with much less aversion to deceit) at quickly picking up on a great deal about a person. After acquiring that information, they then start "reading" the person, making high-probability guesses, such as the medium that said to my family, "Does anyone here have a female they've lost? A mother or grandmother figure, or an aunt?" And though that might seem a silly question to us, I have myself experienced the urge to give the medium the benefit of the doubt and say, "Okay, I do have a grandmother who passed, so let me see where this goes." Psychologists have a term for why cold reading mediums might be successful: The Forer effect. A psychologist named Bertram Forer tried an experiment in 1948 in his psychology class—an experiment still carried out today on college campuses every year. He asked his students to "reveal their personalities" by filling in missing words in a series of phrases. A week later, he gave each of his students a summation of their personality, "tailored to their results." He asked the students to rate the accuracy of the summation on a scale of 1 to 5, and the average rating from the class was 4.26 (an average that holds to this day when the test is given). The class was amazed at what their professor had done by simply using the words they filled in to gain so much insight regarding them. But in reality, Forer didn't even look at the students' answers on the personality test he'd administered. Instead, he took an astrological reading out of a magazine and gave it (the same one) to every student. And yet, even though each student was reading the same thing, a random horoscope, the vast majority believed it was written specifically for them, quite surprised by the "accuracy," which seems to indicate that human beings are prone to taking vague and general statements and applying them to ourselves. Because the statements are vague, we quickly begin to interpret our own meaning, and we take that "meaning" to indicate that the medium is accurate, rather than simply looking at the words he or she said. What sticks with us are the specific meanings our brains very quickly generate from the general statement, not the statements themselves, and this creates the illusion that the medium is being far more accurate and specific than they actually are. Combine that with confirmation bias (which is an established tendency to recall and highlight things that we already believe, and easily dismiss things that might go against those beliefs), and it becomes easy to see why human beings might be duped by a person claiming "supernatural" abilities. A medium doing cold reading might be adept at picking up on whether or not what they say is a "hit" based on the sitter's reactions. If they find they have said something that resonates (often easy to do in what can be a very emotional circumstance where tears might flow), they keep heading in that direction. If something doesn't hit, they move quickly on. Given what we've discussed above, we see that it is then common for people to remember the hits and dismiss the misses.

The human brain is capable of extraordinary things. We know there are rare cases where a brain functions in ways the average one doesn't. For instance, you may have heard of the condition where a person is able to recall literally every moment of their lives. I remember seeing some people on *Oprah* who have this, and I was stunned. I don't remember the day of the week I saw the episode, or even the decade, let alone the amount of cloud cover that day. But the people featured on the episode would. You can ask, "What was the weather like on April 3rd, 1988?" and they will be able to tell you. A quick check of the almanac reveals that they are indeed correct. And they don't just remember April 3rd, 1988, in general: they remember every minute of that day—literally every moment of that, and every single day. So, they can tell you not just the weather for that twenty-four hour period, they can tell you whether or not rain was falling on their purple shirt and blue jeans at 2:17pm that day, while they stood outside being handed a letter from Ray the mail person who'd just come back to work after having his baby named Alfred after his wife's grandfather. A person whose brain works in this way is not someone you want to have an argument with. Personally, I've "won" many an argument by both of us forgetting exactly what was said or done.

There are people with autism who have abilities the majority of us cannot fathom, such as being able to instantly perform complex mathematics without paper or pen or the aid of a calculator. There is a condition known as synesthesia, where the sensory pathways get crossed. Some people, for instance, will hear a different note of music depending on what color they are looking at, or the texture of a surface will cause them to see an image, etc. The variations of the condition are many. There are kids who can play Beethoven at three years old and some who have advanced scientific insight long before it's been taught to them. None of these things are considered to be "paranormal." Though they aren't all entirely understood, they are thought to be properties of rare brain function we'll someday figure out. So, who is to say that a "medium" might not be someone whose brain picks up subtle cues about a person's body language or vocal cadence, or how their pupils dilate in a way the average brain does not allow? To me, this has to be considered a possibility in each individual case.

So, that's a little bit about "cold reading." The other, more simple deceitful practice is known as "hot reading." In this case, the medium somehow gathers information before the reading. They may use, as discussed, the internet, private investigators, or other means. For instance, if a medium is giving a group event at a theater, such as the one my sister went to, they may have people working for them seeded in the crowd in the lobby, overhearing conversations, then relaying the information to the medium before the show begins (and in this case, "show" is indeed the right word). The medium is given a few bits of information about a number of people and then might use cold reading to fill in. You can see this dramatized in the film *Leap of Faith* where Steve Martin plays a conman posing as a preacher who gets "supernatural" information, when in reality, his assistants are feeding him details via an earpiece.

Recently, a story appeared in the *New York Times* in which a medium was caught cheating in a sting operation called "Operation Peach Pit." Over many months, even years, the organizers of the sting created fake Facebook accounts. They regularly posted to these accounts, in effect creating fake people with fake histories. Then, they bought tickets to a medium's show under those fake names. And when one of them was called on by the medium, it was quite clear he had used those Facebook accounts to gather information about people who had purchased tickets. Every "accurate" thing he said was a piece of fabricated information they'd recently planted on the Facebook page of the created person and their created life.

So, we know this stuff has happened and still happens—which is why the idea that you could ask a disembodied person to deliver a specific message, as my sister had done, was immediately latched onto by me. This was a simple way to rule out any type of fraud that I could think of. I could not see any way cold reading had been involved. I mean, what kind of a visual cue does someone need to give for a cold reading medium to pick up on the fact that the person wants to hear about a book they are reading, let alone the name of it? And hot reading was also out as a possibility. Jen had asked my dad to say something highly personal, and that was published nowhere. No amount of internet sleuthing, or going through trash or hiring of private detectives would make a difference in this case. This was a single piece of information known only to my sister. Until after Angelina said, "He sees you reading . . . a manual," she had shared it with no one. Given the apparent success her message request met with, it meant tests could be devised, controlled experiments that should be able to tell us concretely, it seemed, whether or not this was an actual phenomenon. Since Angelina was scheduled to come to our house the following week, I'd be able to casually carry out a personal experiment myself. If my father was truly able to get Angelina to say such a specific thing, and this wasn't a case of coincidence combined with confirmation bias, I saw no reason he shouldn't be able to do it again. Our science requires replicability. Until something is proven to happen again and again, mainstream science won't consider it. "Anomalies" are persona non grata in science, no matter how meaningful they might seem to an individual or individuals. To establish objective reality, science says it's got to happen again. And I was going to need it to happen again too.

I set out to find my word or phrase—my "code." It would be something specific, that only I knew. I decided I wouldn't even share it with my family, as my sister hadn't. This would be only between me and my supposed disembodied dad. If this process is real, the process of interpretation that Angelina describes, I didn't want the code to be a muddy one. I wanted it to be something simple, preferably a single word. For the whole week I thought about it, and on the night that Angelina was scheduled to arrive, I still hadn't settled on it. After all, so much was riding on this. Following my sister's life-changing experience, a hope was born in me. After being in a deep well of despair, I began to see some light. The call from Chris had provided the first glimmer, but the experience my sister had was a spotlight. I felt myself climbing out of the hole I was in. But I also knew it was a tenuous climb, fraught with pit-holes, and with any misstep I might easily slide back. As striking as "a manual" was to me, my mind kept stepping in to say, "But what if . . ." and I couldn't really finish that sentence. I suppose the only "what if" would be that it hadn't happened the way my sister thought it did—that she'd either forgotten something or her broken heart embellished what she heard and it wasn't supernatural at all, but merely a case of a combination of factors coming together to create the illusion of something astonishing and paranormal. Feeling the whispered tugs of that pelagic and bottomless anguish any time these thoughts crossed my mind, I'd carefully go over the facts again. One thing I knew without question was that the facts were clear to my sister and they'd absolutely altered her sense of reality. She knew exactly what code word she had decided on that morning, and Angelina definitely said, "He sees you reading . . . a manual." My mom and brother-in-law heard Angelina say that, as well (not knowing, at the time, why it had thrown my sister into near hysteria). So, I held on to those two facts, and any time my brain tried to lessen their consequence, I recalculated the odds of that sentence being said by chance. But to really be sure, I would need to be the one, the only one with the secret code, and Angelina would have to say it to me.

The day of the reading finally arrived. Jen and I spent it at my dad's as we continued to go through and organize his things. For most of the day, I pestered Jen with question after question about her experience the week before. I wanted to hear every particular of it again. While we continued to pack up my dad's physical life, I grilled her. "So, she came to you first. Did she point at you, or just say, 'Does someone over in this area have a father who passed?' What was the very first thing she said after she pointed right at you? Her exact words? Did you say anything at that point? Show me what she did when she said she saw him reading a manual. You said she mimed flipping pages. Show me that. Are you certain you had said nothing at all to that point about a book or reading or being lost? Are you sure she immediately said, 'I see your dad behind you. He's wearing a Red Sox shirt'? Were those her exact words?"

I continued to probe with query upon query and Jen enjoyed answering them, as it provided her an opportunity to relive the experience. To her, there was no way this was anything other than my dad reaching out to her from beyond the grave to let her know he still existed. Meanwhile, my dad was about to speak to us in his own, heart-breaking words—words we were extremely surprised to find.

Deep in a closet behind all of his old clothes, we found a metal box. In it were pictures of days gone by when he was a little boy with his mom and dad. It soon became clear that this was his "treasure box," holding within it some of the physical possessions he most prized. Of the greatest interest to my sister and me was a poem in his handwriting. Composed in rhyming couplets, it was almost too painful to read. As mentioned, my dad was not the type to express himself verbally and poetic prose was included. Though he was made of a love too deep and beautiful to fathom, it was not one he aired in flowery language. So, it really threw us to find a poem that he'd written, even before we fully grasped its meaning. And once we understood its content, well, the emotions elicited by his precious, private penmanship from long ago were overwhelming. The poem had clearly been put to paper sometime after my parents separated, but before they'd gotten divorced. It was my dad's last-ditch effort, it seemed, to clearly express how deeply he loved my mom and us, and how he'd hoped we'd all always be together. Every cross-out I came upon, as I felt my dad, a twenty-five-year-old kid, searching for the absolute perfect word, the word that would bring my mother back to him, broke my heart. The poem was stunningly beautiful. It was honest and pure. In the twenty lines on that page, my dad, and who he was, was laid bare.

Given the cross outs, Jen and I figured it must have been a first draft he'd written before making the final version he most likely gave to our mom. And the thought of him handing her this poem, this piece of paper on which he'd cracked open his heart and let it spill, was gut-wrenching. Jen and I knew that during that time in my mom's life, she was head over heels in love with a new man. Looking at the world in the skewed way the thrill of a new relationship offers, she could feel only the excitement of what was to come, and would have been unable to process the pain of the one she was leaving behind. We almost all know what that is like. But the thought of my dad putting himself out there in this way and having it be dismissed was a notion that could break me if I let myself think on it for too long. What my dad could not have known, of course, all those years ago when he penned those lines, was that the woman he was writing to, though unable to receive his love at the time, would one day realize that he was indeed, her "soulmate." He would not have imagined that there would come a time in the distant future, as his body lay limp on the ground, that same girl whose love his poem would not win back, would for hours hold his cold hand and run her fingers through his hair, and wail and sob and think herself unable to go on at his passing.

Because my mom was so utterly distraught, my sister and I decided we would not give her the stinging relic we'd found, thinking it would be the thing to push her grief over the edge and threaten her sanity. Besides, since he'd clearly given her the finished version years ago, we didn't think bringing it back up now was necessary. So, we placed it back in the treasure box and continued the difficult process of wrapping up our dad's life. In just a matter of hours, Angelina would be arriving, and I would have my own conclusion as to whether or not "wrapped up" was the correct way to look at it, and whether these crushing words my dad had written all those years ago on this now fragile page would be the ones he left us with.

As evening neared, my excitement and nervousness continued to grow. After witnessing what Jen's experience had done for her psychological state, and me getting a "contact high" just from hearing her story over and over, I wondered how I'd be able to contain my emotions should this evening go anything like hers had. So many thoughts were bumping into each other in my mind. I wanted so badly for the night to go well, given how my sister's life had been changed. If I were to detect some sort of cheating, I didn't think I'd be able to share it with Jen. *How could I possibly say anything that might negate her newfound sense of a larger reality?* At the same time, I needed to know that she could not be cheating. Knowing how my obsessive compulsive mind works, if I did not have some sort of ironclad evidence that this woman was getting information in a way that the greatest and most careful scientist in the world would have to agree was out of the ordinary, I knew that I'd eventually end up doubting things, no matter how much the scale seemed to tip at the time towards a genuine ability of some kind.

As the hour of Angelina's arrival approached, I still hadn't settled on the code word. With just forty-five minutes before the scheduled sitting, I realized I had left my phone at my dad's house. Since we were meeting with Angelina at my mom's house only a few minutes away, I drove back to retrieve it. It was time to pick the word that would hold such power, either to devastate or elate. As I stood alone in my dad's garage and looked around at the remnants of his life, it came to me. My parents had gotten divorced when I was about three or four and they split custody. We spent the weekdays living with our mom, and the weekends with our dad. He didn't have much money, so after the split he'd moved back into his parent's house. There wasn't a bedroom for him, so he stayed on the couch in my grandmother's living room, and on Friday and Saturday nights, my sister and I would sleep on the floor beside him. It was sometimes hard to fall asleep on those nights. The novelty of the situation hadn't worn off, and we were just so excited to be with our father. To help us calm down and slip into slumber on the bunched-up quilts, my dad would play with our hair—something I'm sure he wished he'd not started, because we never let him stop afterwards. Every weekend, until his hands were positively cramped up, he'd play with our hair. "Five more minutes, Dad," was my constant refrain. "Five more minutes." And he never stopped until I was fast asleep, no matter how many hours of five minutes it took.

That memory had come back to me with force. So, alone in the garage of my dad's house, which stands on a back-lot in the middle of the woods in Connecticut, I said, "Okay, Dad. This is it. This is the deal. If you are really there tonight, if this woman is actually able to pick up on spirits, I want you to have her mention my hair." Not only was the code word "hair" connected to a deeply personal memory that had just unexpectedly flooded my brain, but it served another purpose, too: my hair is exceedingly ordinary. It's not in any way a feature one would use to try to describe me. Just thoroughly average, brown hair. A person pretending to have mediumistic powers would have no reason to think, "Oh, there's got to be a story about this dude's do." So, I decided that if this woman in any way referenced it, said the word "hair" to me, I'd know my dad was still around, and all that stuff that was him hadn't simply evaporated. I was willing to allow it in any context, too. She could ask me about the hair on a rabbit I don't have and I'd take it. She could even talk for ten minutes about the rabbit I don't have, being wrong about the nonexistent rabbit's name, it's color . . . how it had a funny hop. Whatever. For my personal experiment, I decided I didn't care what the context was. I just wanted to hear the word "hair" somehow directed at me. The fake bunny couldn't belong to any of the others in the room and she'd have to specifically reference bunny's hair. And, by the way, there would be others in the room.

When my sister set up the appointment for Angelina to do a "house call" at my mom's, all Angelina wanted to know was where to meet and approximately how many people would be attending, as her pricing fluctuates based on the number of participants. She did not ask for anyone's name (including my sister's) so, all my sister told her was the address of my mother's house and that there would be "4-6 people attending," as she wasn't sure yet if a friend of ours and her sister might come. This range of people was fine with Angelina, and she asked nothing further about who the people were or how they might be related (or not). Which meant that Angelina did not know I was going to be there. However, given an address and the internet, finding the name of the owner of that address seems quite possible. Once you have that name and Facebook (Facebook was the main social media platform at the time and my mom had just created an account, though very rarely used it), one can imagine much information might be garnered about a family. Not knowing anything about Angelina at this point, I had to allow for all possibilities, even if it seemed they were unlikely. So, of the six people who ended up attending, let us suppose, for argument's sake, that Angelina used the address and the internet to find my mother's name, and used that to find out on Facebook that my mom had two daughters and a son, and that one of the daughters was married. At this time, my mom had not designated any family members connected to her on Facebook, as she was using the platform in the most rudimentary way back then, but again, we're considering Angelina was able to gather all of this information just to cover all angles. So, we'll assume that when my sister greeted her at the door and she walked into the room, she knew by face, my mom, my sister, my sister's husband, and me. On top of that, Angelina had given Jen that stunning reading just two weeks earlier. Though Jen said nothing about it when Angelina arrived, and Angelina showed no recognition of Jen, it is entirely possible she could have recognized Jen's face. In fact, if Angelina was a cold reader, she might be expected to be adept at paying close attention to faces and the cues they may inadvertently display, and to have a rather good memory, which a person posing as a medium might use to bring bits of information up later in a reading that you, the sitter, have forgotten you may have subtly offered. So, let's assume that Angelina had done all the internet research she could, finding names and birthdays and seeing, perhaps, family photos, and that she recalled giving Jen a reading two weeks earlier at the theater, and remembered all of the "hits" she'd gotten then. That covers four of the six sitters. What she could not have been prepared for, however, were the other two—my sister's friend Amie, and Amie's sister, Sara. There would be no way Angelina, using only my mom's address and name, could have connected Amie and Sara to her. Not in any way that I can fathom. My mom and Amie were not connected on Facebook, and though Amie and I were, there is no reason to think, out of the hundreds of random "friends" I am connected to, that Angelina would have singled her out to learn all about her and what departed person she might be hoping to hear from. Unless, of course, we allow for the possibility that Angelina's brain works in one of the extraordinary ways we discussed earlier. Perhaps she has an eidetic (or "photographic") memory and was able to look through every contact I and my sister and mom have on Facebook and memorize at least the recent posts from their pages, or go through their photos. Again, this is highly unlikely given the low frequencies with which things like photographic memory occur, but for this scenario, let's allow for that. So, Angelina theoretically could have known the names, birthdays and interests of all six of us, and the fact that my dad had passed, depending on what was on social media. She also could have had access to my dad's obituary, which listed his children, grandchildren, devotion to the Red Sox, and the fact that he worked for many years for FedEx (it did not include anything about how he died). So, for me, any information publicly available would have to be discounted as proof. Given how I felt about the unlikeliness of her having done this sort of research, or having the sort of memory she'd need in the case of Amie and Sara, if she hit on the fact, for instance, that my dad was a delivery man, it would probably still provide an exhilaration for me and make me even more intensely curious about how it was happening, but it certainly could not be considered ironclad evidence by any means. The only "control" I had on the evening was the one bit of information I'd privately asked my dad to deliver that I knew there was absolutely no way for Angelina to know.

When she arrived a few minutes late, she apologized saying she got stuck in traffic. And, of course, I silently said to myself, *Didn't you know there was going to be traffic? Not a great psychic, so far.* I let that thought go, though, and did my best to figure out who this woman was as a human being. Did she seem like the kind of person who would take money from grieving people while peddling lies about her "communication" with their loved ones? This, obviously, is an entirely subjective piece of the puzzle, absent polygraphs (which, of course, are far from foolproof themselves). And truth be told, I didn't know what a person who did that would look like. I guessed they'd look like everyone else, which is what makes them so good at it. They probably didn't dastardly twirl their mustache with their fingers and laugh in a cartoonish way. Angelina had no mustache to twirl, but she seemed quite nice.

I paid a great deal of attention to what she was focusing on, at least with her eyes. *Was she examining the house? Did she look for photos on the refrigerator?* (There were none, because I'd removed anything I thought she might be able to get easy information from). But when in someone else's house, a person can get a lot of information in other ways. *Was she going to ask to use the bathroom where she might quickly rifle through the medicine cabinet? Would she ask for a tour? Would she want to chat for a while?* To me, it did not seem as though she was attempting to gather information before we started, either by speaking with us or carefully inspecting the house. Instead, we immediately went into the living room where we'd set up places to sit in a circle and she began. She went through the same opening talk that she gave when Jen saw her at the theater where she explained a bit about what she does and how she does it. One of the things that caught my attention was that she wanted us to "say only yes or no," if she asked a question. She said people have a tendency to offer up more information, and once that happens, that information obviously can't be used for "validation." So, for instance, if she said, "I have a male here who fell off a horse, does that make sense?" She wanted us only to say, "No," or "Yes," not "Yes, that was Sandy when we were at my grandmother Martha's farm." If the answer was "No," she said she would then try to ask for more information and clarification from "the other side" to figure out what they were getting at. So, that was a plus for me. She told us she was an "evidential medium," meaning she relied on that evidence to prove she was doing what she said she was. Therefore, she said she wanted no information to come inadvertently from us—which was why she insisted on us responding with nothing but a "yes or no." For our own peace of mind, she said, she wanted us to be certain later on, should we get information we considered to be evidential, that we had not given it to her. She was aware of the things skeptics say, and she wanted to do whatever possible to assuage any skeptics that might be in the room. That was good to hear. In the negative column she said, "And if something doesn't make sense, just keep it in mind. Spirit will bring up things that have happened, are happening, or might happen in the future." I thought, *Well, that would seem to make your job pretty easy, if all you have to do is say, "If you don't understand, it just means it hasn't happened yet."* But, for the most part, I had a positive feeling about her after hearing her speech. She seemed like an empathetic woman (she talked a lot about grief and what it does to us) who hoped she could offer "at least some comfort by being a microphone for your loved ones." At this point, if she were lying, I felt she might be the sort who'd convinced herself she was doing it to be helpful.

After about ten minutes of explaining what she does and how we should respond, Angelina asked, "Does anyone have any questions?" We told her we didn't, and she said, "Okay, I'm ready to begin." I took out my notepad, and prepared to record our session. And within seconds, I realized this was going to be an experience unlike any I'd ever had, and that my steady, scrutinizing, scientific wits would be seriously challenged.

She started by immediately telling my mom that her parents were "stepping forward." My mom was in her late fifties at that time, so it's a fairly good bet that one or both of her parents might have passed. However, unlike the experience we had with the first medium all those years ago who spoke almost entirely in generalities that could apply to many, if not most people, Angelina began to tell us about the personality of the person she was sensing. This was interesting, because certainly none of this information could have been available to her in any "normal" way. She talked about the sort of people both of my grandparents were and what their relationship with my mom was like. However, there were also things said that were not correct, such as "Did your mom like crossword puzzles?" As far as we knew, she did not. And if she did, it was certainly not an identifying feature about her, the way it might be if I was talking about Stanley on *The Office*. Chances are, if you and I were discussing *The Office* (and we both knew the show), as soon as I mentioned "crossword puzzles," Stanley would enter your mind. If my grandmother was really in that room, out of body, trying to identify herself, saying "crossword puzzles" would be an odd way to do it. Angelina also asked if my grandmother "had many pairs of glasses?" And, again, she did not. However, the rest of what Angelina said about both of my grandparents was accurate. She got a number of factual, easily verifiable things correct, such as discussing how much my grandmother "loved to cook," (this was a big part of my grandmother's life). However, considering that my mom is of a certain age, one might guess that cooking would have been a big part of my grandmother's life. At that time, there were not a large number of women working outside of the home, and emphasis was placed by society on women being able to cook while the boys "brought home the bacon."

Angelina also said that my grandfather "worked with his hands," (he worked for my stepfather's carpentry business. Of course, if my grandfather had spent his life in an office wearing a shirt and tie and trading equities, and Angelina said, "He worked with his hands," it's entirely possible my mind would have gone to the fact that he liked to garden, for instance, and still considered it "a hit." Again, we must remain ever vigilant of the Forer effect).

She correctly stated the ways they each passed, noting that my grandmother was "sick for a long time, her passing was a long ordeal." My grandmother had Alzheimer's disease, and indeed her passing was a drawn-out process. She said my grandfather had "a lot of indigestion" and "ultimately passed because of fluid in his lungs." Here, too, she was correct. Beyond these "yes or no" facts, she also spent quite a while speaking about the personality traits of my grandparents and the different relationships each had with my mom. This stuff is more subjective than "he died because of fluid in his lungs," but my mom found it all remarkably accurate. She said things to my mom like, "Your mom says she is glad you got tough on her about doing what she needed to do when she was sick." My mom saw this as true. She did what she had to do to help my grandmother's life be as pleasant as possible, including getting her to take her pills and go to her doctor appointments, and she often bathed her. My mom had my grandparents move into her house for the last few years of their lives, so she was a primary caregiver to my grandmother for quite a while.

Angelina also said, "Your parents left you on your own to make decisions. You had to be independent." My mom saw this as referring to the fact that she had to put herself through college, as this was simply not something my grandparents pushed, or even discussed. My mother became a nurse only after somehow putting herself through college while having two children and a full-time job with no financial help from anyone. She did it "independently" indeed, and again, my mom feels this as a major aspect of her life and who she is.

As all of this was going on, I wondered how Angelina could have gotten this information. *Is it possible she found my grandparents' obituaries? If so, could this information have been gleaned from them?* But at the same time the knee-jerk skeptical part of my brain posed this question, another part of me knew that some of this highly personal stuff would not be found in any obituary or published anywhere else. So, if Angelina was faking "mediumship," I surmised that what I was witnessing right then must be a mixture of research and luck. *Some of this stuff she must have been guessing at, hoping the Forer effect would connect the dots, if not gathering it in a "paranormal" way.* There were ways, certainly, to make the guesses "educated." For instance, it would have been a good guess, based on the time period, to ask, "Was your father in the service?" Many, if not most guys that were around my grandfather's age were somehow in the service (this was not something she mentioned, however). Once a guess like this is made and the answer is "Yes," the sitter, I personally found, very quickly starts to help the medium, in a sense, trying to make the other pieces that might not be so accurate fit. For example, having gotten that my grandmother "loved to cook" and then accurately describing how she passed, I found myself going back to the comment about the crossword puzzles and thinking, *Well, maybe she meant just "puzzles," and Angelina misinterpreted the type.* Our brains, as we discussed, can quickly start to make allowances and draw connections where none actually exist—especially if we so badly want a particular something to be true. Confirmation bias is a powerful thing and I was already noticing it in myself—five minutes into this sitting with a medium. But I was at least aware of it, and I tried my best to remain hyper-aware of what Angelina was doing and saying and how my brain was reacting to it. Overall, by this early point of the reading, I knew I'd need to do more research. And I was already planning readings with other mediums (if I could find any—*How common are these folks?* I wondered), where I'd plug the holes I was now noticing, such as the potential for a person to do research if they have an address. The next medium I'd see would have only my first name, a fake last name, and a new email address connected to that fake name that I'd already picked out in my mind, when Angelina said to my mom, "Your mom and dad have a younger male energy with them, and he is now stepping forward."

My heart instantly began to race. But not nearly as fast as it soon would.

# CHAPTER EIGHT

# Holy Shirt

"This younger male energy comes across as being like a son to them—not necessarily their actual son, but he feels like a son to them, and he, this younger male, has great respect for them. It's like, he has been waiting and waiting to come through, but such is his respect for these two people, your mom and your dad, that he wanted to let them go first. There is a "b" connection to him, like "Bob.""

That is how Angelina introduced the third "spirit" she claimed to be sensing. As she calmly related these messages to us, often looking at the floor or gazing straight ahead, as though she was seeing something in her mind's eye, my system was thrown into an adrenaline induced haywire. Wanting to show no emotion, to give nothing away to her (even though she wasn't looking at me, *Who knows, maybe one of her little understood "superpowers" isn't just a photographic memory, but tremendous peripheral vision?* I thought), I sat still, while internally I was vibrating at an ever-increasing rate. And when she said, "Bob," which happened to be my dad's name, my mind and heart began to race out of control. I needed to consciously begin to breathe more slowly and focus on writing down what she was saying. My mom, on the other hand, was having no trouble giving absolutely nothing away. Perhaps tainted by the experience we'd had with the other "medium," she had been taking everything Angelina said with a stoicism so pronounced that I actually felt uncomfortable. At one point, Angelina said something about my grandmother, and my mom responded, "Well, I'm not sure. I guess that could be true." And in that moment, I felt awkward for Angelina and jumped in to say, "Mom, yes, that is definitely true." And my mom thought for a moment and then conceded, "Yes. Okay. I see what you mean. That's true, yes."

As Angelina moved on to this next spirit that, of course, everyone in the room was assuming was my father, my mom's resolve to not be bamboozled became even greater. She offered no smiles or indications of recognition, instead just staring straight at Angelina. My sister, though, was not as good at concealing what was happening internally, which I realized at the mention of "Bob" when I looked up at her to see tears coming to her eyes. After Angelina asked, "There is a 'b' connection, like 'Bob,' does this make sense?" It was my sister who said, "It does." Angelina then immediately added, "He passed very unexpectedly and very quickly. He's telling me he was here and then gone. He's saying it came out of nowhere. He didn't realize there was anything seriously wrong with him. He says he was not the type to go to the doctor. And he wouldn't have shared with anyone if he was feeling off anyway, because he would never want to worry anyone. This is an extremely loving man." And at this point, Angelina became a bit emotional as I saw tears form in her eyes. She didn't speak for a moment as she looked up at the ceiling, then said, "I'm sorry, this doesn't usually happen to me, I'm sort of detached when I receive these messages, but his love is sort of overwhelming." She wiped her eyes and then looked at my mom, saying, "He is telling me how sorry he is about the way you found him. He was there, and he felt all of the craziness that was going on, and he knows how unbelievably upsetting it was."

At this point, we had said nothing to Angelina about who exactly this "Bob" was, or how he might be connected to anyone in the room. The only words we'd so far offered were from my sister, her simple answer to Angelina when she'd asked "Does this make sense?" And Jen responded, "It does." So, my mind was entertaining endless questions. If this had all been fake, it would mean Angelina had somehow gathered from whatever research was available connected to my mom's address, that my mom had lost an ex-husband named Bob (who she hadn't been married to for thirty years). As we've discussed, the possibility exists that she could have used my mom's name (discovered through her address with a bit of effort), to then connect her with my sister and me, and through us discover my dad's obituary. From that, she would have obviously known his name, his job, that he liked the Red Sox, and that he loved his children and grandchildren. The obituary said absolutely nothing about how my father passed, nothing at all, and did not mention my mom. From that, if one were faking this stuff, one might guess that my mom and this man she'd divorced all those decades ago were not very close other than through the connection of their grown children. To fake the "stepping forward" of my father, and then look at my mom, rather than the two people in the room appropriately aged to be his children (or the faces of the people she knew were his children through pictures on Facebook), would be an odd choice it seemed, for a fraudster. Moving straight to my mom, a woman he'd been divorced from for thirty years and who was not mentioned in his obituary—unlike the names of his parents, his kids and grandkids—would seem to be a low-probability move. And if she had recalled the reading she had given my sister two weeks earlier, she would have already known that my sister was a high probability (and emotional) target (that reading, by the way, had happened from approximately forty feet away—Angelina never left the stage, so my sister was a face in a crowd, from her perspective—not ideal for picking up on subtle cues). So, why focus first on my mom? There could be no reasonable way for Angelina to be aware of the unique relationship my mom and dad had—that they had somehow remained friends even after all of the pain, and that though she has been married for thirty years to the man she left him for, she never stopped loving him, and in fact, now considered him to be her "soulmate." There is absolutely no way Angelina could have known my mom would have "found him there," or that there would have been "craziness" happening around her. The obituary said nothing whatsoever about the fact that my dad had passed unexpectedly at home, that he hadn't shown up for work, that a coworker had gone to his house to check on him given how unusual that was, that the coworker called the police, and that when my mom arrived and was the first to find him on the floor, the police and paramedics were canvasing the house, attempting to make certain no "foul play" might be involved, as this rather young man lay inexplicably dead on the floor, almost as though he'd fallen asleep there. And beyond accurately hinting at the situation my mother had been in, something else that struck me was the way Angelina reacted to the information herself. When she paused while looking at the ceiling, her eyes becoming wet with tears, then eventually apologizing for becoming emotional, as an actor myself I thought, *If she is faking this, she could easily have a second career. Her response was a subtle one. It was only because I had been scrutinizing her every move that I even noticed why she was pausing in the moment. It was clear to me that her choice would have been to quickly reign the emotions in and continue. There was nothing about her reaction that felt like it was part of "the show." It seemed organic, that it surprised her, and that she was a bit uncomfortable, as though there might be something unprofessional about it.* Obviously, this is all entirely subjective, but they are the thoughts my skeptical outlook produced at the time.

Angelina then looked at my sister and said, "And you were there, too?"

"I was."

"And he says, 'Dad.' He just told me 'Dad.' So this must be your dad."

And Jen gave a tearful nod, her emotions making it difficult to speak.

"He is so, so sorry about what you both went through. But he saw you there, and he was with you there. At the same time that he wishes how you found out could have been different, how he wishes there was a less traumatic way, he also says that he is glad he passed the way he did. Not in the way of the shock that it caused for your family, but in the way that, if he had survived—which he is now telling me he could not have, he is telling me that there is nothing anyone could have done, it was his time, and he had to go, so he doesn't want anyone thinking 'What if I'd done this or what if I'd done that,' like 'If I'd paid more attention and made him go to a doctor' sort of thing—he says no, there was absolutely nothing anyone could have done, so put that out of your mind—but he is saying that in some cases like this, when someone does survive, but their body is then very compromised, and they can't live the way they always have and they need help, he says he would never have wanted that. He knows that you would have done anything for him, no matter what, but he says he wouldn't have been happy having to be taken care of. So, in that sense he is glad. He is glad he passed quickly with "no fuss," he's saying. And he needs you to know that there was no pain for him. He says he had felt a little tired before he passed, like maybe thought something might be up, but he had no idea it was that serious. But when he passed, it's like he felt something behind his eyes, like he got dizzy. It's like he got dizzy and laid down, almost like he was just going to take a nap. And then he closed his eyes and opened them again, and he was out of his body." This was all coming as a stream of consciousness for Angelina, uninterrupted. "He also tells me now that the transition was very easy for him. Sometimes, if for instance, a person has a very strong religious belief, or an expectation of what death is supposed to be like, it can be a little hard for them if it's not exactly like that. But your dad tells me that he wasn't religious. He says he never really thought a whole lot about it, so because he didn't have specific expectations, it was very easy for him when he found himself there. I have to also say this: I really like your father. When you do this work, a lot of it for me, is through feeling, and I feel the energy of the person. And sometimes when I do readings, the energy of the people on the other side isn't one I want to stay in for longer than I have to. When someone leaves the earth plane, they don't instantly become different people—they might have a greater perspective, but if they were kind of jerky in life, they might still have that energy on the other side. Your dad's energy . . . I could sit with your dad's energy forever. He feels like a very evolved soul to me. Like, even though I know I just said he wasn't religious, he's like the guy that if, you know, if everybody was like him, the world would be beautiful. So, I have to say, and again, this isn't something that is always the case by any means, I have to say that I just really like your dad. I can feel how sensitive he is, and he is also very charming, and he's funny! I can feel now this funny side to him—this dry sense of humor. And his energy is so calming. He's this no-frills guy. He's like, 'I don't care what kind of clothes I wear, I'll eat whatever . . . ' he's like a 'don't worry about me' kind of guy. He wants everything to be easy for everyone. He's like, 'Take it easy. Just take it easy.'"

And that was neat to hear. Angelina had no way of knowing this, but that phrase, "Take it easy," was extraordinarily meaningful to us. Remember that video I mentioned I took a few weeks before my dad passed where I went around the table, asking everyone what they'd learned about life? When I turned the camera on my dad and asked him the question, before he could answer, my niece, who was about ten at the time, jumped in the frame to say, "Poppy Bob wants you to take it easy." She said that because this was something my dad always said. He never said, "Bye." It was always, "Take it easy." And, as Angelina noted, my dad was, indeed, easy. All he ever worried about was making life easy for those around him. If our lives were good, if we were happy, he was happy. So tied up in who my dad was, in fact, as Angelina said he was saying, "Take it easy," those words were being etched into the granite that would become the headstone of his grave. No one, beyond the engraver, knew that his headstone would read, in quotes, as a summation of what we figured my dad would want to leave the world with, "Take it easy."

Angelina's description of who my dad was as a person and what he felt like, was extraordinary to me. Even if she had gotten all the facts she could have about him by doing research, this qualitative summing up of my father was nowhere to be found online, or anywhere else. My father never joined Facebook—being as "no frills" and unselfish as he was, and he would never share anything about himself, even if he had. The things Angelina said about him were the things I would say about him if asked to sum up the totality of my father. Her sense of his "energy" was thorough, and there is nothing about it that I would find the need to alter or add to. Listening to her that night, it was as though he was standing there. I could feel his embarrassment at being talked about, as he would never, ever want to be the center of attention (something Angelina also later noted). This whole portion of the evening, the ten minutes or so that she spoke uninterrupted about what she was feeling about who he was, was nothing like anything we'd experienced with the previous medium. If the evening had ended right then, at "He's like . . . 'take it easy. Just take it easy,'" I would have had quite a lot to think about. But Angelina wasn't done. She paused following "take it easy," and then looking towards the floor, she said to no one in particular, "He doesn't want you to focus on the craziness of his passing or the pain. He knows that's much easier said than done, of course. But he wants to take me to the backyard, here." When she said that, she motioned towards the backyard with her hand. When Angelina had arrived, it was about 8pm and dark, so she didn't have a sense of the landscape. However, it's easy to ascertain, even at night, that the neighborhood is one that has backyards. It was what she said next that I found remarkable: "Was there . . . did you have a cookout, recently?"

Three weeks before my dad's passing, we'd had the "just because" cookout in my mom's backyard, where I took all of the photos of my dad and recorded the video of him giving me his advice to "Have patience, good things will come," and where the butterfly had shown up and stayed for what seemed like an inordinately long time. But beyond that, this was now the second time a person professing to be delivering messages from my dad mentioned the backyard.

"We did," my sister said with a smile.

"Your dad wants you to focus on that. He wants to take us back to the feelings of that day, of being together with the family . . . there is something important about that day and the feeling of that day. He wants you to hold that day front and center in your mind. Because he is still . . . even though, I know, believe me, I lost my mom, I know how hard the physical loss is, but even though you can't see him, he is with you just as much now as he was on that day. He hasn't changed. He is still the same man he was on that day. He is still your dad, and he wants you to remember him like he was on that day."

You might recall a phone conversation I mentioned earlier that I had with my cousin, Chris' medium friend, Christina Treger. She was talking about my dad and said, "I keep seeing a big, yellow butterfly." She then added,

"He wants to take me to the backyard where this butterfly is, maybe where you or your mom saw this butterfly, and tell you to remember what the feeling of that time in the yard was like." Which sounded remarkably similar to what Angelina had just said. So, Angelina had echoed in starkly similar words a private conversation I'd had with a different medium . . . and again, it was a conversation that was posted nowhere. So, unless Angelina had the wherewithal to tap phone lines, her repeating this message short-circuited my logic board as it tried to come up with a normal explanation.

And if she *was* a huckster, she'd clearly done her job, at least as far as my sister was concerned, as she now openly wept. Another visibly satisfied customer. But . . . I was increasingly feeling like this woman didn't have "huckstering" in her. Obviously, again, this is an entirely subjective take on my part. However, the way she had paused to tell us about losing her mom (which is true—I'd eventually discover that everything Angelina told us about her life was the truth) felt like an attempt to offer genuine comfort to us. The effect of authenticity is not easily achieved without actual authenticity (though, of course, it is definitely possible), and to me, Angelina felt authentic. Beyond that, some of the things she was saying simply could not have been gathered by deceitful means. There was nowhere for her to have learned about that cookout, or the importance it had for us. There's zero way she could have sussed out that three weeks before my dad passed we'd had this family gathering in the very backyard she was now motioning to with her hand where I'd felt compelled to take photos of my father and where I took a video which is now the most important few seconds of video on the planet to me. Yes, people have cookouts, and this might be considered another high-probability guess, but the importance of that cookout to us, in that backyard, and the fact that another medium also mentioned the "backyard with the butterfly," made it difficult for me to entirely dismiss that particular "guess." With my sister crying on the couch on the other side of the room, Angelina turned, now, to me.

"And this is your dad, too, yeah?"

"Yes," I flatly said.

"Got it. So, he wants to focus on you for a minute."

And if I'd thought I was already having trouble remaining calm, I hadn't seen anything yet. Angelina paused, again looking up, apparently interpreting something she was being shown. I soon had a Pavlovian response to these pauses, quickly learning that some of the best evidence, the verifiable, black and white sort of evidence of an objective nature, came after these pauses. She'd look up at the ceiling or down at the floor or gaze straight ahead and get quiet, and then speak to a specific person such as my mom and say something like, "You were the one who found him," and then look at my sister and say, "And you were there, too," then go on to the more subjective stuff, like how my mom and sister had been feeling in those moments. But the objective, "yes or no" sort of stuff often came right after Angelina took a moment to "listen," or do whatever she was doing. After taking a pause like this latest one, she looked back at me and said, "Your dad tells me that you have been playing his voicemail messages, you've been listening to his voice on your phone."

Whoa. I *had* been listening to my dad's voicemail messages—over and over. I said, "Wow, yes, I have," immediately wishing I hadn't offered the "wow," which added more than I wanted to as a "blank slate," but feeling the instant rush from hearing her say something that was true. As she looked again at the ceiling, I calmed myself, thinking, *Well, I'm sure that is true of many people who've lost someone. I'm sure we all start to look at photos and listen to voicemails and watch videos and pour over whatever physical remnants we might have, the last vestiges of concrete evidence that they had ever lived at all.* At the same time, though, it was meaningful to me. As I've mentioned, I had been listening to my dad's voicemail greeting over and over, calling his number every spare chance I got just to hear his voice, and then becoming quite panicky at the thought that this greeting would be gone as soon as the phone company cancelled his service. My sister and I entertained the thought of continuing to pay the bill forever, just to have those three seconds of my dad's voice saying, "Hi, this is Bob, please leave a message." Luckily, I realized I had a number of messages my dad had left me on my voicemail. And this was lucky, indeed, as it was incredibly rare for me to not drop whatever I was doing and answer the phone if I saw "Dad" on the screen. I had saved four messages from over the last few years and now needed them more saved. I purchased an app which allowed me to record them, and then I sent them to my mom and sister and saved them on my hard drive (and now in "the cloud"), fighting my dad's dissolution by spreading his voice wherever I could. Even though I conceded that this might be a high probability guess on Angelina's part, the fact that there had been so much energy expended on those voicemails was striking in the moment. Angelina then lowered her gaze from the ceiling, again looking at me.

"Your dad tells me that you have been sleeping with his sweatshirt."

*Holy shit.* Sorry, but in the moment, that was all I could think, and when I bring back the memory now, the result is the same. *Holy shit.* "Yes," I responded as cooly as I could, still attempting to not betray how any of this was hitting me, or not, struggling still to be a tabula rasa, allowing Angelina nothing to play off of, and recalibrating my stance back to neutral with each of her utterances. I wanted the information to come from wherever she was getting it, either her own mind or my dad's, but I did not want to offer any assistance. So, as steadily as possible I said, "I have been, yeah."

"You have?" My mom asked.

"I have," I answered, and for the first time, my mom began to cry. The thought of her thirty-five-year-old son sleeping with his dad's shirt broke her heart. And to be honest, I was embarrassed. I had told absolutely no one about the fact that the "Wayne State Dad" sweatshirt I'd bought my father after I'd gotten into an MFA acting program, and that he often wore when he knew he was going to see me, had become a grown man's blankie.

When I found it in his closet, I immediately buried my face in it hoping to still smell my dad, and I'd slept with it every night since. It actually took me a moment before answering "Yes," because it felt so silly. This was extremely private information unbeknownst to anyone but me. Or, so I thought.

Again, taking the skeptical point of view that this woman has to be cheating somehow, this seemed to me like another low probability "guess." In that moment, I quickly asked myself the question, *How often do grown men sleep with a clothing item of their dad's when they pass? Is this more common than I think?* Angelina didn't allow me a great deal of time to ponder that, as she continued.

"Did you and your dad . . . were you . . . did you debate politics a lot?"

*What the eff? How, how in the world could this woman know what she just said?* My brain again reeled, ticking off the ways she could have gotten this information, and knowing there were none, short of having hired Magnum P.I. before Dad died who followed us around for months. Obviously, that did not happen. So, how the eff did she know to say what she just said? The fact that my dad and I had a nearly lifelong habit of heatedly discussing politics, me on the liberal end of the American political spectrum, and he on the fiscally conservative end, was not published on any social media sites, and certainly his obituary didn't note the following, "And, by the way, his son, Mike, worries that the debate they had on the night he died had raised his blood pressure and contributed to his passing." Which is the truth. The very night my dad passed, while watching *Monday Night Football*, my dad and I again had a debate about politics. These debates were always out of love, and we actually enjoyed them, but on this night, we did get even more excited than usual discussing the pros and cons of a universal healthcare system. It had played over and over in my mind, the fact that we'd had this debate just hours before he passed. Thank all that is good, my dad and I never left these debates upset, and we'd hugged and said, "I love you" to each other after our discussion that night, but still, it had been on my mind.

Our political debates were such an integral part of our relationship, in fact, that you'll recall I was surprised on the train ride home the night I learned of his passing to be sitting near two guys who debated for the entire train ride in the same jovial, but spirited way my dad and I had the night before (and over the same topic). Given all of this, when Angelina asked, "Did you and your dad debate politics a lot?" I was simply stunned.

"We . . . we did. Yes, we did," I said, as my mom and sister and brother-in-law began to laugh, knowing that, "we did" was an understatement, and each taking this as sparkling evidence that Angelina was doing something extraordinary.

"He says that you taught him to see things in a different light. Even though you debated, he liked the way you looked at things. He tells me that you took life to a whole different way of living. Like, maybe your dad was . . . maybe he was a little more, 'this is what you do: you go to high school, you get a job, you get married and you have kids' and that's sort of just how he was brought up. Like 'you go from point A to point B,' and it's sort of a straight line. But he says you took life to . . . to a different way of living. Like, he says you aren't, maybe you aren't living a traditional sort of way, or something like that, or you are doing it different, somehow, and he is so proud of that."

Much of this was subjective in nature. Could this have been the Forer effect? Was she saying something general, something that could apply to most people, but that I was then personalizing? Was my brain doing the thing brains do that make horoscopes so popular and had 4 out of 5 students in Forer's classroom believing he had psychic abilities based on how well he'd "described them"? It is difficult to say. All I can report is, in that moment, it felt quite accurate. My dad came from a hard-working, "blue-collar" family. After high school, he quickly realized college wasn't for him, so he took a job working at a grocery store. He and my mom got married when they were twenty, then had me five years later, and my sister a year and a half after that. Soon, he got a job as a delivery man . . . a job he would hold for the rest of his life. He followed "the plan" the way his dad and his grandfather had. He focused on family, and the point of his work was to support them, and that gave his work the value he needed it to have. I, on the other hand, had gone a completely different route. The idea of marriage had freaked me out from the time I was a teenager. And I couldn't imagine spending a whole life doing a job that I didn't love. After high school, I went to college and studied theatre and acting. My dad, before I became an actor, had never been to a play in his life. Theater was simply not his "thing." However, once it became mine, he went to every length to make sure I could pursue it, including helping me, on a delivery man's salary, pay for college. He worked thousands of hours of overtime, every weekend and holiday, so I could pursue a career I loved. And even though he'd never been to a play before, he never, not once, missed one that his son was in. He drove all over the Northeast and as far as Ohio, to see me in shows (he was afraid to fly, so driving was his only option). I had remained single up to the time of my dad's passing, moving from place to place as I continued to act at different theaters. My life was nothing like the life my dad had. I had not gone from "point A to point B in a straight line" as Angelina suggested my dad had. I hadn't followed "the plan" the way he and his dad and grandfather did. The line of my life was of a different nature, with many twists and turns and zigs and zags, with no plan but to see where it went. But no matter how different my life was from his, my father could not have been more supportive—or more proud. I will leave it to the reader to decide whether or not the Forer effect caused me to connect dots that were not there, which is certainly possible. But next, Angelina said something that was not subjective, and which Forer, I think, would not as easily explain away.

"Did your dad like poetry?"

"Um . . . no," my sister and I both said with a bit of a smile. As mentioned, my dad focused entirely on his kids and doing the work it took to make our lives as easy as possible. He wasn't much of a reader, and the only time he'd heard Shakespeare was if the Bard's words were coming out of his son's mouth. So, when she asked, "Did your dad like poetry?" We took this as a very clear miss. One of the only, in fact, "misses" that Angelina had so far offered.

"Okay," Angelina continued. "Let me try to figure this out, then. He's showing me . . . a handwritten letter or poem. Did you find a handwritten note from your dad?"

Oh my. Jen and I looked at each other, totally stunned. You'll recall that earlier that day, in a small "treasure box" at the back of a closet, Jen and I found the poem our dad had written many years ago asking our mom to reconsider leaving him and pledging his undying love for her. Given the cross-outs, we'd figured this must have been a rough draft he'd later rewritten and given to her. Knowing how devastated my mother already was after his passing, we'd decided we'd not show her the draft we found, feeling it would just bring her further pain and possibly disrupt the precarious psychological balance she was trying to maintain. But now, here Angelina was apparently referencing that poem, as her question of "Did your dad like poetry?" suddenly made sense when combined with, "Did you find a handwritten note from your dad?" I was completely taken aback by this and unsure what to say. We really did not want my mom to know about the poem, given how afraid we were of how she might react.

"We did," my sister said, offering no more.

"Okay. Your dad wants you to give that to your mom."

And now any rational explanations went completely out the window. My sister had said only, "We did." She said nothing about the note being for my mother. How this sequence could possibly have been the result of cold reading I simply could not put together. The amount of luck required to achieve this series of utterances, as far as I could see, wouldn't be a more likely explanation than my dad's consciousness having survived his body's demise and now somehow communicating with this woman. The odds of Angelina saying what she did in that order by chance seemed as astronomically small to me as the other possibility. At this point, my mother obviously wanted to know what we were talking about.

"What note?"

Jen and I looked at each other unsure of how to proceed and still trying to protect my mom from what we thought might be further emotional trauma. But given what had just occurred, my sister felt the information was coming directly from my dad and trusted that he knew what he was doing by bringing this up. So, after a long look at me, and me nodding to her, Jen said, "Well, we found something today in Dad's closet. It was something he wrote to you a long time ago that we think he probably gave you way back when. A poem."

"It's a poem?" Interrupted Angelina?

"Yes," Jen said. "A poem that he wrote."

"Okay!" She said with some relief, as if a mystery had been afoot and Mr. Holmes just explained to everyone in the room who'd done it. "That's why he was talking about poetry."

"Oh right!" Jen said, also putting the pieces together. "Yes, you asked if he liked poetry, which he really didn't."

"That's one of the interpretations I was talking about before, how I might get something wrong. So, he didn't like poetry, but he wrote a poem."

Angelina seemed to be enjoying the process of breaking it down herself. Meanwhile, my mom was still looking for answers."

"Well, where is it?"

"We left it at Dad's," I said. "He wrote it a long time ago, after you separated, but before you divorced, it sounded like. We just didn't think . . . we just worried that it might be hard for you to read."

"Well, I'm reading it," she resolutely said.

The following day, my sister and I retrieved the aged piece of paper with my dad's precious scribbles and heart-breaking cross-outs, too-hard-to-think-about-for-very-long evidence of his search for the right words, the words that would put his world back together. We drove together to my mom's, and in the same living room where the previous night my dad seemed to somehow break down the veil between wherever he might be and us, the three of us sat. "Okay," my mom said. "Let me have it." With one more "should we really do this?" look from my sister, she handed it to my mom. In silence, my mom read every word, more carefully perhaps, than she'd ever read anything. Within seconds she was crying, and the fear that we were right to worry about giving it to her began to rise. But she got through the whole thing, then sat in tear-filled silence looking at it again and then touching the words with her hand, trying to get as close to them as possible. She then folded the letter back up with great care and looked up at us.

"I want you to bury me with this," she said.

After a few moments of silence, I asked, "Do you remember him giving a finished version of this to you?"

"No, I never got this. He never gave this to me." And she cried once more. I was, again, trying to take in the whole event and what had led us to this moment. When my dad wrote those words, my mom was head over heels involved in a new and exciting love. Had he made the finished copy of his poem and given it to her, chances are it would have meant little at the time. She was just twenty-eight, their whole lives ahead of them, and my step-father was all she could see right then. Certainly she would have thought that someone like my dad would easily find a new love and, like her, move on. She'd have had no way of knowing back then that she would end up being the only one for him. So, had he handed her that poem, it would likely have been soon forgotten, even perhaps, something of an annoyance—when you are in a new love, you often don't want any encumbrances from the old one. That note may not have even been fully read before she tossed it in a drawer, or even in the garbage. But now though, thirty years later, that poem finally made it into the hands of its intended recipient. And since she received it now and not then, its significance was fully understood and more powerfully felt. And those words he penned all those years ago, ended up being the most important words she's ever read— the only words she wants to be "buried with." And if Angelina had not come that evening, that note would have forever remained unread. Looking at my mom again caressing the piece of paper, I was in awe.

Again taking the skeptical point of view that Angelina *had* to be engaged in deceit, the night had been a resounding success. She'd so thoroughly hoodwinked all six of us, that we were in tears by the end. I won't go into the stories of the other two people who were there, but they, likewise, had received specific information that they believed could only have come from their deceased mom, and they too wept. So, from Angelina's point of view, mission accomplished. Everyone in the room (including me, by this point) was saying things like, "This was the most extraordinary night of my life," and throwing around words like "life-changing" and "amazing." Angelina was going to get a lot more work from these six satisfied customers. Having "fooled" us all, it was time for her to leave. However, she found she had one more message to deliver before we all got up. And the message was for me.

"Your dad says . . . he wants me to talk about your hair."

CHAPTER NINE

# Can You Hair Me Now?

By the time Angelina seemed to be wrapping up, I'd actually momentarily forgotten about my experiment. Going in, of course, that had been the only thing on my mind. I was not going to leave the reading satisfied that anything "paranormal" was going on unless I'd gotten the code word. And for a good part of the two-hour sitting, I had that code word squarely in mind. In fact, the more specific Angelina got about things, and the more "on the nose" her evidence was for my dad's survival, the more I wondered, *Well, if this is true, and he can get her to say such specific things, why wouldn't he get her to say the* one *thing I want to hear?* Angelina had said that the whole point was for her to be "an evidential medium." She said she would try to get information that could be verified and validated, which would be the way we'd know the information wasn't coming from her. Well, in that case, this would be easy, because I only needed to hear one thing. This could be a quick and easy chat with the deceased for Angelina, and she could be home in front of the fireplace, curled up with her cats and some hot chocolate before nine o'clock. But as the evening went on and my code word wasn't being said, I became more and more confused. Some of the information she was coming up with seemed to be most likely obtained in some out of the ordinary way that science doesn't yet have a handle on. *Let's just say, for a moment, that that's true,* I said to myself. *There must be a reason she is picking up all of this specific information, but not the thing I want to hear.* I started wondering about what the process might be. *Perhaps my dad didn't hear my request? Perhaps they can only say what they want to say, and don't take requests?* Obviously, I had no idea what the answer might be. But it did become a challenge, as the evening proceeded, to reconcile the idea that such specific things could be brought to Angelina's mind, and yet, not the only one I was waiting for. And Jen had gotten a specific mention of something she'd been waiting to hear—"a manual." She *was* my dad's favorite, but still, I can't say I wasn't a bit jealous that she had gotten this "no doubt about it" message, one that entirely changed her perspective on what reality is, and I hadn't. Nonetheless, eventually I was so consumed with trying to understand what was happening in that living room that I forgot about my experiment. My brain was focusing on every little nuance of Angelina's, looking for any sign of deceit, no matter how small. And by the time she had gotten to "Did you find a handwritten letter from your dad?" I was utterly baffled by what was going on, having picked up no indication that Angelina was anything other than honest, and further, compassionate. As the evening was drawing to a close, I'd already known I was going to do whatever I could to look further into Angelina and this "phenomenon." Something, *something* had happened, I felt sure, that science can't explain. Of that, I was satisfied. But Angelina wouldn't leave until my life had been totally turned upside down.

"Your dad says . . . he wants me to talk about your hair."

And my heart began to pound.

"He . . . I'm not sure what this is. I think he just likes your hair. He put his hand up on his head, and at first I thought he was telling me that he'd gone bald. But then he was like, "No, that's not what I mean, and he pointed to your hair. He likes your hair."

"OH MY GOD," I said, now unable to contain my awe and excitement. It's difficult to describe what this feeling is like when something apparently "mystical" enters into your space. It's something of a high. The routine of your day to day is shattered and something new is there. In that moment, to me, something undeniably "out of this world" had just happened. I'd asked my dead dad to get Angelina to use the word "hair" somehow in reference to me, and it happened. For no reason—out of the blue, she said what she said. We weren't in the middle of a conversation that led to her saying this. It was its own, individual, self-contained, apropos of nothing message that Angelina said my dad wanted to deliver to me. Short of Angelina having high-tech listening equipment stationed around my father's empty house in the middle of the woods, there is just no way this could have been fraudulently obtained, and the chances of it being "luck" or some kind of cold reading just seemed cosmically small.

"Oh my God," I said again.

"What?" my sister asked?

"Well, remember when you asked about *Emmanuel's Book*? I asked Dad to mention my hair. Today, at his house, while I was all alone, I asked Dad to mention my hair, and that's how I'd know that something real was going on, and this woman wasn't just taking fools' money—sorry, Angelina, but, you understand."

She laughed and said, "I do! But, I have to tell you, it's unusual for that to happen. People do it a lot, ask for something specific, and I have no idea why, but it usually doesn't happen."

I guess my and Jen's ingenious plan wasn't so original. I asked Angelina to speculate on why it doesn't happen more often, as this would be such an easy way to prove, beyond the shadow of a doubt, that something is going on that science says is impossible. This could so easily be the ticket for Angelina, and those who do what she does, to legitimacy in the eyes of the scientific world. "I really don't know," she said. "You're right, it would make my job so much easier. But for some reason, it just doesn't often work that way."

That, among many other questions, swirled around my mind. But one thing was clear to me: the world doesn't work the way my past teachers and professors, and almost all of mainstream science, say it does. I could not imagine how any skeptic who had gone through the exact experience I had could come out not believing they'd been wrong to be so sure that, "It can't happen because it can't happen."

After saying our goodbyes to Angelina (and paying her), my family went back upstairs to debrief in the living room. And the world was a different place. This was not the same living room we'd sat down in at the start of the evening. This living room was in a world of possibility. A world that contained new things I hadn't known were there—wondrous things, things such as the idea that death might not be entirely what we think it is, and "we" might not just be a product of electrical impulses in brains. Mostly though, it was a world that still had my dad in it.

We went carefully over every bit of the evening, comparing the notes we'd judiciously kept. There were so many "validations," as Angelina called them, bits of information she knew that she should not have—if Mr. Vance, my high school physics teacher, was right about the ways we can know things. But one of those bits, for me, had just changed my life. No amount of "but what about this?" or "maybe she did that" could explain her saying, "Your dad wants to talk about your hair." I had to accept that the most likely explanation, in this particular case, was a paranormal one, one that expanded what "normal" means. But if that were true, it didn't necessarily mean the information had come from my dad. I had to rule out every possibility. What if "mind reading" is a real thing? We know that our brains give off an electromagnetic field. And some science now shows our brains can pick up on the magnetic field of the earth. Perhaps it's possible that information, somehow, can be carried in or on these fields. Perhaps a medium is someone whose brain is adept at translating this information into pictures, feelings and tastes, and believes these perceptions are coming from a deceased person, when, in reality, they might be coming from the people sitting in front of them. Perhaps she said, "He wants to talk about your hair" to me and "He shows me that you are reading . . . a manual" to Jen because her brain picked them up from our thoughts. This was just as possible, it seemed, if not more likely, than the information coming from my disembodied dad. So, my first order of business, I knew right away, would be to test this, somehow.

When I woke up the next morning, the world looked different. If Angelina had truly gotten that information, either from my father or my brain, it meant that the universe, or at least our part of it, doesn't work the way we have been told. No matter how "out of the ordinary" my experience the previous night was, no matter how "anomalous," it had happened. I knew no reputable scientist, no matter in what detail I described to them the circumstances, or how certain I was of their "paranormal" nature, who would take what I had to say and think, "Well, I guess telepathy or communication with the dead (or both) is real." But to me, after going over and over again the events of the previous day, it truly did seem that simple. And when I combined it with the experience my sister had two weeks before, I was convinced that something sometimes operates in a way that our current mainstream scientific paradigm does not allow. If I could just get some folks from Oxford or Harvard or some similarly weighted academic institution to sit in on the experience I'd had, I was sure we could put this on the world radar and give it the attention it would seem such a thing would deserve. But, who was I going to call at Harvard? "Hello, Harvard . . . listen, I had an experience that I think points strongly towards information being able to be carried in a way we don't currently think possible, like, for instance, from the consciousness of a previously embodied man, so, you know, basically I mean someone who once was alive, so, you know, someone who is dead, I guess, to the brain of a living person, or I suppose it could also have been from my brain to a living person's brain, that is yet to be determined, but, so . . . can you put me through to the scientist I can talk to about that who will bring legitimacy to this whole thing, please?"

Before making that phone call, I thought it might be a good idea to do a few more personal tests. Having, for the time being, accepted the possibility that mediumship might sometimes be a real thing, and that Angelina may have said "He wants to talk about your hair" because that information came to her by some means other than a person she'd hired with high tech listening equipment who'd been following me around, it quickly occurred to me that there might be two possibilities: one, my dad, who is apparently something other than the body I knew him as, told her to say that, or two, the thought had been in my brain, and Angelina's brain picked up on it by a process we are unaware of. It seemed to me that at least this question was testable, and my sister and I set our plan to test it into motion. The idea was a simple one: we would hire a different medium, and this time only my sister, my brother-in-law and I would go, leaving my mom behind. On the morning of the reading, we'd ask my mom to go to a place where she was totally alone and ask my father to deliver a very specific message to us. Once she decided on what it was and had communicated it to my dad, she would not tell anyone else. In this way, no one sitting in the room with the medium would be holding the code word or code message in their brain. If the medium were to be engaged in telepathy, they'd have to be doing it at long distance—which obviously might be possible, since the attributes of this "impossible" phenomenon have never been ascertained, to my knowledge, because people don't often speculate on the characteristics of a thing that "doesn't exist." Still, if telepathy worked in that way, where a person could get information out of any brain they needed to, even without knowing which brain on the planet that might be, and where the distance of that brain, once they'd found it, made no difference—well, that would be just as extraordinary, in my mind, as my dad still existing without a body. If telepathy were found to be real, that would topple the current scientific paradigm just as assuredly as survival of consciousness, and it would open a whole new realm of study. It seemed less likely to me, however, that a person's brain could get information from any brain on the planet as easily as getting it from those sitting in the same room. If, for instance, information is somehow carried on a "field" the brain emits, and this field acts like others we know about, it would mean the field only had influence over a certain distance, the strength of which is inversely related to that distance.

To conduct the casual experiment, we found a medium named Jonathan Louis who lived in Long Island, NY. He is a friend and protégé of the famed John Edward, the man who'd first made me aware of mediumship with his television show *Crossing Over*. John Edward had become so well-known by this point, that he generally did only large events with hundreds of people. Since getting an individual appointment with him was so difficult, he began to let people know at the ends of these large shows about his friend, Jonathan Louis, saying that he was a phenomenal medium with a much shorter waiting list. I found his website and through it booked an appointment. Jonathan was apparently pretty good, if his prices were anything to go by. For three people to sit with him for an hour, it would cost six hundred dollars, which was double what Angelina charged for six people, and a few times more per hour than some surgeons make. With prices like this, it was easy to see why skeptics would be so . . . skeptical, and from where the motivation might come to fake this stuff and take money from desperate people, no matter how gross a thought that might be. But, since this was for science, we decided to make the appointment. To do so, I had to email Jonathan's assistant. To book a session, she wanted my phone number, my full name, and the first name of the other two people who would be attending. As we've gone over, this information obviously allows for much about me to be gathered through social media—which meant, again, that receiving messages that provided information not published anywhere would be paramount. Nothing this medium said (whether or not

I believed he was cheating in this way) could be considered evidential if he could have found it through "normal" means.

On a February morning, 2012, approximately three months after the reading with Angelina, my sister, brother-in-law and I piled into one car in Connecticut and began the nearly three-hour drive to the medium's office on Long Island. We called my mom from the car and said, "Okay, Mom! Now is the time. Go somewhere alone and talk to Dad, and ask him to deliver a very specific message. When the reading is over, we'll call you and tell you everything he said."

"Okay!" she said, excited to participate in our little experiment.

Upon arriving, we sat in a small waiting area. It seemed that no one was in the office, though we then heard quiet talking coming from down the hall. We discovered that Jonathan had been in a session with someone when the door at the end of the hall opened and a woman walked out looking rather thrilled. "This was amazing. Thank you," she said. She said a quick "hello" as she walked past us to exit. I looked at my sister and brother-in-law and said, "Well, it seems like she had a good experience." The whole time we'd sat in the waiting area, we said nothing about my dad or anything else that could be used—just in case listening devices had been installed hoping to gather some last-minute bits. When Jonathan came down the hall to welcome us, I again found myself scrutinizing this man's every word and facial expression. My brain was still having such a hard time accepting the reality of what he claimed to be able to do, that a small part of me was almost constantly thinking, *How could you? What kind of a person would lie to people in this way? That's so low, dude.* Again, though, this guy seemed so sweet! He was about my age, I guessed, in his thirties, and came across as intelligent, funny and quite nice. Again, as with Angelina, I perceived a gentleness about him, a kindness that went beyond, deeper than "nice." He was someone I was sure I would have been friends with had we grown up together. I thought that maybe afterwards he might be fun to hang out with, even. Then, I could get him good and drunk, tequila after tequila, until he'd spilled the truth of how he does what he does, how he'd gotten that woman's face to look the way it did, filled with an excitement, an "I-can't-wait-to-tell-you-what-just-happened!" expression as she pulled out her phone before even putting her hand on the door to leave.

Jonathan led us down the hall and into a small, undecorated room. Again, I was surprised. Like when we'd first visited a medium years ago, I was expecting the room to be . . . weird or "new age." I think I expected crystal-lined shelves and buddha statues, and sage and incense burning. Instead, there was a small couch on which he sat and four or five armless plastic chairs separated by a coffee table. The walls were so blank that I was struck by them. There weren't any angel pictures hung or buddha statues laughing or spiritual platitudes on hand-carved wooden signs or anything else. Just a dull white paint. The room didn't have any warmth to it, feeling more like a waiting area at the doctor's office. It was just not a space that called out to me, "And in this room, the veil between this world and another will fall, and the sacred and mysterious act of communion with the dead will take place. In this room, what you have known to be 'reality' will break down, the spacetime continuum will dissolve, and truths afforded only those who seek them shall be bestowed." Instead, I kept expecting my dental hygienist to open the door and tell me she was ready for me. However, no matter how sterile the decor, that "mystical" feeling was about to change the look of things.

After a five-or-so minute description of what he does and how the information he gets comes to him (quite similar to the way Angelina opened her session with us), Jonathan said, "Okay, they're ready." I could only guess who he meant by "they," but he wouldn't leave us in suspense for long as he immediately said to my sister and me, "I have your grandmother here. This is on mom's side. So, your mom's mother. Do you understand this?"

119

"Yes," we said. Again, given our approximate ages, one might guess we'd have a grandmother who passed. In this case, this medium narrowed it down to one person, though, saying it was on our mom's side (and our dad's mother had not passed at this time). He continued, "And I have your mom's dad here, too, with her. So, her husband. Both of your grandparents on your mom's side are here, and they have a male with them that is like a son to them, he's younger, and he is also here. He feels like a father figure to you. Looking at my sister, he asked, "Did you lose your dad?"

"I did," she said.

This first minute of the sitting was extraordinary in my mind—not because of the brief descriptions he gave of my supposed grandmother and grandfather and the younger male that was "like a son to them," it was because this was the very same pattern of "appearances" at the reading with Angelina a few months earlier. In that reading, too, Angelina claimed first to sense my mom's parents "step forward," followed by my dad. And, again in both readings, this younger energy was described as being "like a son" to them. Which was true . . . my parents had met when they were twelve years old, so my father was, indeed, like an actual son to them. I was very struck by this pattern being the same. Unless fraudulent mediums have some sort of club where they get together and compare notes on all clients, cross reference names, and send each other what the others have said in previous readings, this was, perhaps, the surest sign yet that something genuine might be happening.

As Jonathan continued to speak, I wondered what a statistician would say the odds were of this same pattern showing up? I couldn't consider this question for long, however, because Jonathan was forging ahead, now focused on this energy he had identified as Jen's father (he specifically asked Jen, and I did not respond, so at this point in the reading, he still didn't know what the relationship of the three people in front of him was). He said, "Your dad went very quickly. Like, here and gone like that (and he snapped his fingers). He needs you to know that there was no pain. It was so fast. He didn't even know it was happening . . . did you find him on the floor?"

"We did," my sister said.

"Okay, that's how fast this was. It's like he was standing up completely fine, and then, swoosh, he was gone. He is emphasizing, again, that there was no pain at all. He says he wants you to let that thought go."

This was stunning to me, as well. Again, as with Angelina, this professed medium correctly stated that my dad died very quickly and also intimated that we had been hung up on whether or not he had been in any pain during the last moments of his life. "He wants you to let that thought go," was one thing we connected to quite strongly, as it had been something we'd played over and over in our minds, imagining the worst-case scenario that my dad had felt pain and couldn't call for help. We envisioned him being terrified about what was happening while he was all alone in his house. We scrutinized every aspect of how his body was positioned and went over the ways it could have gotten there. As mentioned earlier, we'd chosen to focus on the fact that his knees were bent and his arm was by his head, looking as though he'd laid down for a quick snooze. We imagined that, had there been pain, his legs would probably not have been in such a relaxed position. Obviously, we have no idea whether or not that is true, but it was the picture we needed to hold onto. So, to now have two mediums, both unprompted in any way, say that our dad died "very fast," it's like he was "here and then gone," "he didn't even know it was happening," and for both to say, "he needs to be clear that there was no pain," seemed extraordinary. The only new piece of information this time was the fact that we'd found him on the floor (which no one beyond us knew). When I tried to add this to the accumulating statistical analysis in which the pattern had now extended to four items (the order of "arrival" to the session of three deceased loved ones, and then the manner of passing of the third) my mind boggled.

*What was going on here? How could this be a product of fraud?* I understood how individual bits might be (such as hitting on these peoples' names and dates of passing), but this pattern now twice showing up—out of two times—by means of deceit, seemed to be well out of the realm of probability, if not possibility. The stretching of the odds would mount further, much further, in my opinion, when Jonathan next looked at me—still unidentified with regard to my relationship to this deceased man he claimed to be speaking with—and asked, "Do you have his voice on something that you've been listening to? Like a recording of his voice?"

Maybe all mediums ask this? Perhaps it's something you learn on day one of medium camp—"Look, a lot of these suckers spend time listening to voicemails from their deceased pals, so that one is pretty foolproof—except to these fools! They'll just think you're really doing this shit. Hahaha."

The reading had only started a few minutes earlier, and he'd said just a small number of things by this point. It wasn't like he'd given us a hundred bits of information knowing that at least something would stick and hoping "listening to his recorded voice" would be one. He'd said:

1. I have your mom's mom here.
2. I have your mom's dad here, this woman's husband.
3. I have a younger male who is like a son to them.
4. "He feels like a father figure to you . . . did you lose your dad?"
5. He died very quickly. "Like, swoosh, and he was gone."
6. Did you find him on the floor?
7. Have you been listening to his recorded voice?

And again, what really hit me here was that six of these seven things were said by Angelina, as well, and in that order. He then asked, "Was your dad bald?"

"Um, he had lost some hair, but he wasn't completely bald. He had a bald spot on the top back of his head," I said calmly, as though the question meant nothing of import to me. But inside, the mention of the subject of "hair," had further peaked my attention.

"Well, then I'm not sure what this means. He's showing me Mr. Clean. You know Mr. Clean?"

"I do."

"Yeah, he's showing me that guy, just a completely bald guy. So, there's something about his hair, a lack of hair or something."

W.T.F. You tell me, scientists. What was happening here? Was this a coincidence that, once more, though not requested this time, the medium should bring up the notion of hair after establishing that it was supposedly my father that was speaking? Of the eight things this medium had now said, one happened to be the code word I'd used with the first medium. At this point, I was completely flummoxed as to how this guy could be perpetrating a fraud, given how this reading was lining up with the first. He then asked my sister, "Do you have a small dog, like a Yorkie?"

My sister doesn't have a dog that is like a Yorkie. She has a Yorkie. But the next animal reference would surprise me more. It's entirely possible that my sister had a picture somewhere on her Facebook page with her dog. And since Jonathan had access to my full name, phone number and email address, it would have been entirely possible for him to have found me on social media, and through me my sister, and done a little casual research by scrolling through our photos. But he certainly had no photo of what he said next to my sister.

"Were you recently scared by a mouse that ran out from somewhere . . . like in your house, maybe? Your dad is showing me something about you being afraid of a mouse."

When Jen and I had been getting my dad's house packed up and cleaned out one morning, as we cried over brand new shirts we were pulling out of his closet—Christmas gifts that he'd saved to wear "someday"—a mouse ran out from the closet scaring us both, but sending my sister into an all-out panic. She jumped up on Dad's bed faster than I'd ever seen anyone move, where she continued to jump and scream. I became completely hysterical with laughter, as did she, eventually. In the end, we were thankful to that mouse for lightening up an otherwise difficult day.

"I was," Jen said with a laugh.

After this, the messages got confusing to us. It seemed a different energy was stepping in that we soon thought might be the mom of one of our best friends. We jotted all of her messages down, and later called our friend to deliver them. Fascinatingly, it seemed to be the mom of the same sisters that had been with us during the reading three months earlier with Angelina, apparently adding to the pattern in another extraordinary way. When we called our friend after the reading to tell her what Jonathan said, all but one of the messages made sense to her. At one point Jonathan said, "Does some-one have a bad toe? Or maybe a bad toenail or something? They are want-ing to discuss someone's toe." That didn't make sense to the three of us in the room, and it also left our friend scratching her head.

After the messages that ostensibly came from our friend's mom, Jonathan claimed that my dad was stepping back in. "I'm coming back to your dad now. He wants to take me back to his last day. He says that it was like this perfect day . . . like it was a very strategic set-up, that day. Like, if he could have chosen a last day, it would have been the one he had. It would have gone just like it did. He said it was set up that way, strategically set up, set up perfectly for him to go."

Indeed, as described earlier, my dad's last day on earth was a "perfect" day. I was living in New York and saw my dad maybe every other week, on average. The day before he passed, he asked me if I'd be coming to Connecticut on Monday (which was my regular day off). I had something to do that week, so I said, "I don't think so, but I'll definitely come next week." Strangely, my dad said, "Maybe I'll take a ride down to see you, then." Monday was also my dad's only day off, and I knew driving into New York City wasn't high on his list of fun things to do. So, I immediately rearranged my plans in my head and said, "Actually, I will be coming! I thought I had an audition (or something) on Monday, but I just looked and its next week. So, I'll be there!" The following morning, I drove to Connecticut. My dad called while I was driving, but I'd had the windows open and the radio blasting and missed the call. And thanks to that loud music, I have one of those voicemails that two mediums referenced. "Hiya Mike, I'm just going to run a few errands, so let me know when you get here and I'll meet you at your mom's." As it turned out, my mom and my sister also had the day off. It was unusual for all of us to be together like this on a Monday. Everyone met at Jen's house (which is right around the corner from my mom's) and we spent the day talking and laughing. My dad showed me old YouTube videos (he'd just discovered YouTube) of Jack Paar and clips of Sammy Davis Junior and Dean Martin roasting each other. I can still hear him laughing. Then, when my niece and nephew got home (the loves of his life), we all went outside and played basketball and laughed at how much shorter my mom is than the hoop, and how basketball was most definitely not her sport. Finally, we said bye to my sister and her family, and we went back around the corner to my mom's, where she made dinner for us. Eventually, my mom and stepfather went to bed, and my dad and I sat together in the living room debating politics and watching *Monday Night Football*. Interestingly, we started talking about his mom, who was now showing definite signs of dementia, as her previously acutely sharp mind began to finally give way at ninety years old. I said, "I think maybe, for some people, like gram (who had always been so in control of everything), something like Alzheimer's or dementia may make the process of dying less frightening." To which my dad said, "I'm not afraid to die." This was strange to me, even right there in that moment, as we hadn't been talking about him, but his mom. But he somehow found a way to let me know that he was "not afraid to die," about two hours before he shockingly (to us) died.

When the game ended, we got up and hugged each other as we always did before leaving. He said, "I love you," which would turn out to be his final words to me and the final words of his life. The door closed behind him, and he walked across the yard towards his car, which was parked in the quiet cul-de-sac in front of the house. And something came over me. For some reason, I needed to say something else to him, though I had nothing to say. At the urgent behest of an unidentified prodding, however, I found my hand turning the doorknob. *What are you doing?* I asked myself midway through the action. Dad turned around when he heard me open the door and I said, "We'll go see that movie next week." That day, we'd watched a trailer for the film *MoneyBall* in between Dean Martin clips, and thought, as baseball fans, we'd enjoy it (my dad and I had a thing for sports movies—the underdoggy, schmaltzy ones, anyway). So, for whatever reason, this was the thing I came up with, feeling the inexplicable need to say *something* more to him. And he didn't say, "Yes, that'll be fun," or "See you then" or anything else. He just smiled at me, leaving "I love you" as his last statement. And then, as we'd always done since I was a little kid when he would drop us off back at our mom's after spending the weekend with him, I flashed the lights on the porch, and he flashed the lights of his car as one more "goodbye." And after a day spent with everyone he held dear, reminding us to keep laughing and playing and loving, he drove the five minutes to his house, walked in the door, and died, as evidenced by the keys still in his hand. So, when Jonathan said, "It was a perfect day, it was a very strategic set-up, perfect for him to go," it was very meaningful, as we had remarked to each other right from the start, even as we sat in my sister's living room at 3 AM just hours after his passing, how "perfect" our last day with him was. It was a theme we had returned to again and again. Even now, my mom still says, "If Dad could have planned his last day, his last day would have been it." Jonathan's message, therefore, was a definite hit—a hit that was published nowhere.

"He says it was all meant to be," Jonathan continued. "But, he again wants to take me to his actual passing. To how you found out. There is this feeling of apology to all of you. He is apologizing for . . . for how he left. He didn't have a choice, obviously—this was 'his time,' and there wasn't anything that he or anyone else could have done." This, again, was a repeated item that Angelina had given, as well, adding to the increasing pattern between the two readings. "But he knows how terribly you've all been affected. He knows what a shock it was, and how hard it was and is, and he is so sorry about that." Then, Jonathan said yet another thing that Angelina had also said: "I have to tell you, I really love your dad's energy. Being a medium isn't always easy. We come into contact with so many different types of energy, but I could sit with your dad's energy all day. I feel the kind of person he is. I can feel why this has been so hard. I just . . . I just really like your dad."

And we cried. I know it's of little scientific value, and maybe this is taught on day two of medium school, but to have two people separately comment on how much they liked my father (and in the case of Angelina becoming emotional about it) felt evidential to us. My dad was such a special sort of human, such a singularly good guy. And sitting in his energy when he was here was about the most peaceful, calming, hope-restoring thing you could do. Not even a hired Nancy Drew could have given Angelina or Jonathan the right words, in our minds. If you asked us, only sitting beside my dad could have done that. And as this second sitting with a medium came to a close, I was closer to thinking it might be possible that that is exactly what was going on.

We left Jonathan's office and felt the same sort of high we'd experienced after sitting with Angelina. It was positively thrilling to feel as though we'd just spent an hour with my father, and like the woman we'd watched leave the office in a vibrant rush before us, we too, were ready to call family and friends to excitedly exclaim, "You're not going to believe this!" However, the possibility of telepathy was still on my mind. Though I was now feeling quite strongly that at least some part of this phenomenon was happening without the use of fraud, the question of what exactly *was* going on obviously still lingered. Could Jonathan have pulled all of this information from our brains, unbeknownst to us, and perhaps to him, as well? It seemed unlikely, as a good portion of the sitting had apparently come from the mother of a friend of ours, and it wouldn't be until later that we'd find out that "Rose" was, indeed, her daughter's middle name, for instance, or that the "J J" name he was hearing in connection to that daughter whose name is Julianne, was immediately recognized by her mom as referring to "Juju," which was the only name she was regularly called, reserving "Julianne Rose" for times that she'd, let's say, used markers on the living room wall. The majority of the information supposedly originating from our friend's mom was not contained in any of the brains in the room. If "telepathy" was involved, or something of that nature, it would mean Jonathan's brain had somehow decided to pick out a friend of ours who'd lost her mom a couple of years before, and then gathered information from her brain, which his brain somehow located back in Connecticut. And, to repeat, his brain just happened to choose the brain of the friend who'd been with us in the life-changing reading three months earlier.

Once we'd found our way back to the highway, my sister called my mom and put her on speaker so we could all take part in the conversation. Jen began reading her the notes she had taken going over everything Jonathan said, wanting to know if any of the items was the code my mom had asked my dad to deliver. Between us and our friend Amie, there were very few messages that hadn't made sense. If our experiment had worked, it seemed likely it would be one of those. But my sister shared everything with my mom, from start to finish, reading each one of her notes in order. My mom was astounded that Jonathan had said some of the things he had, thinking that he, too, was "the real deal." The three of us in the car excitedly recounted the experience, having already forgotten some of the "amazing" things we had just heard. Knowing how despondent my sister and I had been in the months following our dad's passing, my mom was thrilled to hear us in such good moods, and her own mood had been quite lifted as well by these brushes with . . . something. But the laughing and "wowing" stopped after my sister said, "He asked, does someone have a bad toe?" For the first time, there was silence on the other end of the line. After a moment we said, "Mom?" But again, she said nothing. Finally, thinking maybe the call had dropped, I asked, "Mom, are you still there?"

"I'm here," she eked out, and it sounded as though she was crying.

"What's wrong?"

After another beat she said, "Don't mess with me. Are you messing with me?"

"What do you mean?"

"That was the thing."

"The thing?"

"That was what I told your father to say!"

My sister, brother-in-law and I felt a rush of excitement, and for me, it may have been the greatest I'd ever felt to that point.

"You told dad to say something about a 'bad toe'?"

"Yes! Are you screwing with me?"

"What do you mean? How could we be screwing with you?"

"I don't know! But . . . holy shit, that's what I said!"

She told us that when we'd driven off that morning, she took her coffee and went to sit on her porch by herself. She said, "Okay, Robert. The kids want me to have you say something to the medium today. And you have to say it. Do you hear me? You have to. They need this. So, what should we have you say?"

She'd been sitting there in her sandals, and she looked down at her feet while thinking about what she wanted Dad to say, which is when she saw her crooked toe (which I didn't even know my mom had). "Okay," she said. "I want you to mention my crooked toe. Got it? My crooked toe."

Given how out of left field that message was, my mom had little hope it would actually be said. So, when my sister read her the note saying, "Does someone have a bad toe?" even though it wasn't precisely what she'd said, as he hadn't used the word "crooked," it was close enough to shake her to her core and throw her world upside down, too, the way "a manual" had for my sister, and "He wants to talk about your hair," had for me. To my mom, there was simply no doubt that my father heard her and had gotten this medium to say it.

For me, the experience of this reading, given the unsolicited and accurate messages supposedly from a friend's mom (a friend that Jonathan Louis obviously did not know was a part of our first reading), and the fact that my mom had asked my dad to say one particular thing without telling us what it was and it had been said, the idea of this "just" being the result of telepathy seemed less likely (of course, proving telepathy alone would upend western science). To my great surprise, some things had happened over the course of these two readings that my mind—a mind that tends towards rationalization, especially over time—could not easily explain away. Now what?

# CHAPTER TEN

# Lighten Up

When I was at work the week following Jonathan's reading, the universe felt different to me. If I'd been wading through a thick and heavy atmosphere before, almost needing to concentrate to breathe, I now floated. For a time, my always questioning mind was restful, accepting that what had happened, actually happened, no matter how unlikely it might have previously seemed. As far as I could see, the facts clearly pointed to a reality denied in revered scientific institutions all over the world. Though that thought continued to play in the back of my awareness and cause some friction (*why didn't they know about this? What was I missing???*) every time I replayed the course of events, the conclusion was the same: something genuine had happened. The alternative was too complex. I had to stretch the bounds of feasibility to make it work. It would have meant that Angelina was not only surveilling us (and all those other people who left the theater that night also convinced that she'd been able to communicate with their loved ones), but that she was also in cahoots with the second medium who also had been surveilling us, including my mom that morning, with some high tech James Bond equipment. All of that felt extraordinarily far-fetched. And as unlikely as it might be to so many, the idea that consciousness is not created by the brain and survives beyond it, seemed the most logical explanation in this scenario. And if this wasn't evidence of the survival of consciousness beyond death, or that consciousness is not a product of our brains, it seemed to me, at the very least, to be powerful evidence that it is not trapped in those brains. That alone changes everything.

So, with a new joy, I went back to life and work. My bosses must have noticed, because before long I was given a new job at a much larger theatre than the one I'd been working at. Now, I was the bar manager at the Minskoff Theater on Broadway, which had been home to the *Lion King* for well over a decade. On my first day there, my boss stopped by from the main office to check in on me. "Congratulations," he said.

"Thank you!"

"So, do you have any ideas for this place? Any changes you want to make?"

"I do," I said, instantly nervous since I didn't.

After that conversation, it was clear that my boss was expecting me to increase business somehow, and make adjustments to how things were run. After he left, I took a walk around the theater to look at the four bars. Though the Minskoff is a beautiful and enormous venue in the heart of Broadway, the bars looked as though they were an afterthought. They were old and run down, and you might not even know what they were, if you didn't know, as they sort of blended into the background. One easy, yet very noticeable change I could make was to the bars themselves. A little sprucing up might go a long way and would be progress my boss would easily see. After doing all we could in that regard, I decided to put up some lighting around the bars. The assistant manager and I went to various places, eventually deciding on the lights we liked. It felt to us like a big deal, at the time, adjusting the lighting in a Broadway theater, and since my company technically rented space from the theater for our bars, we needed to make sure it would look acceptable to the "higher ups." We spent the week putting the lights up, finding creative ways to hide wires and make things look as professionally installed as possible. As it turned out, the lights made a big difference, and business picked up (It made such a difference, in fact, that soon our main office would put lights around all of the bars in the seven other Nederlander theaters they owned).

The next day, Jen and I were set to sit with another medium. As you might guess, feeling like you are connecting with your dearly departed can easily become addictive. We were aware of that, and when my sister told me about booking this medium she said, "This will be the last one," then adding with a smile, "at least for now." This woman's name was Robin, and she'd been recommended to my sister by a friend. I had never heard of Robin before. When I first became aware of mediumship, I figured anyone who professed to have this ability, and did whatever it is they do well enough to be believed, must make a pretty quick name for themselves, appearing on television a la John Edwards, or on the radio like Angelina. I imagined they were as rare as the oracles of old, hidden away at Delphi, only accessible by arduous quest. It didn't occur to me that there were others living more or less anonymous lives, and living those lives just a short drive from our house. It was surprising to learn of the sheer number of people who do this—there are hundreds, maybe thousands in America who make a living saying they are connecting people with their deceased loved ones.

Unlike Jonathan (but like Angelina), this medium wanted only Jen's first name and the number of people that would be coming. I'd decided, this time, to not have a code word. I wanted to see what the experience was like when I wasn't waiting to hear something particular. And now that I was feeling convinced that the experience with Angelina was genuine in nature, there was much less riding on this reading. If this woman turned out to be like the first medium we'd seen years ago, no matter. I'd already gotten my evidence. And to be honest, I was rather expecting her to be of the . . . less convincing variety, as her pricing was so far below both Angelina and

Jonathan's. After paying the $600 for the reading a few weeks earlier, the $200—$100 each—seemed paltry.

The strip mall in Connecticut which housed Robin's office was so small and nondescript that we drove past it. When we finally pulled in and got out of the car, we found a woman standing outside by the door smoking. The strip mall had a few businesses in it, and we figured this woman must work in one of them. We were a bit embarrassed about what we were doing there, so sheepishly asked, "Excuse me, do you know if we're at the right spot for 'Readings by Robin?'"

"Yeah," the woman said. "Right through that door on the right. You here for an appointment?"

"We are," I said, half expecting to be laughed at. In the five-seconds we'd known each other, I'd surmised that this woman was of the "no nonsense" sort, and might not be into something as ridiculous as what we were about to do. I was sure she was thinking, *more suckers*, when instead she said, "Take a seat in the hallway. I'll be right in. Gotta finish my smoke. Been a long day."

"Oh, okay, yes. Thank you. Take your time. Are you . . . are you Robin?"

"Yup."

And I was now sure this reading would be used by Jen and me merely as a funny story for years to come, as nothing about this woman said "medium." Nothing in her manner or dress or anything else said "spiritual" or "new age," to my mind. In fact, she felt like the opposite—if anything, I thought she might be the person you'd bring along to sniff out the nonsense and who'd be quite unafraid to let everyone know what she smelled—which made it quite a surprise when she came in, still smelling of cigarettes, sat down, lit a small candle and said to me, "Okay. Your dad likes what you did with the lights at work."

I'm not going to get into the rest of this reading, except to say that my sister and I were in a continual state of shock. Where Angelina and Jonathan had spent a good amount of time describing feelings they were having, and discussing spiritual lessons in between the messages they were getting, this woman was giving us message after message, all supposedly coming from my dad. Her opening sentence is not exaggerated—that is what she said, word for word: "Your dad likes what you did with the lights at work." So, immediately, in eleven words, she said that it was my dad we were there to hear from, that he saw me do something with lights, and that he saw the place where I did it. I was utterly stunned. I sat there, mouth agape, staring at my sister (who knew about my promotion to the larger theater, but didn't know about the lights I'd put up). I had been ready to have this sort of fun time, expecting my sister and I would be kicking each other under the table trying not to laugh as we got sillier and sillier over the vague messages. But instead, I'd just been given the most specific message yet. "Your dad likes what you did with the lights at work."

Finally, the medium broke the silence, rather impatiently asking me, "Did you put up new lights at work?"

"I did. I did. I put up new lights at work. I did. Like . . . yesterday."

"Okay then."

My sister and I spent the next hour in astonishment as highly specific message after highly specific message was delivered. Beyond the many objectively verifiable things she said, I found this statement to also be of particular interest: "Your dad is really good at this. It's a skill, people who have crossed being able to clearly communicate with the physical world, just like we have skills here. Not all spirits are as adept at this. Your dad is . . . I'll just say that it's not going to matter how good the medium is that you go to—your dad is going to be able to get through." Given that the entire foray into mediumship began when we received an unsolicited phone call from someone who believed my dad was trying to reach us through a medium we'd never met, which I gather is a rather rare occurrence, my dad having a certain panache in this area seemed to comport with our experiences thus far.

After the reading, we got into the car and sat in silence for a moment, both smiling. Finally, Jen looked at me and said, "That was our dad. Our dad is still here." And I had to agree. There was simply too much said of a specific and often highly personal nature that was not available to Robin. Most of what she said involved things that had recently happened in our lives—things that were "little," and not published anywhere. And unless an associate of hers had somehow gotten past security in the Minskoff theater and watched me as I worked alone, there is simply no way she could know about the lights at work. That was not information I'd shared with anyone, and it had just happened. I also couldn't see how the Forer effect or patternicity could be involved. I think if you said to most thirty-five-year-old people, "Your dead father likes what you did with the lights at work," the first response might be, "Well, my dad isn't dead," followed by, "What do you mean? What lights?" I didn't need to think about it for a moment and "connect the dots." Her sentence was one that would not apply to most people, as was the case with the horoscope Forer used on his students. This woman also got all of the other things the previous mediums had said, such as that my dad passed "very quickly." There was "no pain." And she asked, "So, your mom and dad were divorced, yeah?" We told her that they were, and she said, "Okay, and she remarried?" Again, we told her she was right. "But your dad says that she remained the love of his life. And actually, he is also the love of her life." This, again, would be a "shot in the dark" unlikely to hit its target, as the relationship between my decades ago divorced mom and dad is an unusual one. When taken all together, the things she could have researched and the things she couldn't, to me this was the clearest evidence thus far that some people are capable of picking up information in ways that scientists do not currently believe exist—and that my dad might still exist, no matter what those scientists believe.

When I got home, I sat alone for a while, amazed at how staggeringly these three readings had changed my life. Instead of the long and painful road of accepting that my dad was forever gone—the road a traditional psychiatrist might advocate and take me on—and learning to live with the loss, I found myself on an entirely different and utterly unexpected path. I now believed my dad was, in fact, not forever gone. The mounting evidence was telling me that simply accepting his loss and "moving on" would not be the rational move. If some part of my father was still around, still communicating with us when given the chance, it seemed the more rational move would be to accept not his complete demise, but rather a shift in our relationship. I felt so good, so thrilled at this prospect, that I found myself wanting to shout it in the streets—"Hey everybody, my dad didn't totally die! He's still here! And it seems to me that might mean yours is, too!" What I'd experienced was so life-altering and grief-alleviating that I didn't want to keep it to myself. During the next year, when people close to me lost someone, I began freely sharing my experience, and it seemed to bring a modicum of comfort, at least to some. But now that I was sharing my experience, it became of the utmost importance to me to know that I was doing the right thing. I only told people what had happened because I firmly believed I'd had a genuine experience, one that pointed to the survival of consciousness. I would never, ever want to be giving people "false hope." A sense of responsibility began to set in. A responsibility—to be sure.

A large part of me wanted to just file these experiences away as "real." I wanted to put them in a box, a box with a lock on it, a box in which the truth that my dad had survived would be stored, and so also safely stored in that box would be a good part of my happiness. If I could just leave the subject alone, I could have that peace and move forward with an enormously alleviated spirit, and in fact, an even greater joy in some ways than I'd known previously. Every time I went over the facts, with each replaying of the events surrounding my sister's initial "a manual" moment, followed by the "hair" and "toe" episodes, and finally "the lights at work" message, I was re-convinced that something "supernatural" had transpired. The complexity of what would have needed to happen to fake these things, to know that those three utterances would carry such weight, seemed enormous. And for a lot of people, that would have been enough to leave that box full of peace safely secured and stowed away. But since my brain doesn't always cooperate, the calming replaying of the facts was no longer enough. I needed more.

So, about three years after that first reading with Angelina Diana, I called her. My fingers trembled as I dialed, unsure of what I was going to say. I knew what I wanted to say, but had no idea how to do it. What I wanted to say was, "Hey, you gave a reading for my family a few years ago that changed my life and I've been telling everyone about it, which has made some people feel better. So, now I want to make sure you weren't cheating, which would mean I have been lying to people, and they are feeling better for reasons they shouldn't be, reasons that I put in their heads because you are so good at doing whatever deceitful and despicable thing you are doing, if, in fact, that's what you're doing, so now I'd like to test you to see if that's what you're doing." But mercifully, what I said was, "Hi Angelina. You probably won't remember me, but you gave a reading for my family a few years ago that changed my life, and I think I'd like to make a documentary regarding what happened and I was hoping we could talk about it over some coffee?" Angelina said, "Oh, well, sure!"

We set up a time to meet the following week, and after the relief of the proposition being well-received wore off, I realized I'd just committed to making a documentary—which would have been fine, had I known the first thing about making documentaries. Here's what happened in my brain: deep down, I knew that what I was actually after was more proof that this phenomenon was real and that this woman was capable of it. Though the "hair" experience had completely altered my sense of reality, and that new sense was further cemented with the following readings with two other mediums, during the years that had since passed, it was impossible for me to completely shut out the "But what if . . ." part of my subconscious, no matter how unlikely the "if" would have had to be. The only way I could be totally sure that nothing underhanded had happened would be if I had complete control over the events leading up to a reading. I'd need to be the person who picked the sitter and be the only one who knew who that person was. I'd set the time and place for the sitting, and I'd have to get it all on camera so I could carefully analyze it afterwards. That was what my brain required to finally let this question rest. And it occurred to me that making a documentary would be the best way to get what I was after. But how could I say all of that to Angelina? As I said, this woman had struck me as kind and compassionate. Coming at her with questions about genuineness made me incredibly uncomfortable. I knew I'd need to frame this the right way.

A friend and I sat with Angelina in a small coffee shop near her home. She was as warm as I remembered and in high spirits, so to speak. It can be an odd experience, sitting across from someone who claims to be psychic and able to hear the dead. I found myself trying to not think about anything weird, like, for instance, the Lucky Charms guy, which for a reason I'll need to unpack someday with a therapist, turns out to be the first thing to spring to mind when I try to not have something in mind. This, of course, had the opposite effect, and for a few minutes my entire inner world was overrun with marshmallow-hording leprechauns. (Afterwards, I asked my friend, Marie, who'd come with me, if she had the same problem. "No," she told me. "Oh," I said). I recounted to Angelina the "hair story," which she didn't seem to recall, but she said she was so happy to know it had helped in the way it did. I then took a deep breath and prepared to make my proposal, a proposal that, for no money, and with no control on her part, she would submit to letting me put her on film doing readings for people that I would choose, and whom I would give her absolutely no information on—she'd not even know whether she was reading a male or female until the person walked in, so I could scrutinize the entire experience. I knew she was going to turn this setup down when I was barely halfway through explaining it. And I understood. From her perspective, there was no reason to do this. Mediums are considered frauds by many people a priori. For her to agree to do this with someone she knew absolutely nothing about, to sign a release form allowing me to use the footage as I saw fit, would be far too big a risk for her, even if she was 100% above board—which made it rather surprising that upon my finishing the pitch she said, "Sure, I'll do that!"

And that was it. She had absolutely no caveats. She asked for no changes to how it would be done. She would allow me to set up the time and the place, and I could choose whoever I wanted in the whole wide world to be the sitters. And it was sitters plural, because I'd told Angelina I wanted to do this with at least ten different people, knowing how important replication would be for anyone who wanted to take a serious look at what we had done. When we spoke at some later time, I said, "I was surprised that you agreed, given the controls in place." Angelina responded, "Well, I'm pretty good at sensing what people are like, and I know your intentions are in the right place." And she was correct about that—I simply wanted to get to the truth and was certainly hoping the truth would be that she actually had heard my still alive dad. That said, I realized she was taking a big risk by allowing this stranger to do what I proposed, and the ease with which she said, "Yes" has always stuck with me.

Given our set up, "hot reading" would absolutely be ruled out. Angelina would have no opportunity for research of any kind, as the people she was going to sit with were to be chosen by me. I also did not share with any of the crew who the sitters were going to be. We would set up for a day of filming, and the schedule would simply say, "1pm: Sitter One arrives." This meant that I was the only person on set who knew who was coming that day and what deceased person they were hoping to hear from. The crew I hired was on the skeptical side. They were each open-minded, but all of them quite intelligent, and each was coming into the process leaning towards the idea that mediums were fraudsters. I wanted to have that, because I thought it would be interesting to see how their perspective might change (or not) over the course of the journey. Angelina would come alone to set, so she'd have no accomplice anywhere, perhaps listening for information as the sitter arrived. The only way Angelina could "cheat" would be to "cold read," hoping the Forer effect would be enough to dupe the sitter—and all of us.

Over the course of six days, taking place over the span of a year, I conducted and filmed 10 readings, each with a sitter who was hoping to hear from a specific deceased loved one. I found each sitter by word of mouth, speaking directly to them either in person, on the phone, or via email, so that there would not be any social media traces of my choices. Some were people I knew through work (between being an actor who has worked in many different theaters, in many different places, and bartending on Broadway, the pool of potential sitters was large, diverse, and geographically spread out), and some were referred to me by people I knew (again, via direct communication—there were no public discussions on Facebook, or any other social media, for instance). The sitters ranged from quite skeptical all the way to believer. This is a subjective assessment, of course, but I would say that most of the 10 sitters fell in the middle of the skeptic/believer scale. All 10 were at least open to the possibility of mediumship. 4 had been to a medium before, and 6 had not. Of the 6 that had not, 1 was quite skeptical, and the other 5 leaned more towards skepticism than belief. The 4 that had been to a medium previously all believed that they'd had a genuine experience with that medium. It can certainly be argued that a person coming into a reading already believing in mediumship, and not just its possibility, might view some information in a positive light, whereas a non-believer, given the same information, might have the opposite reaction. Indeed, studies have shown that belief in the paranormal increases the chances of experiencing it. For instance, in a study done at Eastern Illinois University, it was found that students who believed ESP was possible scored better on an ESP test than students who did not believe it was possible. Why that might be is the subject for another book. Here, I'll simply note that a person's attitude towards mediumship may potentially unconsciously affect their perception of the medium's accuracy. For that reason, the data, the actual rate of accuracy of Angelina's verifiable messages from supposed deceased people would be more important than the sitter's overall sense of the reading's success, at least from the perspective science would take.

Before the sitters had their readings, I spoke with them each privately and instructed them to be mindful of not giving any information to Angelina. They would not see her until the cameras were rolling, and upon meeting, the natural instinct might be to say, "Hello, my name is Edwin," for instance, and they were explicitly asked to not do that, or say anything beyond "Hello." We spoke also about being very careful during the reading itself to not give any verbal information, and to offer only a "Yes" or a "No" if Angelina asked, "Does that make sense?" Angelina also gave this admonition to the sitters before she began, so this request was clear, in the front of their minds, and generally adhered to. Of course, the other means of cold reading would still be available to Angelina, including gathering information from their faces, attire, body language, etc. But we'll come back to that. For now, we'll focus only on the fact that Angelina had no way of knowing anything about the sitters before the readings began, and that sitters were careful not to verbally help Angelina "fish," which is a pillar of successful cold reading.

With the sitters chosen by me (and only me), and instructed as to how the sittings would proceed, the stage was set for me to find out if my mind had created something that wasn't there three years earlier. When the day of the first reading arrived and the crew set up the location, I was both extremely excited, and very nervous. The nervousness was coming from a few places. For one, if the readings turned out to be unsuccessful, I knew I'd immediately begin to question my own experience. I'd be in danger of losing my father all over again, even though I'd had so much evidence by this point, if the foundation that my journey had been built on crumbled, I knew my mind would hold in serious question the journey itself. But what gave me just as much pause was how this would turn out for the sitters. I felt an extreme responsibility to them and their mental well-being. I worried incessantly that I had built up my personal experience so much, that they could not help but be let down. And when they walked onto the set and saw all of the cameras and bright lights, surely they'd think, *Well, something amazing must be about to happen here . . . why else would this guy go to all the trouble?* It was clear to me in that moment, in a very visceral way, that someone faking mediumship would need to be cut off from this sense of responsibility to the sitter, in one way or another. I reminded myself that I'd observed no sociopathic tendencies in Angelina, and had been previously moved by her apparent desire to truly help people move through grief. With that in mind, it was time to begin my little test.

The sittings were carried out in multiple locations, though the majority of them (7) took place at my mom's house, the very house where we'd had the reading with Angelina three years earlier. The room where the readings were held is off the back of the house and secluded from the rest of the home. This meant that we were easily able to keep Angelina and the sitters separate until the moment of the readings. Sometimes, the sitter would already be seated in the room when Angelina arrived at the house, and at other times, Angelina would be seated in the room when the sitter arrived. At no time was Angelina and any of the 10 sitters in a room together or within sight or sound of each other before the readings began.

Once the sitter or Angelina had been led into the room by me, I left and watched from a monitor in another location where Angelina had no way of seeing me. This is important to note, because by the time the sitter came for the reading, I knew a great deal about them and who they were hoping to hear from. Had I been in the room, it's entirely possible Angelina could have picked up on unconscious cues I gave off as information she offered that I knew to either be correct or incorrect, somehow affected me in a visible way. Some have also said, "Well, if you had in your mind what the sitters said, couldn't Angelina pick up the information from you without you being in the room? To which I answer, "Sure, but in the case that a medium is reading minds, it seems it'd be much easier to use the minds of the people sitting in front of her who know a whole lot more than I do about their deceased person." I can also say that I have since tried "shouting" things to a medium using my thoughts, and they have not once mentioned what I was shouting. Though we can't ever be completely certain, this makes it seem more likely that the information is coming from some other source.

In a moment, I will give you a summary of the readings that we carried out, including Angelina's overall accuracy percentage, sitters' response to the readings, and my conclusions. But first, let's go over a reading that I consider to be generally representative of the first 8 readings, both qualitatively and quantitatively. The final 2 readings were methodologically different, so those will be considered separately afterwards.

The first reading was with a woman named Heather and her mom, Anne. Both were open to the possibility of mediumship, with Heather being what seemed like the more likely to believe than her mom. Anne told me that she would require very definitive proof before she believed Angelina was actually doing what she claimed to, and noted that she was wary of being "played for a fool." Of the 10 sitters, it was my estimation that Anne would be among the most difficult to convince, if not *the* most. Heather is an actress and acting teacher, and her mom, Anne, spent her life as an English teacher, then principal, and finally superintendent of schools.

Heather and Anne were hoping to connect with Heather's dad, Anne's husband, Stewart. Stewart was a history teacher, and he and Anne met in their early twenties when they both taught at the same school—the school where Stewart would actually spend his entire professional life, first as a teacher, and then the principal. The love between Stewart and Anne was described as being of the "first sight" variety for Stewart, and came soon after for the woman who would become his lifelong wife and close partner. Married for nearly fifty years at the time Stewart passed, their relationship comes off as being of the fairy tale sort—a lifelong love affair that only grew. As Anne said, "I loved him more when he passed than when I married him." Sadly, Stewart passed from complications related to Alzheimer's disease, meaning Anne and Heather and their family had to watch the slow letting go of a mind that was once so bright. But though he may have lost his ability to clearly think, he never lost the core of who he was. When asked to use one word to describe Stewart, Anne and Heather simultaneously said, "Kind." Unable to leave it at just that, Anne added, "And funny—he was very, very funny. Funny and kind." This description of Stewart, shared through eyes that were becoming pink and glistening, brought my dad instantly to mind, and I soon realized I was going to have to hold my emotions in check as I went through this process. The pain of tremendous loss in the faces of the people across the table from me, and seeing through their tears the faint hope that some connection might bring a part of Stewart back to them that day, hit me hard. I found myself talking in my head to my father saying, "Please, Dad, if this is real, please help Stewart come through today. They need it so badly. Please, Dad."

Wanting to know more about him, I asked what Stewart was most passionate about, besides those he loved. "Teaching," they blurted without hesitation. "He was a fantastic teacher," Anne continued. "Even when it was towards the end and he was in the care facility, he would walk up and down the halls being a teacher. With all of the same kindness he showed throughout his life, all of the same warmth and care, he gently instructed his fellow patients, also struggling with Alzheimer's, on various lessons. For instance, he'd show them how to hold a ball and pass it to him, and he did it with such tenderness, even when his mind was totally gone." And though he could no longer remember who Anne was or how he knew her, he continued to be entranced by her, saying until the end, "My, you are beautiful." Such a man was he and so profound was the love between Anne and Stewart, that Anne is now writing a book about him, feeling the need to preserve the legacy of his life and his life's work as a teacher and principal. I asked Anne if there was anything in particular she wanted to hear from Stewart should Angelina claim a connection with him. Anne said, "Yes. The school he spent his entire career teaching at, and then being the principal for, is being torn down right now to make townhouses. I'd like to know if he is aware of that."

With all of that information in the back of my mind, Angelina arrived and I ushered her into the house, and to her seat across the table from Heather and Anne. I then left to take my position in another room in which a monitor was set up so that those on the crew could watch the proceedings. Though I'd gone to a lot of effort to make this happen (and spent a good portion of the money my dad had left me), in that moment, all I could think was, *I hope this helps. And at the very, very least, I am desperate for it not to hurt.* And it again crossed my mind how fragile a thing people are and how awful someone would have to be to toy with those who are grieving in this way, were they lying about what they say they can do.

Angelina gave the same speech, almost verbatim, that she'd given to my family when we sat with her, describing how she receives the information she says she does, including seeing, hearing, tasting and feeling, and asking the sitters to answer with only a "Yes" or a "No" when she asks if they understand something. Finally, as my heart thundered, she asked, "Do you have any questions?" Heather and Anne said they did not, and Angelina said, "Okay, then I'm ready to begin. The first thing I have is a male coming through, with a very funny personality." She then looked at Heather and said, "Is your father passed?"

"Yes," she said.

"His energy feels very smart and skeptical—very good with the English language—but also very relatable. He is not at all mean in his skepticism. He may not have believed in mediumship in his life, but he is being very nice to me. Was he a teacher?"

Okay. So, folks, as you might imagine, at this point I was feeling that sense of mysticism I'd felt during my own readings. If Angelina was cold reading, we might consider it a high-percentage guess for her to see a woman in her late-thirties, one in her sixties, both with blond hair and blue eyes, and suppose they might be there to hear from a man who was a father to one, and husband to the other. Her next "guess," that he was "very relatable" and "nice" might also be assumed. Someone that people would care to go to the trouble of sitting with a medium to connect with was probably not an absolute jerk that they never wanted to hear from again. But what she said next out of all of the things she could have said next, was, "Was he a teacher?" I don't know how many professions there are in the world, but certainly chance would say the likelihood of hitting on his with her first "guess" must be extremely small. There was nothing I could see in Heather and Anne's physical appearances (and certainly nothing in the only word they'd said so far, one solitary "Yes") that would say to Angelina, "I bet these two are here hoping to hear from a guy that was a teacher." Angelina then said, "He could speak about a topic in depth, maybe even until people were bored." Though Heather and Anne nodded "Yes" to that statement, I considered it too general to count in the mental tally I was keeping. But then she said, "He was a very sensitive man. Very concerned about the people around him. Kind. He was very kind."

That definitely stood out to me. When I'd asked Heather and Anne to describe him, they'd said "kind and funny." And when I asked about his major passion in life, besides family, they said, "Teaching." Angelina, in the course of thirty-seconds had said:

- There is a male here with a **funny** personality
- He is your (looking at Heather) **dad**
- He was a **teacher**
- He was **kind**

Of the six things Angelina had said, four of them were things Heather and Anne had specifically told me on camera before Angelina was anywhere near Guilford, Connecticut where the readings were happening. And though I considered the other two things general enough to be widely applicable, and definitely susceptible to the Forer effect, they did indeed fit Stewart. He was, according to his daughter and wife, "smart and good with the English language," and able to "talk about a topic in depth, perhaps to the point that people might get bored." Had it been my sitting and Angelina had said these same two statements, they would not have been identifying to me. Though my dad was certainly smart, "Good with the English language" is not something that I or my family would say was a stand-out attribute of his. He had what we might call an average command of the English language—it was not the way my dad would attempt, I should think, to stand out from the "spirit crowd," as his use of the English language was on par with most Americans. Stewart, on the other hand, according to his family, had an above-average command of English (as does his wife, Anne, who has spent a large part of her life as an English teacher). In fact, when I was speaking with Anne and Heather before the reading began (again, before Angelina had arrived at the location), Anne made a joke about her sometime "sailor mouth." She said that any time she used language that one might consider to be on the "blue" side, Stewart, who they said *never* spoke like that, would say in mock disappointment,

"Anne . . . you're an English teacher." So, though the statement "He is good with the English language" might be widely applicable, I would not consider it identifying of my dad, but it is particularly identifying of Stewart, and it had just been discussed between us not an hour before. Similarly, if someone said, "This person could talk about a topic in depth, perhaps to the point of people getting bored," my dad would not at all come to mind. In fact, I would have considered it a clear miss. For Stewart, however, this again felt particularly identifying to his wife and daughter. Nonetheless, when I later tally Angelina's accuracy, I will not include either of these statements, as I consider them too general to constitute evidence for an audience wider than Stewart's loved ones (who very much did consider them evidential).

Angelina, after speaking for a bit about how kind Stewart felt to her, and how kind he was in his life, said to Anne, "He wants you to relax regarding his body of work." You'll recall that when Anne was asked about the one thing she most wanted to know from Stewart was whether or not he was aware that the school he'd spent his life teaching and being a principal in, was being torn down to make townhouses. The thought of Stewart being aware of this was extremely distressing to Anne—so much so that it was her main question for him. She'd said to me, "I want to know if he is aware of that and how he feels about that, but at the same time, I hope he doesn't know." It was her opinion that to know the place where he'd spent his entire professional life was being torn down would break his heart. In this light, "He wants you to relax regarding his body of work" takes on, or at least it did to Anne, Heather, and those listening at the monitor with me, a highly significant meaning. I leave it to the reader to consider how general or not this statement might be, how it might or might not apply to loved-ones in your own lives, and how susceptible to the Forer effect it might be. For Anne, who was again likely our most skeptical sitter, that statement from Angelina carried great import. Because it weighed so heavily on her, the thought of "his" school being torn down, Anne was doing what she could, it seemed to me, to preserve Stewart's legacy—in the midst of writing a book about his life and work. She may have felt that every page she wrote about her beloved replaced a "Stewart brick" in the school that was being demolished. This idea came roaring home to me when, directly after saying, "He wants you to relax about his body of work," Angelina continued, asking "Was he a non-fiction writer?"

That statement is incorrect. He was not a non-fiction writer, and when I tally Angelina's accuracy percentage, it will be counted as being incorrect. But though it may count against Angelina's score, as it must for the sake of science anyway, to me and Stewart's family, this again was a highly intriguing statement, given that Anne is writing a non-fiction book about Stewart, and the fact that Angelina's question came directly after the statement about Anne needing to relax about Stewart's body of work—the non-fiction book she is writing is about Stewart's life, Stewart's "body of work." However, in the moment, when asked if he was a non-fiction writer, Anne simply said, "No," and nothing more. Angelina then said, "Okay, well I'll just tell you what I'm seeing. He is showing me writing connected to him. Non-fiction writing." Anne and Heather looked at each other with a smile, saying nothing more about it, and Angelina moved on, saying once more, "He's showing me a classroom again. Everything is a classroom with him. He is always teaching, even now." And as I stood in the other room watching on the monitor, Anne's story about Stewart still teaching his fellow patients at the care facility, even when the majority of his mind had been ravaged by the incessant and cruel march of Alzheimer's, came rushing back to me.

Then, a new supposed spirit apparently stepped in, one I had no knowledge of, and I thought the reading was about to "go off the rails," as I knew the only person Anne and Heather had come to hear from was Stewart. As it would turn out, this new spirit was about to provide among the best evidence I'd encountered that life does indeed go on, and would push me further towards the notion that it was not telepathy on Angelina's part (and certainly not cold-reading or any kind of fraud), but rather seemed to indicate individual agency on the part of a disembodied consciousness.

Angelina, suddenly veering away from these message's ostensibly from Stewart, the one spirit that Heather and her mom had come all the way from New Jersey to connect with said, "I have a young male energy stepping forward who had a difficult life and drug-related issues. The teacher energy now has this young male with him on the other side and is saying, "I can finally help him in a way I couldn't when we were there (i.e., alive on Earth). There is a hard 'C' or 'K' name connected to this younger male that he wants to acknowledge. This young male was a dog lover, and there is a dog with him over there that has passed."

To my surprise, Anne and Heather both nodded when Angelina rattled this description off, apparently knowing exactly who this younger male was, and seemingly quite moved to be hearing from him. They said, "Yes" to each of the descriptive statements Angelina made about this new spirit she claimed to be sensing. I would later learn that Anne's dog-loving nephew, son of her sister Kay, had struggled mightily with drugs. And his beloved dog passed not long after he did. But what was much more surprising to me was when they told me, following the reading, that this young man had been previously claimed by a different medium to unexpectedly show up during a session.

A number of years before Angelina sat down with Anne and Heather, Anne's other daughter, Erin, just happened to be in a room with the well-known medium, John Edward, as mentioned earlier, made famous by his television show, *Crossing Over*. Erin is a very successful actress, having appeared in multiple television and Broadway shows, and having been nominated for a TONY award for leading actress in a musical. Erin and Heather grew up with Broadway star Kristin Chenoweth, and Erin and

151

Kristin are very close, life-long friends. John Edward occasionally gave readings for celebrities on his show, and Kristin was intended to be the subject of an episode. Excited about the opportunity to connect with deceased loved ones and wanting to share the experience, she asked Erin to come along with her to be an observer. Almost as soon as the reading began, Edwards' reading for the star of the segment got interrupted by a spirit attempting to reach not Kristin, but someone else. It was supposedly the spirit of a young man who'd passed well before his time who was barging in, intent on getting a message to his bereaved mother that he was okay. Erin, sitting beside her friend on the couch, soon recognized who this person was that Edward was describing, and eventually raised her hand to say, "Actually, I think this is for me." And then John Edward went on to deliver messages that, just as Angelina's would do years later at my mom's house, convinced Erin the spirit was indeed her cousin.

I pose the question once more: what are the odds that two separate readings by two different mediums, separated in time and space, giving readings for people who were there to hear from someone else, would be interrupted by an energy that both sitters easily identified as the same person?

Angelina eventually came back to the first energy she'd sensed who they'd come to believe by that point truly was Stewart, saying, "The way he passed made him feel mummied-in." Though we can't be sure how Stewart actually felt about the way he passed, "mummied-in" certainly might be an apt description of how Alzheimer's feels from within. And in perhaps the most difficult to explain (by normal means) moment of the reading, Angelina asked, "Did something about his work fall apart after his passing? He's showing me pieces and squares moving away from each other," as she used her hands to indicate pieces being thrown away in different directions from a center point. It was difficult to not perceive those "squares" "moving away from each other" as being the bricks of his beloved school being torn apart, which was happening as we all sat there. Apparently not wanting that distressing thought to be what Anne was left with, worried as she was about him even being aware of it, the supposed energy of Stewart went on through Angelina to say, "But there was something separate from that falling apart, prior to the falling apart, something he established that's all him, that's all that matters. He showed me all of the pieces or squares kind of moving away from each like, 'that's no longer, that's no longer, that's no longer, BUT! . . . there's one left. One piece left. And that's mine. And no one can ever touch it. That's who I am.'"

And with that, tears came to Anne's eyes.

What it is exactly that had happened no one can currently say for certain. Many, I knew, would say that mere coincidence happened. Desire to believe happened. Entirely natural and explainable events happened. But those people will have a hard time convincing Heather and Anne of that. To them, as extraordinary or even impossible as it may seem to the ardent materialist skeptic, the simplest explanation for some of the things this complete stranger said to them was that their beloved father and husband was saying them to her. Which meant that my father may have done the same thing. It meant I remained not crazy for thinking my dad might be standing beside me, watching the monitor while his new spirit buddy, Stewart, made his way back to his beloved wife and daughter for a while.

For those of you who are interested in seeing the actual breakdown of Angelina's accuracy rate, Appendix I contains detailed information regarding her "hits" and "misses" while participating in my experiment.

Obviously, math can only get us so far here. In my personal experience with Angelina, had everything she said been entirely off the mark, had it sounded as though she'd been talking about any human being other than my dad, but then finished by saying, "He wants me to talk about your hair," that statement alone would have caused me to think twice about dismissing the experience. Likewise, when I show Anne that, when broken down in the quantitative way you'll see in Appendix I, Angelina's accuracy was 63%, though that might strike her as impressive, it is the *quality* of certain things Angelina said that are more evidential to Anne, if not to science.

We are left in a situation where math might not be the ultimate road to truth in this particular case, to the dismay of mathematicians and scientists everywhere. In this case, math might tell us one thing, while content might tell us another. For instance, here is a portion of Anne and Heather's reading where math would give us a 50/50 result for accuracy, and therefore, a mathematical wash as evidence of survival: Angelina asked if the older male energy had a humidor, to which they said, "No." Angelina then asked, "Did he have a hobby where he needed to keep things at a certain temperature?" This was a "Yes." An "enormous" yes. Stewart was an avid gardener—to the point that he had an entire garden sanctuary in his basement. Each plant required different amounts of light and temperature, so Stewart set up individual places where temperature could be independently controlled for each type. It was a large part of his life, a passion that came second only to teaching. If Angelina was wrong about anything it might be that "hobby" was not a strong enough word. Therefore, though math weighs the "no" and the "yes" equally, clearly they are not equal qualitatively. Math has provided fantastic insight to humanity. It has helped us peer into complicated knots of information, penetrating and untangling questions in ways that only math is able to. It has helped us know why it takes 365.25 days for the earth to go around the sun, and why the sun's explosive force is equally matched by its gravitational compacting, resulting in stability. Math was the key to finding the double-helix of DNA and the methods to build the pyramids and skyscrapers. Math has been useful in too many ways to count. It's possible, though, that mediumship research is not one of the ways, or at least, not the prime way. That said, to me, the math here is telling nonetheless. Angelina's average rate of accuracy, as calculated combining all 10 readings, was 62.95%. Of the 10 readings, sitters in 6 of them considered the experience to be "life-changing," coming out of it believing that Angelina was actually communicating in some way with their deceased loved ones, and with a new level of acceptance of "life after death." Even Anne, our most skeptical sitter, came out of the experience "a believer," and with a new level of comfort, believing that Stewart truly does still exist in some form. All 11 sitters were sufficiently impressed to believe Angelina was getting her messages in a "paranormal" way, even if they were less sure it was their discarnate (dead) person providing the information.

As mentioned, I went into detail with this particular reading because I consider it to be generally representative in quality and statistical results to the others (and in fact, the accuracy rate in this reading is exactly the same as the average accuracy rate for all readings, 62.9%), but I'll mention just some of the highlights from the others. First, in 8 out of the 10 readings, she correctly identified aspects of the deceased person's passing. In all 8, she was correct the first time she mentioned the passing (so if she said, "They passed from a heart attack," and the sitter said, "No," and she then said, "cancer," it would not have been counted as a hit). This seems remarkably significant, statistically speaking, especially given the fact that some of the modes of death were given quite specifically. For instance, in one case the sitter was hoping to hear from her deceased older brother who passed in an accident after his car flipped over and exploded into flames when he was 19 and she was only 2. Angelina said, "I have a male figure here who was older than you, who acted paternally towards you. I'm smelling gasoline. He passed in a tragedy involving an explosion." The chances of getting that (which she did within moments of the reading's beginning), while making no other "guesses" for mode of death, must be quite small. In another case, she said to a sitter, "He had stomach issues before he passed." As the sitter told us after the sitting, her brother had passed from large tumors in his

155

stomach. In yet another reading, Angelina told a sitter named Sara, "Your mom had lung issues. She passed from cancer." In fact, Sara's mom had passed from lung cancer. A woman named Jackie was hoping to hear from her husband who'd passed in a motorcycle accident, an accident in which the motorcycle had been thrown into her husband, primarily impacting his head and chest. Angelina first said, "His life ended quickly. He was here and gone quite fast," to which Jackie simply said, "Yes." A few moments later Angelina said, "His passing was so fast he didn't even know what happened to him, so it was gentle in that way, even though the scene didn't look gentle. There was a head injury that goes down into his chest. These two areas are majorly affected." Again, all of this was after the one-word answer of "Yes." In yet another reading, she told the sitter, Richard, while speaking of his mom, "She had a head injury—something wrong with her head when she passed." Richard's mother (who was the deceased person he most wanted to hear from) had passed from a cerebral hemorrhage. We've already gone over the "mummied-in" feeling Angelina got regarding the passing of Stewart who had Alzheimer's disease. In another reading, Angelina correctly said that the deceased person had passed after "A long illness that affected her lungs, stomach, kidneys, a lot of things," though she didn't specifically give a name to the illness. And finally, she told one of the sitters that her dad passed "Very quickly. He left the family feeling like they didn't have all the answers about his passing. But it was very quick. Almost like he passed out." This was highly significant to me, because the sitter Angelina was reading at that point was my sister, Jen.

Of course, the astute reader will be saying, "Wait a minute, your sister, if my count is correct, had already had a reading two other times from Angelina, first, at the large event at the theater, and then the next week at your mom's house. Even though that had happened a few years before these filmed readings, surely Angelina might be expected to remember who your sister is! Plus, she looks just like you!" (Sorry about that part, sis). And, astute reader, you would be correct to lodge this complaint. However, by this point in the process, I had decided to throw a curveball Angelina's way. For 3 of the readings, the sitter was entirely concealed behind an opaque, two-paneled screen, which went from the sitter's feet to well above their head. When Angelina arrived on set, the sitters were already hidden behind the screen, so there was never a time before those readings that Angelina had a chance to so much as catch a glimpse of who the sitter was. "But wait," you are saying now, "Angelina may have recognized your sister's voice! And even if not, she could still have gotten clues from the way your sister answered 'Yes' and 'No!'" Yes, again, reader. Well done. However, for 2 of the 3 concealed readings, including the one with Jen, we had a box set up on Angelina's side of the partition holding three screens that individually lit up when a button was pressed on the sitter's side of the blockade. The sitter would answer each question by hitting a button for "Yes," "No," or "Unsure," which lit up the corresponding "Yes," "No," or "Unsure" screen for Angelina to see. So, for these 2 sittings, not only was "hot reading" out of the question, as there was simply no way for Angelina to have prior knowledge of who the sitters would be, but "cold reading" was also ruled out as an option for Angelina to cheat with. She would be given no visual or verbal cues by the sitter or anyone else. It was just her and a cardboard box that lit up with a "Yes," "No," or "Unsure" anytime Angelina asked, "Do you understand this?" Given all of that, as I watched from a monitor in a different room, I was stunned when Angelina again, now for the third time (unbeknownst to her) harped on how this sitter's dad (who is my dad) had passed "very quickly—almost like he passed out." I was convinced in that moment that something real was happening. And I became so excited I began to hit my friend on the head when Angelina next said, "I'm hearing the name Robert," which you may recall is my dad's name.

In a perspective-shifting surprise, the accuracy percentage for verifiable information for the readings where the sitters were concealed and silent was 53%. This was 10% lower than the other readings, indicating perhaps, that some cold-reading may come into play, even subconsciously. Alternatively, the voice of the sitters might be important in some way. That obviously, is entirely speculative. Also, Angelina had never done readings in that way before. It's possible she would have gotten better in this mode of working. The sample size of 2 is entirely too small to draw any conclusions, so I'll simply note that in Angelina's first reading performed in this way, her accuracy was 50%, and then in the second, it was 56%. I'd like to see in the future if this upward trend might continue with her. Though the overall accuracy was 10% lower than the other readings, the "dazzle shots" were still there. For instance, it was in one of those readings that Angelina talked about smelling gasoline and seeing an explosion connected to the deceased person's passing. Meaning, with absolutely no visual or auditory cues, and no knowledge whatsoever of who the sitter was, she very quickly hit on the mode of death of the sitter's loved one—the only mode of death she mentioned at any point in the reading for him. Given that dying in an explosion is a very uncommon mode of death (and one that Angelina has never alluded to in any of the other sittings I have watched her perform), this one moment must stand out as the "extraordinary evidence" skeptics constantly request in their oft repeated quoting of Carl Sagan: "Extraordinary claims require extraordinary evidence" (ECREE). They use it so often, in fact, that in emails to me from skeptics I wrote to looking to get their side of the story after conducting these ten readings, they simply wrote, "ECREE," having grown tired, apparently, of spelling it out, so frequently do they cite it. To me, for Angelina to offer 1 uncommon mode of death for a spirit she claimed to be sensing, and for that uncommon mode of death to match the discarnate the sitter had come to hear from (among other highly specific hits), with no normal way for her to gather information about the person who'd passed, seems like it answers the skeptics ECREE call.

Likewise, in my sister's reading, those dazzling moments were there, too. "Robert," of course, is a big one, since Angelina gave 3 names during my sister's reading, and 1 of them was our dad's. Beyond *again* focusing on our dad's very fast passing (this time when the sitter behind the screen could have been anyone on Earth), she also said at one point, "Did you discover a letter he wrote after he passed?" Again bringing to mind the "hand-written note" she asked about two years before in the living room she was now just fifty feet away from, which led to my sister and I giving my mom the poem we'd found written by our dad. Finally, Angelina (still not knowing who the sitter was) asked Jen, "Did you have a mishap with your clothes today . . . like, a wardrobe malfunction?" Jen immediately smiled and answered, "Yes." She later told us that when she was getting ready to come to the reading, she'd been trying to get a necklace on, and just couldn't do it. She simply could not get it to clasp. Eventually, getting more flustered and worried she was going to be late, she said out loud, "Dad, help me with this necklace!" And it snapped into place. She thought that was pretty neat, but was much more surprised by Angelina asking about "a mishap with her clothes." Since she literally lives around the corner from my mother, Jen was asking for my dad's help with her necklace just minutes before Angelina would ask her question.

So, even when all conceivable modes of cheating had been taken away from Angelina, she still achieved results that I considered to be significant. The other sitter who'd been concealed also felt that way. She is one of the participants who found her reading to be of the "life-changing" variety, and who now believes that life after death is a real possibility. And after going over and over, watching again and again these readings, I came away feeling that my dad "being with us," maintaining his relationship with me in a new but just as full way, was still a distinct possibility, and one that had become even more likely. I'd gone into the proposition quite nervous that my confidence in what I'd previously experienced would be shaken once I was able to perceive the process of Angelina's mediumship from an emotional distance, and once I was able to break it down and examine it moment by moment. But the opposite happened. Now, I was even more convinced that a genuine phenomenon was occurring that somehow the scientific world had overlooked (or ignored). However, I'm no scientist. I needed someone more academically qualified to tell me what I was missing. Because according to the science I knew, I *had* to be missing something. I had somehow been a victim of craven deceit and the failings of my own mind, duped into seeing something that wasn't actually there. Ten times. According to some pretty smart people, that is the *only* explanation.

# CHAPTER ELEVEN

# The Metamorphosis of Bullshit

I decided, with some trepidation, but buoyed by my personal Angelina experiment, to chance my dad's continued existence and seriously examine what skeptics had to say. Two names that kept on popping up in my strolls through the internet were James Randi, perhaps better known as "The Amazing Randi," and Michael Shermer, founder of the Skeptics Society. "Skepticism" has always been a bit of a confusing word to me. It seems that it is meant as a counterbalance to the word "belief," each falling on opposite ends of a spectrum that considers whether or not a thing is true. Indeed, Shermer says he became a skeptic in response to his own bout with belief. While still in high school, he went to a church service where he says, "A very dynamic and histrionic preacher inspired [him] to come forward at the end of the sermon to be saved." Apparently, the effect was profound, as Shermer then went door to door for seven years evangelizing his newly acquired beliefs. And perhaps this is where the disconnect between Shermer and I begins. He, unlike me, had an experience which he eventually felt had led him astray. He believed without proof, and recoiling from that, went in the opposite direction, with his default position set instead to disbelief—to "skepticism." But science, it always seemed to me from the time I could understand what it was, made both of those words, "belief" and "disbelief," irrelevant, along with that entire spectrum between them. Because science isn't about how much you do or do not believe in something: it is simply the search, through observation, for facts. A fact is not something you believe in or are skeptical about. Are you skeptical that a car that advances one mile in sixty-seconds is going sixty miles per hour? Do you believe leaves change colors in Vermont in the fall? No. You *know* these things. These are true things—established facts based on observation. So, to me, to have a "Skeptics Society" is as odd as having a "Believers Society." Neither of those things get us closer to the truth. Observation does. Science does. Instead, skepticism seems to be more of a philosophy. Perhaps Shermer felt duped by first believing in something without evidence, and perhaps that now colors any evidence that goes against his subsequent belief in materialism, a belief which so strongly rebukes religion as superstition. Whatever the case may be, being a skeptic came to define Shermer to a good portion of the public.

In order to keep my newly forming altered relationship with my father, I knew I was going to have to confront Mr. Shermer and the other skeptics who strike me as very smart people. I needed to know if, after a conversation with Mr. Shermer, my dad could still be standing beside me, or if Mr. Shermer would be able to convince me of why he wasn't. To feel confident about what it seemed the results of my experiments and experiences were telling me, it was important to assess whether my explications would hold up under the sort of scrutiny Mr. Shermer would provide. And if not, I needed to know why not. I needed to know whether or not Mr. Shermer and other intelligent folks like him could show me that I was mistaken in my interpretations of what I'd experienced. I'm a fairly good listener. If I am shown why my thinking is inaccurate or drawing misguided conclusions, I'll change that thinking.

Shermer founded The Skeptics Society in 1992. The society states, "Some people believe that skepticism is the rejection of new ideas, or worse, they confuse 'skeptic' with 'cynic' and think that skeptics are a bunch of grumpy curmudgeons unwilling to accept any claim that challenges the status quo. This is wrong. Skepticism is a provisional approach to claims. It is the application of reason to any and all ideas—no sacred cows allowed. In other words, skepticism is a method, not a position. Ideally, skeptics do not go into an investigation closed to the possibility that a phenomenon might be real or that a claim might be true. When we say we are 'skeptical,' we mean that we must see compelling evidence before we believe." To me, this sounds like the definition of an already established word: science. I don't see why we need a new term, but given the description, I'm a skeptic too, as getting "compelling evidence" is the very endeavor of science, and something I am all for.

After closely evaluating our readings, I sent Shermer an email explaining that I was making a documentary about mediumship and asked if he'd participate. He was quite kind in his response, saying that he would be happy to. He then went on to discuss the various ways mediums cheat, which I was familiar with. He wrote, "I'd need to see her working to see how she's doing it," which seemed not the "ideal" that The Skeptics Society extolls about "going into an investigation closed to the possibility that a phenomenon is real." It felt as though he was saying he already knew she was cheating, he just needed to decipher by what method. Shermer's casual answer reminded me that he didn't realize my father's very existence was at stake, hung precariously in the balance over a yawning abyss, and that whether or not my dad was lost to the infinite nothing, revolved around what he, as the most prominent skeptic I'd corresponded with, had to say. I wrote back offering to send him an entire reading, and also explained "the hair experiment," so that he'd be made aware of my personal connection to the question of mediumship, but that message (perhaps to some relief) received no answer. So, with my dad still in view, I continued the dive deeper into skepticism with The Amazing Randi.

James Randi had been a professional stage magician before deciding to devote the majority of his time to investigating and debunking what he called, "woo-woo." Randi didn't like the term "debunker," preferring "investigator" instead, but if you go into the investigation already calling it woo-woo, "debunker" seems more apt to me. To carry out his investigations, Randi founded The Committee for Skeptical Inquiry and The James Randi Educational Foundation, which is the foundation that famously sponsored the One Million Dollar Paranormal Challenge—a challenge that offered a million dollars to anyone who could produce paranormal phenomenon under conditions that Randi set up, and the claimant agreed to. The offer stood until 2015, at which time, according to the foundation, over a thousand people had applied to be tested, none of whom had ever been successful.

Randi was fueled in his decades-long quest by what he saw as compassion for those who were being taken advantage of, victims of fraudsters using gullibility as a weapon. He saw people claiming to be "channelers," for instance, who said they occasionally gave their bodies over to temporary possession by spirits, spirits sometimes claiming to be 40,000 years old, and then charged people money to come listen to the spirit's "wisdom." This so-called channeling was similar to what I'd watched Pat Rodegast claim to do when, according to her, Emmanuel began to speak via her physical apparatus. The difference I could see was the lack of theatricality involved in what Rodegast did. Though the sentiments were poetic, the manner in which they were delivered was quiet and subdued, and usually for just a few people at a time sitting in Pat's living room, looking out over a country road. The channelers of the "ancient sprits" from far away places that Randi took great issue with performed whatever it is they were doing for large crowds, often. Sometimes, hundreds of people would gather into enormous halls and pay good money for the privilege of being in the presence of such a spirit. The channelers often gesticulated wildly and used funny voices, and to be honest, when I watch videos of them, it's sometimes difficult not to laugh. There were also televangelists who claimed to have healing powers granted by God that Randi could not abide. They'd look out into their large megachurch audience and somehow know the names and addresses of people and what it was that ailed them. They'd then put their hands on the afflicted to offer healing, and shout a lot, and slap them on the heads and throw away their canes and literally tell them to dump out their medications, "You in the balcony, you too, just throw your pills right over the side," and the people would often be overcome with the "spirit of God" and fall to the floor and shake in divine ecstasy while the preacher passed around large buckets for people to fill with money. "Whatever you give will come back to you tenfold," he might say. And it was all too much for Randi.

"If there is something to the paranormal, let's find out what it is, if anything," Randi said. "On the other hand, let's not be taken in by the claptrap that is being offered us, and at our expense." It incensed Randi that people he saw as absolute charlatan's were using tricks of his trade in deceitful ways. "Magicians are the most honest people in the world. They tell you they're going to deceive you, and then they do it." But these folks were deceiving people, he believed, by lying to them about an ability they did not have. To try and wake the public up from what he saw as its stupor, Randi perpetrated an elaborate hoax of his own. He invented a personality who claimed to be a channeler. The person he chose to play the character was his partner (a man who would become the love of his life), and Randi trained him in the techniques he saw those people he considered charlatans using. And Randi offered this invented person, complete with fake news stories he'd created, to the world. And the media covered it as though it was real. To Randi's dismay, not a single call was made from any of the television producers to check into the history of this claimed channeler. It would have been very easy to uncover the fraud, Randi says, but no one at the television networks lifted a finger to try. And the public went along with it, assuming that things they saw on the news had been vetted by journalists. The hoax served as a reminder of how gullible we can be.

In another instance, Randi uncovered the methods of one of those evangelists, or "faith healers," named Peter Popoff. Randi had an accomplice working for the reverend who noticed that he wore what looked like a hearing aid. As Randy astutely asked, "Why would a man who is curing deafness (which he indeed claimed to do) need a hearing aid?" Randi hired someone to scan for radio frequencies during one of the reverend's services and found that, when it came time for the miraculous healings and knowledge of names and addresses delivered by God, the man scanning the radio heard a woman say, "Hello Petey, can you hear me? If you can't you're in trouble. Jody Dean, right there on your right side. She lives at 4267 Masterson." God sounded a lot like the preacher's wife. After the message was intercepted, the reverend, sure enough, called on Jody, and to her astonishment recited her address, and then told her that he and God were going to heal whatever her ailment was, which he supposedly was aware of via divine means, rather than from his wife secreted away somewhere, reading into his ear the prayer request forms the attendees had filled out. Randi played the audio of that recording for the first time on *The Tonight Show* with Johnny Carson. The reverend soon filed for bankruptcy (however, as an example of the gullibility that so riled Randi, the reverend was soon back selling "holy water" that did this or that amazing thing, and again, he was making a lot of money doing so). When I looked into these things that Randi was exposing, I felt glad to have had him. But, was what he exposed the same sort of thing that I had experienced? It didn't seem like it. No earpiece would have helped Angelina know that the anonymous person sitting silently behind our screen was hoping to hear from her brother who passed in an explosion.

166

Randi was making quite a name for himself in his quest to debunk people who were "ripping off the public," but what really brought him to prominence in the 1970s was his challenge to the legitimacy of Uri Geller. Unlike Randi, who'd made a career as a conjurer, never claiming his illusions were anything but, Geller was suddenly on television all over the world bending metal utensils with what he claimed was only his mind. In 1982, Randi published a book titled, "The Truth About Uri Geller," in which he elucidates how age-old magicians' tactics and sleight of hand were responsible for Geller's "feats," and nothing more. Geller sued Randi for libel on three separate occasions, losing each time, and having to pay Randi's legal fees. What particularly irked Randi is that Geller was being claimed by researchers at a highly respected scientific institution, the Stanford Research Institute (SRI), to have actual powers, exhibited under controlled conditions that they couldn't explain. To prove he could dupe even scientists, Randi famously inserted two young men he'd trained to bend spoons in a way that looked as though it was paranormal into a "controlled" study at a different lab. And, indeed, the scientists were duped. For *four long years*. Learning this again had me questioning my own "studies." Still, though, what I had witnessed was of a different nature. I couldn't see what amount of training could help a woman correctly guess, with one attempt, that a deceased person's name was Robert, or that his grown son was sleeping with his shirt. Nonetheless, I saw Randi's basic mission as a noble one, and so did many others who took up the skepticism mantle, fighting to expose chicanery for the good of human kind, and seeking to raise the public's general level of critical thinking. Among the most effective disciples of Randi in this mission is the popular magic duo, Penn and Teller.

"Outside of my family, no one is more important in my life," said Penn Jillette. Both he and Teller are self-described skeptics who credit Randi's career for the success of their own. I'd always personally enjoyed Penn and Teller. I found Teller, in particular, to be not only a magician, but also an artist, using silence as a powerful tool in his act, and I appreciated Penn's humor and intelligence. The degree to which skepticism fueled them had not been clear to me, however, until I started investigating mainstream explanations for mediumship. Given my regard for their work and intellects, I saw them as formidable obstacles I'd need to get beyond, were my dad to remain real to me.

Penn was particularly outspoken about mediumship. Following in Houdini and Randi's footsteps, Penn and Teller have long been actively attempting to dispel any and all notions that psychics and mediums might be real. They had a series on showtime called *Bullshit* in which they debunked mediumship (and other examples of "paranormal abilities") by trying to unmask how the "tricks" were done, just as Houdini did. In fact, in their season one premier episode, *Talking to the Dead*, they open with Penn sitting in a cemetery by what is meant to be Houdini's grave as he says, "Harry, can you believe it? The same bullshit you so thoroughly debunked almost a century ago, is continuing. And even enjoying a resurgence." He then turns away from the gravestone he'd been talking to and says to the camera, "See? Anyone can talk to the dead. Getting an answer . . . that's the hard part." The episode goes on to elucidate the various techniques we've discussed, like cold and hot reading. But our process, the one we'd used at my mom's house, seemed to rule out a lot of what was happening on *Bullshit*. During further filming I later did with Angelina, I wondered, *What would Penn say if he were to have witnessed our entire process here? Would he remain as adamantly opposed to the possibility of mediumship if he saw it happening under the circumstances I'd set up? Would he be able to do the things Angelina does if I sat people behind a screen for him? Would his accuracy rate be as high?* The sort of fraud he claimed to be catching in the Showtime episode seemed of a simpler and much less specific nature than some of what I was seeing. I began to wish I could talk to Penn and say, "But what about *this*?" Well, by sheer coincidence, I was going to get my chance.

In my job as a Broadway bartender, I have access to eight of the Nederlander theaters on Broadway. While I was in production for the film, I learned that Penn and Teller were going to be doing a short run of their Vegas magic show at the Marquis Theater on Broadway. Not only that— upon opening a Playbill I'd taken from a stack when visiting a friend at the Marquis one day, I found that one of the acts was called "Psychic Comedian," which struck me as quite lucky. Penn and Teller were about to debunk psychics right in front of my eyes.

Having gotten accustomed to the warm thought that my dad was still around, feeling I'd now witnessed enough evidence suggesting that was true, it was with a secret smirk that I watched Penn and Teller introduce their bit, "Psychic Comedian," during their magic show at the Marquis Theater. Because Penn believes there simply is no such thing as medium-ship, anyone who does it is, well . . . in his own, very unminced words at the top of the Showtime episode on mediumship: "Before we bust up this party—and, goddammit, we're gonna bust it up—we have to make it very clear where our hearts are. We have nothing but empathy for the people who are experiencing the loss and grief of the death of a loved one [. . .] I'm a momma's boy, whose mom died a couple of years ago, and I'll never get over it [. . .] Once you've felt that pure grief, seeing it exploited can . . . take away your sense of humor [. . .] These . . . performance artists are, in a very real sense, motherfuckers." Later in the episode, talking about another man who'd lost his mom and had been duped, as Penn saw it, by a fraudu-lent medium who Penn believes the cameras caught cheating by gathering information before the reading began when talking with the man (some-thing our set up in my film ruled out), Penn says, "All he will ever have left of his mom are his memories, and this pig has pissed on those for a buck, and a little unearned fame." He sums up the episode by saying, "I'm sure these lame fucks tell themselves that they're easing the grief, but skits for money cannot replace loving memories. How low do you have to be to exploit someone's true grief to sell some bullshit book?"

And I understood where he is coming from. Had I not gathered what I considered to be strong evidence that Angelina was actually doing what she claimed, I, too, would think low thoughts about people who preyed on the bereaved. But I felt as though I knew otherwise—as though I was *seeing* otherwise. I felt I'd been given a peek behind a veil that most haven't. So, as Penn introduced the next part of the show that night at the Marquis Theater, I considered his anger to be misguided, and that he just needed to be shown what I had seen. I almost felt bad that he didn't know. Because how different life feels once the possibility of its continuation beyond its apparent boundaries opens up to you. I knew that Penn and Teller were taking photos with people after the show, and I'd already decided I was going to ask him to be in my documentary. With an absurd surety, I thought maybe I'd be the one to change his mind—to shake his *complete* confidence that it was all deceit. But I didn't wait to meet Penn after the show that night. Because instead, by the end, it was *my* confidence that had been shaken.

"Most stage psychics will use plants. They use paid confederates among the audience." As I watched from the back of the theater, Penn said that as he opened up the part of the show they'd called, "Psychic Comedian." And it brought a smile to my face. Because one thing I know for sure is that no "paid confederates" had been used by me to try and trick myself when we did the readings with Angelina. Thus, so far, my experience with her (and my dad's immaterial being) was safe from Penn's acerbic and often vicious debunking. In words reminiscent of the opening to their Showtime series, Penn then prefaced the "mind-reading" and "psychic" tricks he was about to perform.

"Before I go any further, I must make this very clear: *all* ESP, *all* mind-reading, *all* talking to the dead, *all* psychic events and *all* supernatural events are, *without exception*, as we say on Showtime . . . *bull . . . shit*. There is nothing to any of it. The people who claim these powers are liars, cheaters, swindlers, rip-offs, and the tricks themselves are evil, immoral . . . and I know how to do them all," which elicited a laugh from the crowd. The conviction with which he said all of this was rather jarring, even though I already knew where he stood. To so fully dismiss so much in a single utterance with such authority felt arrogant, no matter the noble place from which the dismissal might have come. He wasn't urging people to look into any of it for themselves, he was actually telling them not to, because if you did . . . well, you were an idiot who was actively participating in something he just told you wasn't real. He said so. What else do you need to know? And this struck me as the very reason such little research of the paranormal is being carried out at the university level. Attitudes such as Penn's, full of such scathing, angry authority and condemnation, make people feel less than intelligent for even looking into these matters. People tend to believe a thing more or less based on the level of conviction with which the speaker says it, regardless of the truth of the statement. Similarly, in an area of study known as "processing fluency," we find that people are more likely to believe statements that are relatively easy to process. In a related finding, if the same food recipe is presented in different fonts, the ease with which the font is *read* gets equated in the brain to how easy or not the *process* of making that food will be. *How* something is presented colors the information, and affects what is ultimately *received* as being true. Penn, in his sweeping dismissal of mediumship (and my dad's existence) could not have stated it with more conviction, or in simpler font. His message was exceedingly clear, and said with a thundering clout: just holding the notion that there might be something to the phenomena that some people claim to have experienced makes you a dolt. Because of how brains receive and process information, we might easily be made to feel by Penn and other skeptics' full-throated and unequivocal position that since it's impossible, it's impossible (and looking into impossible "bullshit" is dumb), that there is something wrong with us, that we might be a few "whatevers" short of a full something for even entertaining the notion that Jillette and his ilk could be wrong. "Do you want to be dumb?" is what I heard Jillette asking the audience. It brought to mind a quote I'd read from a scientist speaking about Alfred Wegener's theory that the continents once held different positions, but had "drifted" over many years. With a certainty akin to Penn's, Wegener's contemporary said, "Anyone who valued his reputation for scientific sanity would never dare support such a theory." Not even *dare* it. For just to dare it made you a nincompoop. And almost nobody wants to be the town nincompoop. (Of course, Wegener turned out to be right, as his theory of continental drift presaged the now accepted theory of plate tectonics).

Again, I could understand where Penn's anger was coming from, but it was hard not to think that his total and cemented a priori stance would shield any evidence to the contrary from reaching him. *If only he'd experienced what I have,* I thought. But then, he went on to, once again, throw me into doubt and confusion about what exactly it was that I *had* experienced, because, for the next fifteen minutes, he "read minds" and performed "psychic" feats and put on a display of what is known as "mentalism" that was stunning. For instance, having handed a number of books full of jokes to several audience members, then having the audience members pass those books randomly around until he said, "Stop," he then asked the five or so people now holding the books, scattered around the 1,500-seat theater, to stand up. He told them to choose any joke they liked out of the thousands within each (different) book, and to concentrate on it. Then, one by one, he told the audience members which joke they were thinking of. And he went 5 for 5, leaving each participant in mouth-agape disbelief.

And I was crushed. "He wants to talk about your hair" and "He likes what you did with the lights at work" and "Who has a bad toe?" and "He died in an explosion" all suddenly (logically or not), for that moment, went out the window. The segment quite effectively made Penn's point that if he can do these things, he, a person with no paranormal abilities of any kind, then anyone with enough practice can. According to Penn, Angelina was using the same tricks he employed, combined with unscrupulousness and peoples' desperate desire to believe.

*What did this mean? Could Penn be right? Had I been completely taken by expert mentalist con artists? Had Angelina tricked me into thinking she had a paranormal ability—which I then subjected other suckers to—when in reality she was simply doing whatever it was Penn had just done?* Penn is a professional magician, having honed his craft over decades and an untold number of hours. The effort he had to put in to learn to do what he does is probably immense. I found it hard to believe that Angelina, who'd worked full-time jobs until she turned to mediumship professionally ten years earlier, could have found the time in her life to become so adept at the mechanisms Penn uses. Nonetheless, the magicians' demonstration had thrown me again into doubt. And much worse, sadness.

As I walked out of the theater when the bit was finished and more traditional magical fare continued, like a rabbit being pulled from a hat and cut in half, I was despondent, even more than that half rabbit. I'd entered the theater with my dad, but left alone, with no idea what to make of what I had just witnessed. Granted, there were differences between what I'd observed Angelina do and what Penn had just done. Certainly, he was in control of the situation in a way that Angelina most definitely was not. And the nature of the tricks was not nearly the same in character. What Angelina did seemed to flow in some organic way. What Penn did was all carefully planned. But what I saw was enough to sincerely shake me. For a frightening time, I felt my dad again dissolving away, and the more I thought about it, the more he eroded. I began slipping back into that deep and vasty hole that quick-sanded me just after he passed, at the bottom of which existence was fleeting and ultimately meaningless. The hole that I'd climbed out of with the rope that, just a moment before, I'd begun to truly believe my dad had thrown me.

Since the Marquis is a theater owned by the company I work for, I could walk in any time, and I'd resolved, as hard as it would be to watch the bit again, to go back the next night. I wanted to see if I could pick up any piece of how he does what he does—if I could discern any clues as to his method. I knew I was setting myself up for pain, as with each trick Penn did, the sand rose, the hole grew deeper, and my dad dimmed. And when I walked in the next evening, I was worried he might push him to a place beyond recovery. I started to wish I'd left that box locked safely away. Still, I *had* to know.

The theater was again full, and as people laughed and clapped and oohed and ahhed, I slouched against the back wall waiting for the rug to be pulled the rest of the way out from under me. Soon it was time, and the theater got quiet as Penn readied to introduce the bit that held such sway over my mental state. With extreme alertness, I watched as closely as I could, every hand-movement or adjustment of his gaze holding a potential key to how he (and, therefore, Angelina) performed his "mind-reading." It was immediately clear how scripted the show was, as word for word, and action for action, the events from the night before played out again. Once more, he began his warning to the audience, again demonizing anyone who claimed an ability that he knew for certain was not real. Whereas the night before I'd listened to this portion with a smile, knowing something Penn did not, or so I'd thought, tonight his diatribe landed heavy on my heart, each sentence driving a wider wedge between me and my father. Then, as he began the sentence, "Before I go any further, I must make this very clear: *all* ESP, *all* mind-reading, *all* talking to the dead . . . ," something above him caught my attention. I thought I saw a flicker of the lights. But as he got to the line, "as we say on Showtime . . . *bull* . . . *shit*," literally in the momentary pause for emphasis he placed—exactly as he had the night before—between the words "bull" and "shit," what the flicker was became clear: a large butterfly. A large butterfly was darting this way and that, in and out of the shafts of light. And lest I begin to think it was the delusional imaginings of a desperately breaking heart, hoping beyond hope that my idea of my new relationship with my dad could somehow survive the onslaught of Penn's evisceration of mediumship, some in the audience noticed the butterfly, too. If I was deluded, so powerful was my delusion that it spilled over to others. A small titter swept through some in the crowd as people noticed it, surprised by the extremely unusual sight of a butterfly in a Broadway theater.

I was stunned, perhaps more than I'd ever been. I could no longer hear Penn, my eyes now focused entirely on this butterfly. All of the butterfly instances I'd had that I'd connected to my dad, whether through the simple functioning of my brain and its use of patternicity or something else, flooded my mind. I actually could not quite believe what I was seeing. And a euphoria engulfed my entire being. Literally one second earlier, I'd been feeling the despair vengefully rushing back. All the work I'd done to come to believe I had not forever lost my dad had been seriously threatened, and I could feel the foundations of my new belief beginning to shift and crumble. But then (and I cannot emphasize this enough), at *the moment* Penn was pointedly saying the word "Bullshit," this butterfly flashed into the light fifteen feet above his head. What in the world are the chances of that? I'm sure there's a number. But it won't mean anything to me. Were a statistician to tell me they'd spent much time and computing power, every bit of RAM and Gigahertz and whatever else a supercomputer might use to make billions of calculations, along with their Nobel Prize in statistics-winning brain, to get an answer to the question, "What are the odds of a butterfly, an insect that you'd connected to your dad, rationally or not, being inside the Marquis Theater—which is located inside the New York Marriott Marquis hotel in Times Square, through the hotel's front doors, up an escalator to the windowless second floor, then through a second set of small theater doors—and appearing above Penn's head at *the moment* he was declaiming why your dad is gone?" And the answer would make no difference to me. As hard as it might be for my scientist friends to hear, math can't describe everything. In twelve years of working on Broadway, I'd never seen a butterfly in a theater. I asked everyone I worked with, some of whom had been working in theaters since they were sixteen, if they'd ever seen one, and no one had. I went to watch the show a third time to be sure no butterflies were used over the course of the entire performance. None were.

Not long after, I was back at my theater, the Richard Rodgers, talking about the experience with a coworker, explaining the euphoric effect the moment had, and how it was impossible not to think my dad—or at least something paranormal—had a hand in it. When, out of the corner of my eye, I saw a flutter.

Yup.

I mean, *come on*. At this point, it felt like my dad must be standing beside me, sweating, if such a thing is possible wherever he was. I pictured him as a spent athlete, hands on his knees at the end of grueling game, utterly drained, saying intermittently through exhausted panting, "What . . . does a guy . . . have to do . . . to show you he's still alive, man?"

The pictures below show the incredulous look on coworkers' faces once the butterfly had alighted in a chandelier. And for the icing on the cake (sweet as it already was for me), just days later, Penn was standing under that same chandelier, having come to the Rodgers to see *Hamilton*. As his large and imposing frame stood two feet from me perched on a banister by my bar waiting for someone he was with, I thought about describing to him what had happened and asking him all the questions I'd planned to ask. But something told me this may be a moment where the wall of skepticism might have kept out not just the noise, but also some signal, and so I let him continue on his way, not knowing that his very speech *against* the paranormal had been turned into, for me, a most powerful *for.* And maybe, just maybe, it had been done so by my dad.

And so, that moment, that one moment with Penn, reinvigorated my quest to know more. Where before I was thinking *there must be something I'm missing*, given how all of these highly intelligent people with IQs much, much greater than mine, say that *all* mediumship is fraudulent, I was now thinking it was Penn who is missing something. Namely, the butterfly above his head. My college physics class came to mind, where I'd learned how much we don't know. Penn's certainty that *all* things paranormal are "bullshit" in a universe where 95% of that bullshit has yet to even be detected, and another 65% has been invented to explain how fast that bullshit is expanding through the universe, seemed ill-advised.

So, I kept searching.

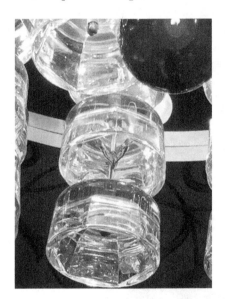

# CHAPTER TWELVE

# Groundhog Day

The "high" that you get when things happen that break through the border of what you think you know, of what you think of as reality, offering a glimpse of a larger reality that your own reality is sitting within, again set in with Penn's butterfly. *How much*, you start to wonder, *is beyond that border? And how many new borders might I come to?*

It's difficult to describe this feeling, but there is a rush that comes with it. A wave of excitement that reminded me of the climb of the roller coaster, just before its greatest loop. An exhilaration. For some, I suppose it might be frightening to have these holes poked in the walls outlining the edges of our conceptions, suggesting there might be far more that we don't know than what we do; but for me it was thrilling. For, if my dad hadn't ceased to exist, that truth must rest somewhere beyond my border of truth and in a greater one well past it. With every crack, I saw more and more fully that, indeed, the world I was shown in high school physics and college astronomy and geology, was not the whole world. So, we were Magellan, my family and I, and with every wave ridden, our new world was expanding.

It was both a shock and a comfort to find that we were not the first, though, as I began to widen the scope of my investigation. Many, many others had been this way before. These walls had been knocked down many times. They still stood only for some. For others, they'd long ago fallen. My high school physics teacher (and the rest of "mainstream science") didn't know about the world beyond their walls, simply because it was hard to believe. And so, no matter the brilliance of the minds that had sailed this sea before, mapping out larger and larger bits of the known universe, a cognitive dissonance made their words difficult to hear by those who were not open to a larger reality. As though they spoke through water, their reports came back muffled and diluted, and were easily forgotten or swept aside. Or, worse, laughed at. Much like Copernicus was derided. And Galileo. And Alfred Wegener.

Today, if the head of the psychology department at Harvard or leading scientist at Oxford or a Nobel Prize winning physiologist made a detailed study of something, and in doing so made a discovery, we'd surely give it the weight it deserves.

Right?

Not always, it turns out. Depending on how far she or he goes beyond the outlines of what we accept as the limits of our reality, even a brilliant mind we'd previously trusted outright might find derision, and even if other aspects of their work stands the test of time, as that Nobel Prize of theirs gets passed down from generation to generation, the parts of the world they discovered beyond our walls get lost to history. But not entirely. Luckily, they are preserved for those willing to take a trip beyond what they "know," as uncomfortable as it might be to need to reshape the limits of our mind. And it can, indeed, be uncomfortable. It is much easier, often, to believe that what we know is what there is to know. It seats us solidly in existence. We know our place in it all, and even if that place isn't always great, there is a definite consolation in being familiar with it's topography. To find there is more to the story unseats us from that place, leaving us unsure as to where we stand, where on the map we are, because suddenly the map isn't complete. To go on this journey means accepting we don't know where the map ends, or where on it we reside, relative to the "whole." If you don't mind that click click click up the coaster, and actually look forward to the twists and turns and the new views you get with every click higher you go, even though each click might make it scarier, well . . . strap in.

~⟶

After having had my own experiences with mediums and then testing one under various levels of controlled conditions, combined with the spontaneous events like hearing "Believe" on the radio and seeing the butterfly during Penn's performance, the possibility of consciousness being more than an aspect of our brain seemed quite real, and more and more clearly I was envisioning my dad, smiling ever brighter as the realization was dawning on me. I imagined the relief coming over his face as all of the effort it seemed he'd expended since finding himself bodiless, desperate to ease our pain, began to bear fruit. If it were so, that he really was still here, I began to wonder what other lines of evidence might exist suggesting that consciousness can operate separately from a brain. Just as I wanted to send his voicemail messages and photos to all of my family members, and store them in multiple places as a safeguard against their ever disappearing, so too I thought the more varied the evidence for survival of consciousness, the more secure Dad's different, but very real relationship with me would feel. If Angelina was really communicating with my dad's disembodied awareness, meaning that there *are* such things as disembodied awarenesses, one might think mediums may not be the only ones providing evidence of their existence. If incorporeal fathers are indeed an aspect of our reality, in what other ways might this aspect present? And upon asking that question, answers came rolling in. "Near death experiences," or NDEs, "end of life experiences," or ELEs, "after death communications," or ADCs, "extrasensory perception" or ESP—just all sorts of three-lettered acronyms identifying various phenomena seemingly pointing to the idea that our awareness can exist without a body, travel to other places independently of it, and sometimes even affect the physical world. And not only did these things seem to exist, but I quickly learned that each of these areas of inquiry could easily individually fill a book, and that, indeed, they've each filled *many* books. I learned that respected scientists, including Nobel Prize winners, highly significant inventors, heads of academic programs at the most prestigious colleges and universities in the world, and some of the leading scientists of their time have investigated these topics, and many have come to the conclusion that the "paranormal" isn't "para" at all, that there are events that occur that are not allowed by our current mainstream paradigm, but occur nonetheless, making them natural indeed, no matter how little we understand (or accept) them. These things, many, many studies and experiences have shown, do happen. They. Do. Happen.

Did you know that the United States Government once had a whole program being run out of the CIA, and then the Department of Defense (DOD), costing millions of dollars, to study "remote viewing," or what might be more commonly called "clairvoyance"? I didn't. Did you know they did that in response to their belief that the Soviet Union under Stalin was doing it? I didn't. But, it's true. Eventually known as the "Stargate Program," the United States seriously investigated psychic abilities and concluded that they were a real phenomenon. The CIA even started training people to do it. The first application, of course (and quite sadly), was a military one, where they tried to use remote viewers to spy on top secret soviet programs, even trying to look inside their file cabinets using nothing but the "third eye" of an American spy thousands of miles away in a Faraday cage at the CIA. One of the more famous subjects they investigated was Uri Gellar, mentioned earlier, whose propensity to destroy cutlery had gotten the attention of the CIA. Using only his mind, he claimed, he bent and twisted spoons, sometimes until they broke in two. Wanting to know more about how he was accomplishing these feats, the CIA contracted the Stanford Research Institute (SRI) to test him. And it was when the scientists there concluded he had genuine paranormal abilities, that The Amazing Randi really went to work, positively beside himself that such a respected lab—the second largest independent research facility used by the DOD—could have fallen for Geller's tricks. To Randi, SRI's backing of Geller posed a significant threat to critical thinking. Had the United States Government completely lost its mind? Certain that Geller was simply using sleight of hand to bend things, or to "see" inside closed metal canisters to find which one was holding a ball-bearing, for instance, or what side of a die was facing upwards inside a box that had just been shaken before it was opened, Randi went on a crusade to expose a man he was convinced was lying about how he did what he did.

After the SRI's proclamation that Geller was the real deal, word quickly spread, and soon Geller was being invited on American television shows to do his metal-bending, watch stopping, mind-reading thing. However, Geller was famously thwarted in his attempt to produce any paranormal phenomenon while on the most notable and popular of those programs, *The Tonight Show* with Johnny Carson. Carson, who'd been a bit of an amateur magician himself, knew Randi well and had his own suspicions about Uri Geller. So, the day that Geller was to be on live television with Carson, Carson's prop department was put in touch with Randi who told them everything they needed to do in order to ensure that if any phenomenon occurred, it would be paranormal in nature. When Geller came out to join Johnny on stage, he seemed surprised to find the props set up for a demonstration, telling Carson he thought he was there to be interviewed, not perform his abilities. The entire episode (available on YouTube for all to see) is very uncomfortable to watch, as Geller squirms for many, many awkward minutes under the spotlight. When he could not perform any of the things he was known for, he finally said, "I'm sorry, I don't feel strong." And the show ended without a single event, paranormal or otherwise, having happened, beyond a slight bend in a spoon (and it is very difficult to tell if the slight bend may have already been there).

However, though Gellar spectacularly failed that night and apparently couldn't fool Randi, if he is a fraud as Randi would have it, he sure did fool the scientists at SRI in some way that *remains* unexplained. Luckily for us, the Stargate Program was recently declassified, meaning that we are free to search through the files in the CIA archives. When I did so, I came across the assessment made by the CIA after millions of dollars had been spent in an effort to prove or disprove paranormal abilities: "A large body of reliable experimental evidence points to the inescapable conclusion that extrasensory perception does exist as a real phenomenon." That's from the Central Intelligence Agency, folks—an agency with "intelligence" in its very name.

The government, via various departments within the military, has not only been testing human beings for abilities involving "anomalous perception" for over sixty years, but they have used it. In a now well-known case, for instance, one of the Army's remote viewers was able to locate a downed Soviet bomber that had crashed somewhere in the jungles of Zaire, after repeated attempts to locate it via spy satellites were unsuccessful. The remote viewer somehow "saw" the precise location where the plane was, gave the coordinates to her handlers, and when a satellite was pointed there, sure enough, they saw it. Former President Jimmy Carter, while speaking to a group of college students in 1995 of the psychic who had divined the location, said this of the astonishing incident that had occurred during his presidency in 1976: "She gave latitude and longitude figures. We focused our satellite camera on that point and the plane was there."

Among the files that have recently been declassified by the CIA, there is one experimental result that, on its own, to me portends the existence of an ability we do not yet understand or largely accept as real, no matter what Randi says, or what happened on *The Tonight Show* that evening.

On August 4th of 1973, Dr. Hal Puthoff and Dr. Russel Targ, two extremely credentialed physicists (with security clearances), at the behest of the CIA, sealed Uri Gellar "in an opaque, acoustically and electrically shielded room. This room is the double-walled, shielded room used for EEG research in the Life Sciences Division of the Stanford Research Institute (SRI). It is locked by means of an inner and outer door, each of which is secured by a refrigerator-type locking mechanism." "Electrically shielded" means that no form of electromagnetic field could penetrate the small room Gellar was locked in. Therefore, if somehow he had an accomplice outside of the room (a prospect the two lead scientists in the study continue to claim is ruled out), and a walkie-talkie or wireless receiver of some kind hidden in his . . . wherever, it would have been of no use. He would have quickly realized he'd put one orifice or another in a good amount of discomfort hiding the walkie-talkie, since no signal would have been able to reach it. Aside from bending spoons, one of the other faculties claimed by Uri Geller was the ability to perceive items obscured from his vision. Even inside of a lead box, he appeared to be able to "see" what the hidden object was. For this experiment, once Geller was sealed inside the small, shielded room, Dr. Puthoff opened up a dictionary in another room to a random page and looked for the first word that could easily be represented by a drawing. In one test, the first word was "bunch," and Dr. Puthoff decided to draw a bunch of grapes, which you can see in the first figure below. Once the picture had been completed and taped to the outside wall of the enclosure, Geller was alerted via intercom (which worked only from outside to inside) and asked to attempt to perceive and draw what he was seeing. Gellar was being continuously monitored by a one-way audio circuit, and he immediately said he saw "drops of water coming out of the picture," and then mentioned "purple circles." He then said he was "quite sure" that he had the picture—which apparently he did, because he did indeed draw a bunch of grapes. But, he didn't just draw a bunch of grapes. He drew the very same number of grapes in the bunch as had been depicted in the "target" drawing. The experimenter had drawn a bunch of grapes randomly using 24 circles. Geller's bunch, too, was drawn with exactly 24 grapes. I'm no statistician, but I have to imagine the odds are remarkably, perhaps incalculably long, against a person randomly selecting the word "bunch" from a dictionary, then randomly deciding to depict the word in terms of grapes, then randomly deciding to draw 24 grapes in the bunch, and then having a person inside an electrically and acoustically sealed room draw the same thing within moments of the first drawing being made outside of the room. You can guess, a fair amount of the time, whether or not the New York Giants are going to beat the Patriots by less than a touchdown, but I don't know that Vegas would ever attempt to put a number on this:

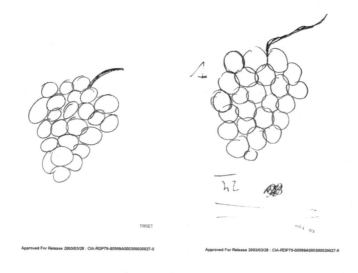

TARGET

Approved For Release 2003/03/28 : CIA-RDP79-00999A000300030027-0          Approved For Release 2003/03/28 : CIA-RDP79-00999A000300030027-0

And lest you think it was simply an *extremely* unlikely coincidence, here's another one of the tests. In this case, they locked the person who would create a drawing inside the sealed room, and Uri Geller was outside with Dr. Puthoff. The person drew a representation of the "solar system," which she labeled as such. When she said, "I'm done," through the intercom, Geller began to draw, in front of Dr. Puthoff, what he was "seeing." Geller's picture is very clearly a space scene as well. Which feels appropriate to end this discussion on, as the odds of this happening by chance again seem astronomic in scale:

In her book *Phenomenon* (which I consider to be essential reading if you have an interest in this topic), Annie Jacobson writes about her 2016 interview with the then eighty-seven-year-old James Randi, who, as mentioned previously, remained steadfastly devoted to the debunking of all manner of claimed paranormal abilities until his passing in October of 2020. When Mrs. Jacobsen asked Randi if his anti-Geller crusade had softened by that point, he shouted, "Never! When I die, I want to be cremated and have my ashes blown into Uri Geller's eyes. There is no such thing as the paranormal. Uri Geller is a magician . . . his life is a lie!"

I personally believe Randi's intentions were magnanimous. I think he meant to rescue people from being had. However, given cases such as those noted above, which he and other skeptics simply ignore, instead choosing to focus solely on instances that *could* have normal explanations, I wonder if such a hardened stance might have acted like the shielded room Geller performed this experiment in, blocking out not just the noise, but perhaps, also some signal. Annie Jacobsen met Uri Geller, and spent a lot of time with him while conducting research for *Phenomenon*. He continues to passionately claim (and has never claimed anything different) that what he does is not a trick. He says he is using an actual human ability that is not yet understood. During their time together, Jacobsen witnessed Geller perform many feats that she cannot easily explain, including "reading her mind" in a test for telepathy, and bending metal utensils almost wherever they went, including a large set of sturdy tongs meant for handling hot coals (and so forged to withstand high heat) that a random fan handed him at a restaurant, which bent with the touch of just one of his fingertips, as far as she could see. If they are indeed the "tricks" Randi and other magicians claim they are, they are *very good* tricks, especially when seen up close. Towards the end of her marvelous book, in which she has remained objective throughout, presenting all the sides that she is able to, she discusses in detail her interactions with him and what she observed him do right before her eyes. Even though she'd taken great pains to learn the ways magicians perform the illusion of bending metal, still she was impressed. She, of course, never claims that what Uri Geller is doing is real or an illusion. She remains steadfastly open to all possibilities. But here is what she writes that most got my attention:

Of all the things I saw, and all the people I interviewed regarding Geller (including the Nobel Prize Laureate Brian Josephson), the most telling revelation about Geller's abilities came from the legendary former curator of mammals at the Zoological Society of London, Desmond Morris [. . .]

"Uri Geller came to see me in 2005 to talk about art, but when he was leaving he asked if I would like him to bend a spoon for me," Morris recalls. "I fetched a heavy teaspoon, and he rubbed it between his forefinger and thumb and it did, indeed, start to bend. I watched the process very closely but I could not see how he did this. He asked me if, as a biologist, I could explain to him how this strange ability of his could have evolved. I pointed out that iron was only discovered about three thousand two hundred years ago, so his special ability would have been useless before that date." Morris was well aware of the controversies surrounding Geller, the legions of magicians who 'claimed that he uses clever hand pressures to make the spoon bend,' Morris said, so he asked Geller to do something unusual for him, as a test. "I asked him if he could do it [bend metal] using only his big toe."

Morris says he fetched from his kitchen the heaviest teaspoon he could find and set it on top of his library table. Geller "took off his shoe and sock and lifted his foot up." Morris recalls. "He found it awkward to rub [the teaspoon] with his big toe but managed to do so, and again the spoon started bending. During this second bending his hands were nowhere near the spoon, and he did not have enough leverage in his toes to use them to apply force to the spoon. So, I was completely mystified by his ability."

Could Randi's magicians that he planted in that later four-year study (not at SRI) have done what they did with only a toe? I leave that to the reader to consider. What seems much, much more difficult to fake and impossible to dismiss if you give the experiments a fair consideration, are the remote viewing drawings produced by Geller, and others who were eventually tasked with real world missions by the military, with results so stunning at times, they still remain classified today. If it were a bunch of magicians making lucky guesses, it's hard to imagine they'd still be immune to Freedom of Information Act requests in 2020. And to this day, Russell Targ and Hal Puthoff still stand by their determination that, at times, Uri Geller was able to produce phenomenon in a way we cannot yet explain. And if some part of Geller is able to perceive things without his body being there, perhaps that part doesn't need a body at all. Perhaps that part is the part my dad used to reach out to his family, once his body stopped functioning.

Some of the evidence compiled by the SRI studies, such as the drawings of the grapes and solar system, I find rises to the ECREE standard proposed by Sagan, and oft repeated by Randi and Michael Shermer and The Skeptics Society. Even if only this evidence existed, and it was discovered that every time Geller bent a spoon, he was just bending a spoon, it would be enough, I should think, to keep an open mind. But I would soon find out that was hardly the only evidence that exists of paranormal abilities. Little did I know at the time, but I was about to discover that science had weighed in quite a bit on mediumship, as well. For over one hundred years, it had been studied by some of the greatest minds in recorded history, minds that line the walls of the scientific hall of fame.

And those smarty-pantses had some pretty interesting stuff to say.

# CHAPTER THIRTEEN

# Veritas

Williiam James was an intellectual heavyweight. Widely considered to be the "father of American psychology," in 1875 he taught one of the first college psychology courses in America, and then went on to form the Department of Psychology at Harvard. *That* Harvard. The one my high school guidance counselor suggested I have some less Harvard-like backups for, ones that my grades might permit admittance to. A great man of science and philosophy was Mr. James, and he hung out with lots of other smarties, too, like Freud, Jung, Mark Twain, and Oliver Wendell Holmes. A few years after he presided over the first Doctorate of Psychology at Harvard, James got wind of a woman who people said displayed an ability no one could understand. Though James was extremely skeptical of the reports he was hearing, his curiosity eventually got the best of him. The woman lived in Boston, not far from the prestigious and revered university. "Veritas," the school's motto carved into the buildings that lined his path, might have been in mind as he left the university grounds, intent on putting his great intellect to the task of living up to it. James was on his way to try and uncover the truth of what this twenty-five-year-old housewife was doing to have caused such a stir.

Leonora Piper, born in New Hampshire in 1859, was eight years old when she was playing in her yard and felt as though she'd suddenly been hit on the ear by some unseen force. She then heard a voice say, "Aunt Sara not dead, but with you still." Alarmed by the experience, which I think is the appropriate response when an invisible hand knocks you upside the head, she ran to her mother. I'm in my forties, and if I get slapped today by an invisible hand, and you are looking for me, check my mom's arms. This, of course, happened in a time well before rapid forms of communication, like telephones, had been invented. Therefore, it was not until two days later that Lenora's mom found out that at the approximate time her daughter claimed to get her ghostly slap-induced message, her sister Sara had unexpectedly died. And so began Lenora's apparent communication with the dead. At some point in her mid-twenties, in around 1884, Lenora's ability to "hear" a few disembodied words suddenly morphed into a more dramatic form of communication, when she went into her first "trance."

"Trance" was a recent phenomenon that had rapidly spread through America and England, especially. People had started to hold what came to be called "seances," where they held hands around a table in a darkened room, and tried to contact the dead. At first raps and taps might be heard, as though some unseen force was knocking on the tabletop, and soon the raps turned into tables tipping this way and that. People would put their hands lightly on the tabletop, and somehow the furniture piece would shake and shift, going up on one side, then the other, and sometimes all four legs appeared to lift entirely off the floor. From there, the supposed spirits directed their focus to people rather than furniture, attempting to communicate using the human apparatus rather than inanimate objects. And this is where trances came in.

In "trance mediumship," as opposed to the "mental mediumship" of Angelina and John Edward, the medium is supposedly taken over by a deceased person, who sort of borrows the medium's body for a spell. In this way they gain access to the medium's vocal apparatus and are able to speak for themselves, rather than the medium interpreting the impressions he or she is getting. Once the controlling spirit departs, the medium wakes back up, often claiming to have no memory whatsoever of what transpired once she "lost consciousness." Now, if this were a real thing, you'd think it'd be pretty easy to know. This would take all interpretation out of the equation, and you wouldn't need an intermediary trying to translate. Theoretically, my dad could just say, "Hey, I heard you ask me to talk about your hair today. I thought that was a bit odd, out of all the things you could have picked, but anyway, let's talk about your hair, if that's the thing it's going to take to prove to you that it's me." and that would be that. Life after death (or at the very least telepathy) verified. Surely, though, if any evidence like that existed, I'd have heard about it, and so would have Penn, and he wouldn't be shouting from Broadway stages with such venom and surety about the lack of any paranormal thing *ever*, anywhere, at any time being even remotely possible. Which made it quite a surprise to read of William James' conclusions regarding Leonora Piper.

In 1884 Leonora had been feeling a bit...weird, experiencing some "twitching" in her body, before passing out face down on a table. "Excuse me Mrs., are you okay?"

"Oui oui, I'm fine," said the young woman, sitting back up—except it wasn't her voice that spoke, but that of a French gentleman. "Mon Ami, I'm fine, and I have your deceased granny here, Martha, the one who loved bird-watching and had a dog named Buster. She says she loves you very much."

Sounds to me like a case for America's first psychologist. If it had been my wife or dad or mom or son who'd had this happen, I'd say, "You take this one, Bill." And Bill did. To William James' great bewilderment, after a great deal of testing he saw no way that Mrs. Piper could have known the things that came out of her mouth by normal means. So fascinated was he by what she was doing that he founded the American Society for Psychical Research (ASPR) in order to undertake systematic study of her, enlisting other scientists to assist in the decades-long investigation.

Somehow, when Mrs. Piper went into this trance, self-claimed dead people gave information that Mrs. Piper should not have known. And figuring out whether this information was gathered in a paranormal way was much less ambiguous than in the case of Angelina. Because in this case, the spirit was speaking in complete sentences, and in their own words: either the spirit knows things, or they do not. And many times, spirits speaking through Mrs. Piper did . . . and to an *astonishing* degree of accuracy and detail—even under conditions when there was no conceivable way Mrs. Piper could have known who the dead person was that a living sitter was hoping to hear from. It'd be like me bringing a complete stranger, randomly chosen, in to sit with Angelina, and suddenly that sitter's aunt is suddenly speaking, able to have a full-on conversation, and saying things only the aunt could know. It wouldn't be Angelina saying, "I'm smelling gasoline . . . I have someone here who died in an explosion." It would be the person who died saying, "Please be careful driving. I speak from experience."

Professor James was awestruck by the knowledge his deceased loved ones displayed, including very private details of his life that he was absolutely certain no one but he could know. By the time his first sitting with the young housewife was over, the Harvard Professor of Psychology tentatively surmised there could be only two possibilities: either Lenora Piper had supernatural abilities, or she was working with a team of skilled informants. So, he had twelve more sittings with her, becoming more and more certain something unexplainable was happening until he finally wrote, "This lady can at will pass into a trance condition [. . .] This is the ordinary type of trance-mediumship at the present day . . . I am persuaded by the medium's honesty, and of the genuineness of her trance. I now believe her to be in possession of a power as yet unexplained." And, though scientists of the day had no access to the brain monitoring equipment now available that might tell us with some degree of certainty that her brain was in an altered state of consciousness, the trance state that James was so persuaded of seemed to be strong indeed. Scientists jabbed her suddenly with pins, put a toxic chemical on her lips, and held ammonia right under her nose, all of which produced no effect on the medium while in the purported altered state. We know now that hypnosis can be used to create circumstances where the human body reacts this way. The brain can be convinced, it appears, that a part of the body will not feel pain, and when a pin is stuck in, the person reports no pain. The placebo effect is another well-documented phenomenon wherein the simple belief of effectiveness can create effectiveness. Whatever the answer to Mrs. Piper's non-reaction was, it was clear to the scientists that her trance was a state of consciousness quite different from the waking state, where being suddenly and unexpectedly jabbed with a sharp object will cause the body to react, even involuntarily, at times, such as when you touch a hot stove and your body responds before your brain has registered that it was hot. This happens because the neural signal goes through the "Reflex Arc" pathway, traveling from your hand to your spinal cord and back to your hand before finally being sent to the brain for processing. To overcome this defense system of the body is highly unusual. Not quite as unusual as talking to the dead, perhaps. But the evidence for that, too, was noteworthy enough to convince many well-regarded scientists (one of whom had been initially intent on debunking Piper from the outset, as he had done with multiple other "mediums") that she knew information she had no normal way to possess.

So determined were researchers to discover if she could be using trickery of some kind in obtaining the information she gave, at times detectives were hired to follow her. Her very steps were traced, and her interactions documented. Even still, they could not figure out how she was doing it. The researchers found that while she was in trance they could hand Mrs. Piper an object, say a watch, that had been owned by a deceased person, and that person could show up and rattle off information for an hour about themselves—even when it was a complete stranger to her, someone the researchers were certain she did not know. To further isolate her from any deceit she might be engaged in, they took her to England to study her. Mrs. Piper had never been there, so had no potential network of assistants. Still, she produced results that so boggled the minds of the researchers most closely involved in the examinations that they concluded she was either unwittingly using telepathy, or people without bodies were speaking through her. It could only be one (or both) of those two things.

Perhaps more interesting still, over the course of the quarter century investigation into Mrs. Piper, members of the scientific team died, and then came back to speak through her. The living investigators were gob smacked by how thoroughly the personalities of their deceased collogues were represented when they came through Piper. At times, the deceased scientists would say things like, "Hey, remember that private conversation we had, just me and you, that day in Brighton, when you said that thing about turkeys?" And the living team member had no explanation for those highly specific and entirely accurate words, recounting a private conversation, coming from Piper other than they were not coming from Piper, but indeed, their departed co-investigator.

So certain of the paranormal nature of her ability by the end of his examinations, William James famously said, "If you wish to upset the law that all crows are black, you mustn't seek to show that no crows are; it is enough if you prove one single crow to be white. My own white crow is Mrs Piper. In the trances of this medium, I cannot resist the conviction that knowledge appears which she has never gained by the ordinary waking use of her eyes, and ears and wits."

And it wasn't just Professor James who'd been led to believe a genuine phenomenon was occurring. A sister scientific society to the ASPR had been formed called the British Society for Psychical Research (SPR), and over the pond other great scientists were jumping into the mediumship fray—scientists like Alfred Russel Wallace, co-originator of the theory of natural selection with Charles Darwin, and a person with enough insight and vision to be among the first to worry about human-caused climate change—in 1850—talk about being ahead of the curve. Among his scientific contemporaries also moved by observation to seriously study the phenomenon of mediumship were Sir William Crookes who invented the Crookes Tube, which changed the courses of both physics and chemistry, and physicist Sir Oliver Lodge, who is one of the people credited with the invention of the radio. And here's what I found to be nuts: all those guys ended up believing mediumship was a real thing. After years upon years and countless efforts to unmask fraudsters (which they sometimes did), each of those people, people intellectually alert enough to found new areas of study, understand nature enough to invent technologies that would significantly alter the trajectory of humanity's story, and unravel mysteries of the impossibly complex human body, all came to the conclusion that some people, some of the time, display an ability for which they had no explanation. The guy who was astute enough to discover the element thallium all the way back in 1861 by using flame spectroscopy concluded, when he put those same skills of experimentation to the study of mediumship, that it actually happened. I was excited when I discovered a faster way to put my shirt on by putting both arms in before my head, instead of arm, head, other arm. I'm not the guy to be studying mediumship. But Sir William Crookes and his colleagues were. And they concluded I am far from crazy for thinking I am seeing evidence of my dad trying to get my attention, bodiless as he might be, as that's what the evidence told them, too. However, because the paradigm of materialism had taken such hold of the collective psyche, a psyche perhaps scarred by the not too distant past when church doctrine held so much sway, and scientific pursuits and discoveries were so often thwarted, much of the work the SPR did with regard to mediumship research was simply swept under the rug. Today, the copious and meticulously kept reports of those studies are filed away in back rooms, covered in the dust of one hundred and fifty years. Skeptics, if they are even aware of this research, often conclude without hesitation that the studies must have been flawed or the scientists duped or biased or, just wrong. In their minds, no matter how evidenced their scientific and intellectual prowess might be by other discoveries and contributions they made, these scientists, in this *one* particular area, for some reason, lost their wits and made grave methodological errors—hundreds and hundreds of times. So, no matter how thorough and well-documented William James' studies of medium Leonora Piper were, today those studies are routinely dismissed (or not even known about, which is much more often the case), relegated to a long ago past, a past when scientists were not, I have to conclude, as "on their games" as modern scientists are, in the opinions of today's skeptics. What is the word for this? It's got to be some sort of "ism." "Old scientistism?" There should be a term for the prejudice we have, the predisposition to give the advantage for clarity of thought to modern thinkers. This does not make great sense. Though our base of knowledge has certainly grown, and that knowledge can inform discovery, surely world-renowned scientists of yesteryear were no less smart than today's. They may have had less figured out, but their ability to do the figuring, their capacities for insight, I would think, must have been in the same ballpark. Evolution does not work that quickly, where the general aptitude of cognition could appreciably increase within the population inside of two centuries. In fact, if we could bring Charles Darwin and Alfred Russel Wallace back somehow, and show them an hour of reality television, they might have cause to reconsider their theory. Perhaps evolution doesn't always go in one direction, after all.

It may have been that these great people of science would have had their work taken more seriously by history, were it not for a major wrench thrown into this entire topic of study: things weren't perfect. You might logically expect that if dead people can take a person over and give extremely accurate information, talking to you as they did in life, making it extremely clear to those who knew them best that they are who they say they are, then this should be the result every time. Why, if this were real, would information sometimes be wrong? And very wrong? This is an extremely complicated question, and to gather an understanding one must dive deep into the research. I very highly recommend *Resurrecting Lenora Piper* by Michael Tymn, who has done the tedious work of slogging through thousands of pages of detailed reports, rescuing from obscurity the reasons why such intelligent people believed that Lenora Piper was the "white crow." Because, if you look up Lenora Piper on Wikipedia, for instance, you will read about the instances where information was incorrect, instances for which scientists, who did not closely look at the whole of the evidence, have thrown out the whole of the evidence based on the much smaller number of instances where paranormal ability was not evident. Which is like throwing out the possibility of a rainbow because there isn't one every time it rains. Over twenty-five years of intense research carried out by multiple scientists, scores of instances were recorded, pointing very strongly to the conclusion that disembodied personalities were sometimes speaking through Lenora Piper, or that, at the very least, some form of telepathy or "super psi" (a catchall term to describe how a medium might know things without the help of spirits providing it from some other realm) was at play. But you'll need to do more work than reading one very incomplete Wikipedia page to get a clear understanding of the facts. Michael Tymn has done that. And I hope you will, too. It's important stuff.

Complicating the issue further is the fact that there *were* many instances of fraudulent mediums, people who, for whatever reason, be it financial, psychological, or otherwise, used chicanery to appear as though they were communicating with deceased people. In fact, some of the same scientists who could not (and not once did they) uncover Mrs. Piper cheating, found many other "mediums" to be doing so. The SPR and ASPR were out for the truth, and were quite happy to expose fraud when they found it. Houdini (perhaps the template for The Amazing Randi) took great exception himself to the idea of mediumship, having failed to hear from his mother when she passed, and railed for years against the phenomenon, in general, believing it to all be the product of illusion, and spent much time debunking specific mediums himself. So thorough, in fact, was his work, that being known as a medium, and perhaps worse, deigning to study them as a scientist, became disreputable undertakings. And so, for over eighty years, research into the phenomenon, no matter how *very* strong some of the evidence was, nearly vanished from the face of the planet.

The very vast majority of scientists after Houdini's debunking (whether the debunking was complete or not) gave up on "psychical" or "paranormal" investigations into mediumship, as the word "paranormal" took on a non-serious connotation, and so since the 1920s almost none have been carried out. I was very pleased to find, however, that a few scientists in recent years have been brave enough to pick the torch back up as the observations that once spurred the brightest minds of the time to further investigation continue to occur. Dr. Julie Beischel is one such scientist.

～つ

"Can you tell me a little about how you test to see if mediumship is a real thing?" I asked.

"Well, we us a quintuple blind protocol when we do our mediumship studies—"

"A which tuple?" I asked with some amusement.

"Quin. Quintuple."

"So that's four levels of blinding, yeah?"

"Nope," said the voice, in a tone suggesting it might have been asking itself, *What have I gotten myself into?* After a moment, though, the voice forged ahead. "Quintuple is five levels of blinding."

And I kicked myself for the mistake. I was on the phone with Dr. Julie Beischel, who was the head of the Windbridge Institute (now the Windbridge Research Center), trying to convince her to be a part of my film. And I was off to a not so auspicious start.

"Of course," I said. "I always mess up Quin and . . . the other Q one. Can you explain what quintuple blind means?"

"In laymen's terms, [somehow she'd figured out I was a laymen] it simply means that everyone involved in the experiment is blinded to certain aspects of it," she told me.

"Uh huh. And can you give me a sort of summation of what you've found using this protocol?" I asked.

"The statistical analysis can get quite complicated, but basically, the resulting data, accounting for Bonferroni adjustments, indicates anomalous reception of information."

To which I said, "I see," as I very incorrectly spelled the word "Bonferroni" on a pad, trying unsuccessfully to sound it out, and thinking, *I'm not smart enough for this conversation.* Even in "laymen's terms."

I was thrilled to find that at least one living scientist was still toiling away at mediumship research. And, perhaps to her dismay, I needed to talk to her about it. I read her books and the summations of her studies on scientific journal websites, and subscribed to her research center's newsletter. But none of that was enough. Given the lengths it felt my dad had gone to in order to make it clear he'd somehow survived the breakdown of his body, and so to bring us peace, the least I could do was track down some scientists, and beg them to spend hours explaining stuff to me. Which, as I'm sure you might imagine, scientists just love. Nothing, I found, makes a scientist happier than to answer this question from a bartender/actor/mostly bartender: "Are you sure you didn't screw this experiment up somehow? Like, *really* sure? Because though I'm a bartender, I majored in Biology for two weeks in college (before I realized I'd rather be an actor), so you can talk to me like I'm one of your colleagues. In that light, aware now of my flirtation with Biology in undergrad for fourteen days, can you tell me how certain you are that you didn't make an error in your studies, or in the analysis of them? My class did a DNA gel electrophoresis experiment when I was in high school, and as careful as my team was, we messed it up, getting only got a B+. So, you know, it can happen to anyone. Any chance you messed up?" Luckily for me, this particular scientist is very gracious, and after a number of emails, she set aside a time to speak with me and answer every question I had.

Heading towards the lucrative potential of a career in the pharmaceutical industry, Dr. Beischel's scientific interests took an unexpected turn after a profound experience following the death of her mom. So arresting was what unfolded that it entirely altered the course of her intellectual pursuits. As I read more about Dr. Beischel, some of the similarities between her story and mine were marked. Like me, the first she'd heard of mediumship was via John Edward and *Crossing Over*. She found it interesting, but being a scientist, she would, of course, put no stock into what she saw unless she had the opportunity to test it for herself— a prospect not at all on her scientific radar at the time. It wouldn't be until her mom's unexpected passing that her mind would bend that way. Recalling the emotion she saw on the faces in the studio audiences of Edward's, she decided to see a medium.

Dr. Beischel, in another parallel with me, wanted to design an experiment to test the woman claiming this fantastic ability, and so she came up with a code word before the sitting. To her very great surprise, the medium (named Angela, just for a little more coincidental fun) referenced her code word at one point—though not as precisely as Angelina had done with mine. This incident was stupefying to Beischel, and she was unable to let it go. Unlike my situation, however, Beischel's relationship with her mom was not a positive one. Therefore, her sitting with Angela would be, to this day, her only personal sitting with a medium. Whereas I sought out medium after medium after Angelina, trying to be sure my dad was really the agency behind what was happening, Dr. Beischel was only interested in observing the phenomenon itself. Her goal was to decipher whether or not mediumship is a part of nature. As she would later tell me, "My relationship with my parents was such that it would be easier for me to think that death is the end. However, what I observed when I sat with the medium did not bear that out."

Dr. Beischel had been in a Doctorate program, earning her PhD in Pharmacology and Toxicology, with a minor in Microbiology and Immunology/Immunopathology at The University of Arizona (UA) when her mom passed. As sheer coincidence (or not?) would have it, she learned that John Edward had been studied by a psychology professor at the university, and through that professor she was directed to Angela, a local (and with a shorter waiting list than Edward) medium. The scientist in her concluded that something unexplainable occurred at that encounter, and that it deserved further scrutiny. As she writes in her book, *Among Mediums*:

> When I went back to school/work on Monday, I shared my experiences with the medium with some of my professors and other students. As good scientists, most thought it was interesting and believed that the facts I conveyed reflected what had really happened. A couple, however, were too mired in their cultural, religious, and/or materialist worldviews and literally told me that what I was describing couldn't have happened. As someone with a tremendously strong sense of justice, I thought it was entirely unfair

for trained scientists to conclude that a whole phenomenon was impossible even in light of testimony provided by one of their colleagues. I think that it was then and there that my future as a mediumship researcher began.

What is good for us about the fact that she decided to study mediumship in earnest, at least with regard to the scope of this book, is that Dr. Beischel is, you know, a doctor, and not a bartender/actor/mostly bartender. Beischel found out that, as luck would have it, the professor of psychology who'd studied John Edward at her school came to conclude something worth examining more closely was involved, and now led an ongoing mediumship research program (so, perhaps the only serious mediumship study in America at that time happened to be taking place at the university she was attending). And the study was reporting positive results: results signaling to Dr. Gary Schwartz (who, for good measure, I also called and spoke with for hours, and then pestered with emails) the study leader, that some people are able to obtain information about deceased people in some "out of the ordinary" way. In a further serendipitous turn of events, Schwartz had a post-doctoral fellowship position available in his lab, which he offered Beischel, and which she accepted. Dr. Beischel abandoned the pharmaceutical path she'd been headed down, and joined the UA study, eventually becoming its primary hands-on researcher. Though the results were reported as significant, many other scientists and skeptics soon took issue with some of the protocols Dr. Schwartz had employed during his early experiments. So, over her four-year tenure in the position as co-director of the VERITAS Research Program at UA, Dr. Beischel figured out better ways to carry out the experiments, sealing any protocol gaps she could find, and still positive results were being obtained. When funding for her position at UA ran out, so taken was Dr. Beischel by the data that she ventured off on her own, forming what is now The Windbridge Research

Center, where she began to employ a "quintuple blind" experimental protocol. That sounded, to me, like a whole lot of tuples, and when she first
said it, I was pretty sure she was making it up, perhaps offering a deadpan
joke. However, these mediumship studies (ongoing now for eighteen years)
are the farthest thing from a joke, and have been accepted and published
in multiple peer-reviewed scientific journals—and are slowly shifting at
least some attitudes "mired in the materialist worldview." If I thought my
idea of hiding a sitter behind a screen and devising a way for them to not
need to speak was nifty, I was nowhere close to what an actual scientifically
controlled experiment looks like, as Dr. Beischel gently reminded me when
she said, "I wouldn't use the word 'experiment' for what you did. It was a
demonstration, maybe, but not anywhere near the level of control a widely
accepted experiment would need to have."

During our first phone conversation, I asked Dr. Beischel if I could take
a trip to Arizona with the film crew to get footage of her doing her work.
To which she flatly responded, "No." After a pause fumblingly filled with
my attempt to tactfully ask why not, Dr. Beischel said, "There is nothing of
interest to film. We are collecting data. You'd be watching me type data
into a program. I'm guessing your audience might have more fun watching
paint dry." I came to quickly appreciate that the good doctor has a fantastic
sense of humor. As she later said, with a wonderfully straight face, during a
discussion on why mediumship research is a worthy endeavor, "In some
studies, death has been found to affect 10 out of 10 people." And I knew
right then that Dr. Beischel was my kind of scientist. But her point about
not wanting me to spend all of that money for a film crew to come to her
lab made something clear: this was numbers-driven, statistically-centered,
"boring" science. When Mr. Sawyer wanted to get us interested in chemistry, he threw a cube of sodium into a bucket of water, causing a reaction
that ignited not just an explosion, but our curiosities. In real mediumship
research (as opposed to the casual "demonstrations" I'd been filming with

Angelina), there are very few sodium-thrown-into-water types of moments that work well on film. Instead, it's data, data, data. And by the time she'd finished telling me about the quintuple blind protocol they use, I had to agree . . . this is not film-friendly stuff. It's math. Cold, indifferent, truth-pointing math—the math that has shown us the way to the universe's workings so many times.

Luckily, Dr. Beischel is a very patient person, and speaking to me by phone until all of my questions were answered, I got the gist of how the Windbridge studies work (at least I told her I did). What was made crystal clear to me is that the experimental protocol is set up to do everything within their control to eliminate the possibility of fraud by the medium being tested. Not only does it eliminate fraud, it also eliminates things like "rater bias" and "experimenter bias," catchall explanations skeptics have used in the past to dismiss studies from both the early days of mediumship research at the SPR and ASPR, and more modern studies, such as the initial ones at UA. At the Windbridge Research Center, they have addressed the skeptics' complaints and closed every conceivable loophole through which any normal means of information gathering might leak. Here are the basics of what they do: from a roster of 20 self-described mediums who have been prescreened and shown able to get accurate information in an anomalous way, one is chosen to be tested. Two sitters, chosen from a database of thousands of people who have requested to participate in the Windbridge studies, are asked to "talk to" their deceased person and say, "Mark, tomorrow at 3pm, some medium, somewhere in the world, is going to be looking for you. Find them." Dr. Beischel tells me she has no idea how this might work, but the results, as you'll see, speak for themselves. The next day at 3pm, the medium is given the first names of two "gender matched" specific dead people, such as "Mark" and "Mick," one at a time. Over the phone a different scientist (who does not know who the dead people are, or who the living people are that want to contact them) says something like, "Okay, medium, please tell me all the information you can get about 'Mark.'" The medium does so, and a list is made of all the things she says. "Thank you, medium. Now please do the same for 'Mick.'" Again, a list of her statements is transcribed. As you'll note, the medium is never even in the same building as the sitters—who could be anyone in the world. Then, *both* transcripts, redacted of any mention of the names "Mark" and "Mick," are sent to each of the two sitters. So, one reading they receive really is for the dead person they are connected to, and one reading is a decoy that is meant for the other deceased person. The sitters are asked to grade each statement of both readings as being either correct or incorrect for the person they were hoping to hear from, and to choose which of the two readings was meant for their deceased person.

Because the sitters have been given two random lists of statements, the Forer effect is effectively washed out. Since the effect says that we easily personalize general information we think is meant for us, having people not know which list is meant for them addresses that tendency. So, were there no paranormal aspect to the experiment, the sitters would be expected to choose the correct reading 50% of the time. If only chance were involved, odds dictate that, just as in guessing which side a flipping penny will land, half the time you'd pick the reading meant for your dead person, and half the time you'd pick the other reading. You have an even chance of guessing correctly. A significant statistical deviation from those percentages would indicate something other than pure chance is at play.

Here is what is remarkable, and to me clear evidence that Penn Jillette, even beyond butterflies, should be less certain in his declaration that, "*All* talking to the dead is bullshit:" the sitters in Dr. Beischel's peer reviewed studies 66% of the time chose the reading that was intended for them. Pause to really take that in. Given two lists of statements made by two sup-posed dead people, lists generated by a medium who had no way of know-ing who the sitter or dead person was, the statements were evidential enough for the sitter to identify which reading was for Mark and which was for Mick 66% of the time. This result is statistically highly significant, to say the least, coming in well above the 50% expected by chance. Including a smaller study done in 2007 at UA (which the 2011 study was a replication of), Dr. Beischel was involved in 74 such experiments using a more than double blind protocol (described in detail in Appendix II at the back of the book). And the statistics in both studies said the same thing: some people sometimes know stuff they shouldn't be able to. The same math that helped us get to the moon and send probes to Mars and land on asteroids and build the world says so.

How could this be if nothing paranormal is going on? When cold reading is ruled out, and hot reading is ruled out, and "rater bias" is ruled out, and "experimenter bias" is ruled out . . . what is left? This, in Dr. Beischel's words: "When I applied the scientific method to the phenomenon of mediumship using optimal environments, maximum controls, and skilled participants, I was able to definitively conclude that certain mediums are able to report accurate and specific information about discarnates without using any normal means to acquire the information."

Welp, there we have it—Dr. Beischel thinks the math bluntly says it is not only possible that my dad is still around, but that the scientifically-gathered evidence is pointing in that direction. And she isn't alone in that interpretation of the results. In a 2011 study carried out at the University of Virginia (UVA) by Dr. Emily Kelly, she was forced by the statistics to come to that same conclusion. Dr. Kelly's experiment was similar in its set up, in that the mediums never met the sitters, and an experimenter sat in as a proxy for them. However, in this case some mediums gave 6 readings each, and *all 6* readings were given to *all 6* sitters, who were asked to, again, choose which reading they thought related to their discarnate. The results, like Dr. Beischel's, were highly significant, indicating an objective reality to the phenomenon of mediumship, even when the sitters only had a 1 in 6 chance of correctly choosing the reading meant for them, and not a 50% chance as in the Windbridge study. And in the case of 1 of the mediums tested at UVA, all six sitters chose, after looking at all six of the medium's readings, the reading that was intended for them. And it can't get much more statistically significant than that.

Now my dad and I were really getting somewhere. While going over all of this with Dr. Beischel, I realized that *this* was the verification I really needed. I needed a living, breathing, super smarty, who knows about things like Bonferroni adjustments in statistical analysis, and has multiple scientific degrees, using multisyllabic words I don't understand and equations that look to me like my cat ran over the keyboard, to tell me that my dad was trying to talk to me.

Beyond the studies to test whether or not anomalous reception of information sometimes occurs, Windbridge has carried out other research as well, such as the monitoring of brain function. They wanted to see if the grey stuff between a medium's ears behaved any differently while they were engaged in the process of mediumship than it did when they were talking about what they had for breakfast, for instance, or if they were asked to make up a story. Did their brains exhibit the same neural activity when they were creating a tall tale as it did when they were supposedly speaking to the dead? Here, too, the results indicate there is much more to this mediumship thing than Penn would have us believe. As Dr. Beischel stated, "Using EEG, or electroencephalography, we concluded that the experience of communicating with the deceased may be a distinct mental state that is not consistent with brain activity during ordinary thinking or imagination." Dr., you had me at "electroencephalography." I would sincerely like to know if Penn believes he would be able to alter his brain waves, then, while under quintuple blind conditions, achieve via mentalism and magic alone the same accuracy results the mediums at The Windbridge Research Center have? Again, I leave it to the reader to ponder.

Finally, it might be worth noting here that my statistical results, as not quintuple as they were in being obtained, nonetheless reflect the results Dr. Beischel's studies predict from a person who actually has this ability. And learning that, I found the reality of my dad's continued existence get closer still. The Hollywood movie I'd written in my mind of him suddenly finding himself outside of his body, able to see us but not make himself heard, then frantically trying everything he could to somehow yell loud enough to pierce the divide, felt like it was getting closer to a documentary, the re-creation of actual events. I started to imagine the relief Dad might be feeling as his messages began to get through. This path that felt more and more as though he'd guided me to, was perhaps, beginning to have the affect he hoped it would. I could feel him thanking Dr. Beischel for taking the time to so thoughtfully explain to his bartender/actor/mostly bartender son why it was okay for him to believe it really was his father doing all of this.

I highly recommend that you read Dr. Beichel's book, *Investigating Mediums*, which much more thoroughly covers some of the research they've done. Likewise, because they believe it is important for people to know this information, given its potential impact on our sense of reality, you can visit windbridge.org, where, for free, you can read the summaries they post of their ongoing studies. The work being carried out at Windbridge is currently the only ongoing serious scientific investigation into mediumship that I'm aware of. I hope they are able to continue in their quest to document and understand a phenomenon that may shed light on a universal aspect of being human, one that "affects ten out of ten people."

All of this "real science," as opposed to the demonstrations I was doing in my mother's back room, brought me peace that the skeptics, as intelligent as so many of them might be, were either unaware of these studies, or were blinded to their significance by the staunchness of their unyielding positions. Still, though, the idea that this could all be the result of some type of telepathy or "super psi" continued to nag at me. I was convinced by my own experiences and by the data from Windbridge and other places that something of a paranormal nature was going on. But what exactly it was . . . well obviously, that was a question still not completely answered for me. I began to wonder if there was existing evidence suggesting not only that Angelina was picking up information in an anomalous way, but that it was more likely that the information originated from my discarnate dad than from living brains or the clairvoyant sensing of obituaries and Facebook feeds?

And the answer, to me, was pretty clear.

# CHAPTER FOURTEEN

# When I Was Big

The modern research on mental mediumship is sparse and often assailed by skeptics who point to various methodological issues they believe to exist (whether or not they do is another question, and I leave it to the reader to decide for themselves based on the individual studies). But there is one area of research also pointing to the survival of consciousness beyond death where the volume and rigor of study is vast, and the best evidence, when finally examined, is not in great dispute: cases of children who have memories that are often found to match, in many specific details, the life of someone else, someone who lived and died before the child was born.

After receiving his M.D. and graduating at the top of his class in medical school in 1943, specializing in biochemistry, the medical world was wide open to Dr. Ian Stevenson. By the time he was just thirty-seven, he'd been published over sixty times, mostly in highly regarded, peer-reviewed journals, as well as many times in Harper's Magazine. So successful had his academic career already been, so well-respected his research, that at the remarkably young age of thirty-eight, he became the chairman of the Department of Psychiatry at UVA in 1957. So, you know . . . no dummy was Dr. Stevenson.

Up to that point, Stevenson had thrown his considerable intellectual heft behind the better understanding of biochemistry, medicine, and psychiatry, publishing papers that advanced each subject. However, to the dismay of UVA, his attention was soon diverted away from the "respectable" study of the human body and brain to something quite outside the scientific and academic establishment's sense of propriety. Namely, the possibility of reincarnation.

In 1958, Dr. Stevenson published an article in Harper's Magazine titled, "Scientists with Half-closed Minds." In it, he lamented the fact that "science," which is the *method* by which new knowledge is obtained, becomes too frequently equated to the body of shifting knowledge it accumulates. He implores the scientific community to see how our handling of that knowledge is often detrimentally subject to the same human foibles that plague the rest of our existence. He writes, "When humans become scientists they continue to experience some of the less rational qualities of being human. And with this part of them they can get in each other's way, and in the way of progress." He discusses his observation that, often, scientists become so entangled with their work that it becomes a part of their identity, and so they protect it with a truth-opaquing ferocity: "Like lesser human beings, scientists have a proprietary affection for their own contributions. Having given the best of their lives, as many have, to new observations and concepts, they may defend these as devotedly as those who give their lives to material possessions. And this kind of psychological investment can carry the investor into the most ridiculous positions." He recounts some of the many times in history that a psychological shortcoming has thwarted the advance of science, as scientists held too fast to old ideas, often refusing to believe, without a shred of investigation themselves, that some new discovery or another was even possible:

A common and astonishing feature of the opposition to scientific advance is the certainty with which it is offered [Penn Jillette's "all" comes again to mind]. For the moment, and sometimes for years, the doubter forgets that he could be wrong. At the first demonstration of Edison's phonograph before the Paris Academy of Sciences, all the scientists present declared that it was impossible to reproduce the human voice by means of a metal disc. One man proposed to throttle the demonstrator. 'Wretch!' said he. 'Do you suppose that we are fools to be duped by a ventriloquist?' [. . .] Resistance to the new can reach into the highest places. We owe to Francis Bacon much of the foundation of scientific method. He said: 'We have set it down as a law to ourselves that we have to examine things to the bottom; and not to receive upon credit or reject upon improbabilities, until these have passed a due examination.' Yet Bacon could not believe that the Earth goes around the Sun. Galileo, who could not persuade fellow astronomers to look into his telescope, could not himself accept Kepler's evidence that the planets move in ellipses. [. . .] A scientist is—perhaps fortunately—only capable of scientific thought for a small portion of his time. At other times he usually allows his wishes, fears, and habits to shape his convictions. The wish not to believe can influence as strongly as the wish to believe. Most of us most of the time practice Paley's recipe for obstruction: 'There is a principle, proof against all argument, a bar against all progress . . . which if persisted in cannot but keep the mind in everlasting ignorance—and that is, contempt prior to examination.'

Stevenson was obviously determined not to be one of those closed-minded scientists who shunned new data for fear of its potential to shift well-established and accepted structures. He understood that belief has nothing to do with science: science is about observation of what happens, regardless of one's belief about what "should" or "could" happen. So when he came across what looked to him like potential evidence that some people have memories of previous lives, he did not dismiss it out of hand as an impossibility, the a priori stance the very vast majority of his colleagues took (and continue to absurdly maintain). For Dr. Stevenson, there would not be "contempt prior to investigation."

In various published works, including books, newspapers and magazines, Stevenson had come across accounts of young children who claimed to have memories that did not belong to the life they were currently living. Often these children were merely 3 years old or younger, and almost always younger than 10. Once you come to know the body of Stevenson's work, the meticulous and, one might even say obsessive nature of his research, you will realize that there were reasons he found these cases intriguing enough to take seriously. Stevenson had a brilliant mind, and not one that would waste time on frivolity. As he continued to discover these cases, published at different times and places, he was struck by the patterns he was seeing. As with my investigation into mediumship, it was these patterns that Stevenson found quite telling. Why would children from all over the world, at such young ages, be reporting such memories, and doing so in such similar ways? And it wasn't just kids telling fanciful stories of having lived before—a good percentage of these children were reporting memories later *verified as accurate* to some previous person's life that in many instances the child could not have known. So compelling were these particular cases to Stevenson that when The American Society for Psychical Research (the same one that had studied Leonora Piper) held a contest in 1958 to find the best essay on paranormal phenomena, particularly regarding the possibility of life after death, he submitted an entry titled, "The Evidence for Survival from Claimed Memories of Former Incarnations," which was a review of forty-four of these published cases. The essay was declared the winner, and in 1960, it was published. Stevenson would later say, "These forty-four cases, when you put them together, it just seemed inescapable to me that there must be something there. I couldn't see how they could all be faked or they could all be a deception." Stevenson began to further investigate cases himself, and doing so right from the beginning in the rigorous way that would be the hallmark of all of his research to come—and eventually sway even some of the most ardent materialists. *Twenty Cases Suggestive of Reincarnation*, published in 1966, was the fruit of his initial studies. The book was reviewed positively by the American Journal of Psychiatry at the time, and it stands up to scrutiny today. Had that been the only book Stevenson published on the topic, he would have left us with much to think about, but Dr. Stevenson was just getting started.

Due to a generous donation made to the University of Virginia, Dr. Stevenson was able to continue his unique investigations and, among other works, published a two-volume, 2,200 page tome in 1997 that carefully dissected 225 cases in which a child talking about memories from another life has a birth mark or birth defect that matches the wound or wounds on the person who died whom that child remembered being in the previous life. The book is called *Reincarnation and Biology: A Contribution to the Etiology of Birthmarks and Birth Defects*—a body of evidence that is enormous both in scope and meticulousness. As I've said, in order for a man as intellectually gifted as Dr. Stevenson to be so taken with this subject, there must have been solid reasons. He certainly did not devote what turned out to be the rest of his life, he did not dedicate almost the entirety of his mental resources until he passed in 2007, he did not give fifty years of himself to this line of inquiry because it was merely interesting to him: he did so because he found the evidence to be overwhelming, and the portent of what that evidence meant profound. And he wasn't alone. Dr. Stevenson soon convinced other bright minds that there was something to this phenomenon, including that of a psychiatrist named Dr. Jim Tucker.

About twenty years after the Division of Personality Studies (Now the Division of Perceptual Studies, or DOPS) had been formed, while Stevenson was now deeply involved in his reincarnation studies, Jim Tucker, having completed his M.D., moved from North Carolina to Charlottesville to complete his general and child psychiatry training at UVA. Though he never met him, Dr. Tucker learned through the campus grapevine about Dr. Stevenson's research. Growing up, and throughout his medical training, Dr. Tucker had never considered reincarnation to be a serious possibility, and certainly not a topic science might be able to shed any light on—until, that is, he read one of Dr. Stevenson's books. "What impressed me was the approach he was taking to the topic," Dr. Tucker told me.

Having been taken aback by what I'd found, so floored was I by what seemed to be the facts, I decided I needed to hear them directly from the "horse's mouth." The horse, in this case, was the world-recognized leading researcher in spontaneous past life memories in children, Dr. Jim Tucker, who, fifty years after DOPS was established, now sits at the head of it. I took a film crew down to Virginia, and after exploring the stunning campus designed by Thomas Jefferson, and wandering around the hallowed halls of academia, each ivy-covered brick wall subtly intimidating me with its astuteness, as though the edifices themselves carried knowledge my SAT scores prohibited the acquisition of, I sat down with a man who, within these storied boundaries of scholastic achievement, was seriously asking— and answering—the question, "Does reincarnation happen?"

I began, of course, by asking Dr. Tucker if he was "a quack." The stifled gasps from the film crew alerted me to the fact that my question may have been one atypical of what Dr. Tucker is queried with during serious interviews. At least not right off the bat. However, in my mind, the question made sense. I mean, if people aren't paying attention to such astonishing evidence, it must mean the people gathering it are "quacks," right? Luckily, Dr. Tucker took my question in good humor, and then assured me that he wasn't one. And by the end of the interview (which can be viewed at mikeanthony.com), after he'd explained to me the nuances of quantum mechanics and the particulars of wave probability collapse (fields supposedly outside the scope of his expertise, though it sure didn't sound like it), I believed him. Dr. Tucker, first of all, is a doctor. Like, you know, a real one. He isn't a Doctor of Recreation or a Doctor of Church Music (which are real things). He is an M.D.—a medical doctor. That means an accredited school (The University of North Carolina—Chapel Hill) trusted him enough to have peoples' lives in his hands while a degree from their university sits prominently over his shoulder. To become a medical doctor takes an enormous amount of intellectual might, I imagine. (I'm sure being a doctor of church music does, too—I meant no offense to church music doctors—it's just that the stakes might seem to be of a different nature).

Dr. Tucker is an extremely level man. I was instantly struck by the measure with which he spoke and even walked. Just the way he moved suggested to me deliberateness and thoughtfulness. When I asked a question, he always answered in what felt like a deeply considered way, no matter from what depth (or shallowness) the question came. Even in my silly questions, he found ways to teach me something. His entire disposition, his steady, quiet and meticulous manner, was completely at odds with the fantastic notions coming out of his mouth. If the meaning of words matched the way in which they were delivered, I'd have expected calls of trumpets, splashes of confetti and the ringing of bells, all alerting those within earshot of the profound nature of what was being said. For, if Dr. Tucker's words are true, it means that the universe does not operate the way the vast majority of the world, at least the scientific world, thinks that it does. These are words that completely knock out the foundations of so much of what we think we know, leaving a new chasm of undiscovered country beneath our daily lives. So, yes, I should think some trumpeting would have been in order, as what he was telling us heralds a brave new world to be discovered and understood. But, to the contrary, these facts were transferred to us in the room with solemnness and slowness and calm. Unadorned. Just the facts, ma'am.

Having established that he was not a mad scientist working out of his mom's basement, and that this was therefore not the reason the research was not being given serious due, I asked Dr. Tucker why a man such as he, with all of those letters after his name on the wall behind him, a guy who could make a living studying anything he wanted, decided to spend his academic life researching children claiming to have these memories? After all, before reading Stevenson's book, Tucker had a successful private child psychiatry practice in Charlottesville, and he and his wife (a clinical psychologist) were doing well. What about these cases Stevenson was researching was so provocative that he would give up his private practice, and then give the bulk of his mental energy (and the next thirty years) to them instead? He said, "I think the question of, 'does part of us survive after death,' is one, obviously, that a lot of people have an interest in. What drew me to this work was the scientific approach to the question, where it's not based on faith or wishful thinking or anything else, but just trying to explore the question, explore phenomena that address the question, and see what the results are."

To Dr. Tucker, the many years of Dr. Stevenson's research, as well as the thirty of his own that he'd conducted by that point, clearly show results that are highly significant. "If that is true," I asked, "why is your work so easily tossed aside by mainstream science?"

"Many people know next to nothing about our work, so they just dismiss it when they hear about it and think it's not something that's serious. With mainstream science there is this fundamental paradigm of materialism, the belief that the material world, the physical world, is all that there is. When you're challenging a premise like that, people have a tendency to dismiss the evidence without really considering it, because if accepted, then it means it challenges everything that you think you know. So, the scientific community as a whole has simply ignored this work. Most scientists have never even heard of it."

And that's too bad, because hidden within the data at DOPS, on the campus of one of the most prestigious universities in America, a university that has played a role in major discoveries such as a brain-immune system link, the Higgs Particle, mass spectrometry, and using visible light for wireless communications, another major discovery, perhaps the biggest yet, one that might portend an entirely new understanding of what it means to be human, has been waiting for fifty years to see the light of day, ever since Dr. Stevenson first came across those 44 cases before winning the essay contest he entered in 1958. The reason those cases so intrigued Dr. Stevenson (and subsequently Dr. Tucker, among other researchers around the world eventually convinced by Stevenson's initial work) is because they displayed common features, patterns he could not dismiss.

In a "typical" case, at a very early age, usually around 2 or 3, the child will begin to speak about a past life, often as soon as they are able to use language. As their language skills increase, they get more clear about the memories they are having. Often, they will say something along the lines of, "When I was big, I used to have a car like that." In some cases, this is a one-off scenario. The child will say this one thing, and never speak of it again. A parent might think, "That's odd," and that is the end of it. However, in the cases studied by UVA, the children typically talk over a period of years about their "other life," often repeating over and over again the same details. Dr. Tucker told me, "Many of the children keep talking about it, and a lot of them will show great emotion as they are describing it. So, it's not like a fantasy about a castle or a dragon or whatever, or a sing-songy voice . . . the kids get quite serious about it."

And, usually, one of the memories is how the previous person met their end. "Most of them talk about dying in that life," he said, "So, this is not just a fun game of make-believe. And in 70% of the cases, the previous person died in some sort of unnatural way, so it's murder, suicide, accident, combat, that sort of thing, that these very young children are describing."

221

A child might say, for instance, "I was shot in the war." Dr. Tucker continued, "A lot of the children also show behaviors that seem connected. With the unnatural death cases, over 35% of them show a phobia toward the mode of death, so they'll have an intense fear related to how the previous person died." In a fascinating case of Ian Stevenson's, a child, since birth, became extremely distraught at bath time. Long before she could speak, she would absolutely scream when her parents tried to bathe her. As she got older and stronger, it became more and more difficult. Eventually, when she began to learn to use words, she told them she had drowned in an accident in her previous life.

"That's the kind of thing that we see frequently. Or we'll see in the children's play themes that relate to the previous life, either the previous death, or most often the occupation of the previous person. These kids will be seemingly driven to compulsively play the previous occupation for hours on end. For instance, there is a case of a child where the previous person he claimed to be had been a biscuit shopkeeper, and this kid would play at being a biscuit shopkeeper for hours on end, he refused to do anything else, including schoolwork, and fell behind. There was just such a compulsive quality to try to reenact, seemingly, what the previous person did."

I don't know about you, but when I was three years old, I maybe pretended that I could fly, or that I was a lion, or an astronaut. If a friend had said, "Let's play biscuit shopkeeper," I think I would have said, "Um . . . what?" And when he began to insist that this was all we play, all day, every day, it would not have been long before I would have said, "This has been, you know . . . fun . . . and everything, but, gosh, look at the time. I think I hear my mom calling. I've got to go. I've got a thing. I have a non-biscuit related thing I really have to get to."

"You are a child psychiatrist," I said. "You know what 'normal' behavior, 'normal' play looks like. Is there a chance these kids are disassociating from reality?"

"We've actually looked at that question with psychological testing. With a group of American kids, we used different rating scales that are accepted in the field of child mental health, and what we see is the kids are not dis-associating. They don't show any sort of psychological disturbance or any psychotic indicators. The one thing that came through in the testing is that they tend to be very intelligent, and very verbal. Some of them will show some anxiety often related to things that happened in the past life. Otherwise, they seem psychologically healthy."

So, these kids are normal in all the other ways, with the exception that they used to be somebody else who was "big," and that they are often of above-average intelligence.

This sort of compulsive play and pre-language behavior indicative of a phobia is notable, to be sure, but what's most important is that eventually, enough details are given by the child to determine who the previous person was. Like, they find a *real* dead person whose life matches the details the child gave—details there is no way the child could have known. For instance, a child who displays an intense fear of tractors, say, even before verbal communication is possible, and even though he was born in a big city where tractors are quite rare, later claims to have been run over by his dad's red tractor when he was big. One day, when playing with his little sister, his mom might overhear him say, "When I was big, I lived in Massachusetts." Later, after his dad called him by his name, let's say "Eric," Eric gets oddly and earnestly angry with his dad—"I keep telling you! I'm Brian! My name is Brian!" Often these pieces of information don't come all at once, but rather over time, usually when the child is calm and relaxed, such as at bedtime or after a bath. One night as mommy is tucking Eric in, he might say, "I miss my mommy." And his blonde-haired mother will say, "What do you mean? I'm right here." And Eric will answer, "I mean my *other* mommy. My brown hair mommy on the farm. I miss her. Can you take me to her please? Her name is Barbara." Sometimes, the child will become *extremely* emotional, and beg, over and over again, over months and even years, to be taken to their "other family." The parents are often at a loss, at this point, and that is when they will start doing some Googling, eventually coming across Dr. Tucker and UVA, and contact him desperate for help. Dr. Tucker asks the family to keep a notebook and make dated entries every time the child says something. In one case, he received emails from a mom nearly every day for months on end with new things her child was saying (55 things, to be exact. All of which matched up to a real dead person that Dr. Tucker eventually found, after enormous effort). Then, in our example, one night Eric might even give the name of the road he used to live on, "Robinson Road, and I had a little sister named Maria and we had a dog with white spots." And then, the final piece, a last name is given, say, "Levy." Once enough details have been compiled like this, Dr. Tucker is able to find that, indeed, a little boy named Brian Levy who lived on a farm on Robinson Road in Massachusetts, and whose mom was Barbara and whose little sister was Maria, was killed in an accident five years before Eric was born, when he got caught under his dad's red tractor.

When they find a previous person that matches the memories the child is having, and the child has been begging his or her parents to take him or her to their "other house," so much so that the desire to do so is disrupting their current life—the children may speak about these things non-stop, even in school, where their teachers sometimes become confused by what the child is talking about—the child will, indeed, be taken to the previous location. "The average length between the death of the previous person and the birth of the child is 4.5 years," Dr. Tucker said, "so they are usually very recent lives." Therefore, then, often family members of the previous person are still alive, and they and the previous home might be visited. "And what happens when the child finally gets there?" I asked. "Sometimes they seem rather overwhelmed by it all. There are other times when they will be recognizing people and calling out to them by name. What often happens is the child will be extremely emotional about the previous family, begging to be taken to the previous family, sometimes *every day*—they are crying and begging their parents to do it. Then, after the trip, often that will die down." Dr. Tucker told us about one of the cases where he personally accompanied the family and the child to the previous home that they'd identified.

"There was a little boy in Glasgow, Scotland who started, again at a *very* early age, he was 2, to talk about a life on the Island of Barre."

"He specifically gave that name, the Island of Barre?" I asked.

"He did. And he gave some quite specific details that seemed unusual. For instance, he talked about seeing airplanes landing on the beach. And it turns out that Barre is the one airport, perhaps in the world, but certainly in the UK, where the beach is the runway. There were other details the boy gave similar to that. He also described some things that we were not able to find a fit for. He talked about how his father had been killed when he was hit by a car, and we weren't able to match that part. There was a very strong emotional component. There were some things that he was dead on about, and other things, as far as we could tell, we weren't able to find a match for. It got complicated because we couldn't completely nail down when he was talking about. He did talk about rotary phones, and we talked to a historian on the island about when there were rotary phones there, so we thought we had it narrowed down to around the 60's. It was not conclusive in the sense that we found a definite match to a previous personality. But he did show information about life there that it seemed quite unlikely he could have learned through any sort of normal means."

"Did he have an emotional attachment to these memories?" I asked.

"Yes, he desperately wanted to go see his 'Barre mom.' He started talking about it in pre-school, as well, so his teacher got confused and asked his parents, 'Do you have a vacation home, or what's the story about Barre?'"

I asked, "You accompanied this kid to the island, and you found a home that you think was the home he was talking about?"

"We think so. It certainly fit the details he gave, but those were general enough that we couldn't nail it down completely. He gave the name of 'Robinson' as his last name, and that was not a name of anybody on the island, so at first we thought it was just a zero. But then the historian did more research and they found that there was a family from Scotland named Robinson that would summer on the island, and we looked at their home, and a lot of the details that the child gave were accurate for that home. But we couldn't find anyone that had been killed the way that he described his father had."

"You had trouble finding the name 'Robinson,'" I interrupted. "Even the local historian didn't know it and had trouble finding it. So, if this little kid is committing fraud, he's a pretty good researcher."

"Yes. And it wasn't like it was a very common name, like 'Smith' might be here. There was just this one 'Robinson' on the island."

"Did he recognize the house?"

"He seemed to and he had quite an interesting response to it. He almost looked . . . sort of shaken, or kind of frozen. We took him inside the house, and he was just . . . he just seemed kind of overcome. His mom comforted him, and he was fine afterwards."

Dr. Tucker shared video footage of this kid and him arriving by plane on the island and then going to the home. Discussing the video later I said, "Now before, when he's coming in the plane and they're landing, he's all excited, he gets off the plane and says to his older brother 'I told you, I told you!' like he's been wanting to prove this to his brother and his family that this is real. He is extremely excited. And then he gets into this house, and he's a *totally* different kid. He sits and looks into the fireplace, and he looks so far away. His energy totally changed. To me, it speaks to some type of reality, at least to this kid—this kid was not messing around."

"Yes," Dr. Tucker agreed. "And it did seem like it really hit home for him. He'd been talking about all these things, and wanting to see this and that, but then when he was actually there, it kind of hit home that no one else was there anymore, and that seemed to be stirring up memories of another life that he didn't have anymore."

I said, "You've written that you've seen this before, where a kid will be having this, desperate sometimes, desire to connect with this previous life and previous family, and then when they do give enough details to find out who this person might be, and they are taken there, they are then somehow able to see that that's in the past, and it sometimes resolves some of their emotional issues."

"Yes, often *considerably*. Some of the kids are literally crying every day, saying, 'I want to go to my other mom.' They are *that* emotionally invested. There can be a very strong emotional attachment to the materials that they are describing. The intensity that they're expressing and feeling, and missing people, that typically will go down substantially once they do visit the previous place. This child in Barre . . . one thing that was helpful to him was that it seemed to validate his memories. When he got off the plane, the first thing he said to his brother was, 'I told you this place was real.' So, the children's memories are validated, but then also, they see that life has gone on, so they see that these families are still there, and have continued on with their lives—they see that the past is the past, and that seems to help them then get more fully accepting of the family they have now, and they kind of go on with their lives."

"So," I responded, "we see that this is extremely meaningful to many of these children. It seems to have a deep psychological impact on them. This is clearly not a game. And after finally being brought to the family and home they'd begged for, and seeing that life has changed in those families and homes, it can have a powerful effect on the child's happiness and acceptance of *this* life. We would not expect to see such impact were this all make-believe, right?"

"That's right."

"So, if they've made it up, they have really started to believe it," I said.

"It's certainly not just a game of fun make-believe to them, that's for sure," Dr. Tucker responded. "I think it's clear that the vast majority are not intentionally faking it. And parents will typically say they can see the difference between when their child is just kidding around vs. this material, where they are typically *much* more serious about it. The bigger question would be, 'Could it be fantasy that they believe, and it matches by coincidence,' but then when you look at the strongest cases, coincidence really seems quite far-fetched."

This question of "faking it" is very important because, for the best of the UVA cases, the *only* answer the skeptics have is fraud. The evidence is so strong that the *only* explanation *must* be, according to them, since reincarnation is impossible in their understanding of things, that the families are lying. I asked Dr. Tucker about this, and he said, "We're hearing from parents all the time about children talking about past lives, often getting multiple cases per week, and there's no reason to think that parents are making it up. You can look at some of the strongest cases and say, 'Could the family have committed this fraud?' and fraud can be difficult to rule out 100%, but there are cases where it would be *extremely* unlikely, if not impossible."

I asked Michael Shermer, noted skeptic and founder of The Skeptics Society, as noted earlier, and chief editor of its magazine, "Skeptic," (and the person I'd communicated with the year before about mediumship, who is often quoted by people who haven't thoroughly investigated evidence for themselves in "debates" about "paranormal" topics) what his thoughts are on the area of study focusing on children with apparent past-life memories. He kindly pointed me to his book, "Heavens on Earth," in which he told me he "thoroughly debunks Stevenson's claims for evidence of reincarnation." However, I found more of what Dr. Tucker had told me: most people just aren't aware of the evidence. In Mr. Shermer's "thorough debunking" of the fifty years and 2,500 cases worth of UVA's work, he cites but one (probably the most well-known, at least in America) which is that of James Leininger, a young boy found to have many memories matching the life of a WWII fighter pilot named James Huston, Jr. In the short space provided the "debunking," the most difficult to explain aspects of the case are entirely left out, and the ones left in are, in my opinion, not at all adequately explained. The old standbys of "methodological problems" in the studies, patternicity and faulty memories are invoked as explanations. It seems to me that Shermer isn't aware that Dr. Tucker has in his possession copies of the web searches James' father was doing *at the time* that his son's memories were unfolding. Every time he found something on the nascent Google search engine, he printed out the web page, for fear he wouldn't find it again. We know the exact dates, because at the bottom of the printouts the date and time is automatically produced and printed. So, we know precisely when Bruce, James' father, was searching and what he was searching for.

Much of Shermer's quick dispatching of the case revolves around his own questions, such as, "We might inquire where James Huston's soul was before little James was born? Was it occupying someone else's body, or floating around in the equivalent of a soul purgatory awaiting re-implantation? How does this work, exactly? How does the soul of someone else enter the brain and rewire the memory synapses? Does it do it by turning genes on and off, altering protein chain sequences, and repositioning synapses along the dendritic spines of newborns and their connections to other neurons, as happens when new memories are formed?" He frames his questions further in the words of philosopher Paul Edwards, "When someone dies, his disembodied mind and/or nonphysical body (whatever that means) still somehow 'retains memories of life on earth as well as some of his characteristic skills and traits'; after a period varying from a few months to hundreds of years, this pure mind or nonphysical body, which lacks not only a brain, but also any physical sense-organs, picks out a suitable woman on earth as its mother in the next incarnation, invades this woman's womb at the moment of conception of a new embryo, and unites with it to form a full-fledged human being. More problematic still, most of those reincarnated should seem to prefer 'to enter the wombs of mothers in poor and over-populated countries where their lives are likely to be wretched." Mr. Shermer continues in his own words, "When you put it that way the very idea of reincarnation is barking mad." To which I say, you can put it any way you like! The questions of why or how reincarnation might take place are well beyond the scope of what UVA can (or attempts) to answer. Once, we could not fathom how the sun rose, so gods were invented to lift it up into the sky—but we did not deny the sun was rising—no matter how it was happening. Dr. Tucker and his team are not starting the way Mr. Shermer seems to be, citing all the reasons reincarnation makes no sense to him as a concept, and why, to his logic, it doesn't line up. Rather, they are simply noting what is being observed. We saw fire before we understood what it was or how it happened. We observed rainbows in the sky before we answered how they got there. Just because a thing baffles us and threatens our sense of "how things are supposed to be" does not mean it isn't happening. Children are having these memories. Often, they are later verified to be accurate. Dr. Tucker is happy to leave what it all might mean to the philosophers: he is simply documenting the observations. If you'd told Newton his apple fell faster or slower depending on each individual observer, he might have thought you mad. But the equations, and now experiment, show us that we are not. Sorry, Newton.

Finally, I asked Mr. Shermer if he was aware of the Ryan Hammons case. He told me he was not. Which means that he is simply not aware of the best evidence. I won't get into Ryan's case here, as it is quite involved and published elsewhere in full, but suffice to say it is extraordinary. Unlike Mr. Shermer, I took the time to get to know Ryan's mom, Cyndi. Over the last four years or so, we have maintained a friendship, as their story continues to unfold. What I can say is that I believe Cyndi and her husband are very honest people, with no ulterior motives. From my many personal interactions with Cyndi, it is clear to me they are dealing with something extraordinary, and their only goal is to understand it. Dr. Tucker unravels the specifics of this amazing case in his book, which I highly recommend, *Return to Life*. And as I queried in my interview with him, "The evidence here is *so strong* that, in this case, either *you* are committing fraud, or this really happened. Did this really happen?"

"It did."

Another example of cases where fraud is extremely unlikely, in Dr. Tucker's opinion, are some in which "recognition tests" are given to the child by the researcher.

There are some cases where the child is given a controlled recognition test, where different people from the past life are shown to the child to see if she or he will recognize them, and included in that are people that the previous person didn't know. For instance, there was a little girl in Sri Lanka. At 2 years old, she started saying that she had a mother and father, along with two brothers and many sisters in another place called Talawakelle, and that she wanted to visit her former parents there. She gave the name of only one person, which she sometimes said was "Lora," and sometimes "Dora." Eventually, they found that the details the girl gave matched the life of a boy who had died two years earlier in Talawakelle. The researcher, Dr. Nissanka, decided to do an unannounced recognition test with the child, where he would introduce her to various members of the previous boy's family without saying anything about who they were. The child, now 4 years old, sat in a room on her mother's lap while Dr. Nissanka (who made an audio recording of the test), paraded a number of people in front of her. Everyone that the previous person knew, the four-year-old recognized, and often gave details about each that she could not have known just from looking at someone. For instance, not only did she say, "You're my

231

older sister," she said, "You're my older sister, the sister to whose house we go to sew clothes." The first person to walk into the room was the mother of the boy who had died. Dr. Nissanka asked the young girl if she recognized the woman. Dr. Nissanka says the girl became excited, but then shy. The woman then asks, "Can you tell me who I am?" The girl, wanting to make sure her own mother (again, whose lap she was sitting on) couldn't hear, leaned over to Dr. Nissanka's microphone and whispered, "Talawakelle mother." It was as if the girl didn't want to offend her current mother, so told Dr. Nissanka in confidence who the woman was. While hearing Nissanka's account, I was thinking, *So, this girl is either an incredible actress at this very young age, or something real is happening.* But it got only more extraordinary. She next identified her "Talawakelle father" when the next person, a man, was brought in. Then her sister, the one she "went to school with," which was correct. When asked how they got to school the girl replied, "By train." This, also, was accurate. Then, one of the controls entered, a man that moved to Talawakelle after the boy had died, and so did not know him. He asked her, "Who am I?" The girl says, "No." Dr. Nissanka then asks, "Do you know him? Look again carefully? Who is he?" really trying to get the girl to give an answer. She then says, "No, I don't know him." The very last person to enter was the brother of the boy. According to the family, the two brothers had constantly quarreled, and therefore had a strained relationship. When the girl was asked if she knew him, she twice answers with anger, "No! No!" Dr. Nissanka, picking up on her clear (and sudden) upset, tells her that she "can tell her mother if she wants to." The girl then whispered to her mother, "My brother from Talawakelle." Dr. Nissanka then asks if she would say it louder so everyone would be able to hear and she said, again, "My brother from Talawakelle." In all, there were 11 people that knew the previous person the little girl was claiming to be, and 4 people used as controls who the previous person did not know. The young girl correctly identified not only the 11 people that the boy had known, but also the boy's relationship to most of them. 2 were the previous person's teachers (one a regular teacher, and the other a Sunday school teacher), 4 were his sisters, his father and mother, a brother, and 2 friends. When asked about the 4 people who were not acquainted with the boy, the girl said of each, "No, I don't know him/her."

"So," as Dr. Tucker said to us, "in this case, if it was deceit, it was a very young child who would have been at the center of this *huge* fraud for some completely unknown reason." What seems to make that even less likely is this: Dr. Stevenson, who had not been there for the initial recognition test when the girl was 4, eventually, years later, found a girl named Lora that had been a classmate of the boy who died. Since "Lora" (and sometimes "Dora") had been the only name the young girl had ever mentioned, Dr. Stevenson saw an opportunity. Lora had not been located by the original research team, and therefore had not been used in the initial recognition test. So, in 1970, Stevenson flew to Sri Lanka and interviewed Lora. Lora did, indeed, know the boy who'd died all that time ago. Unannounced, Dr. Stevenson took Lora, now 30, and a female friend of hers that did not know the boy as a control to the home of the young girl who'd so brilliantly performed in the recognition tests when she was 4. Now, at nearly 15 years old, Dr. Stevenson asked her if she recognized the two women. One of them she did not. But to the other she said, "Dora from Talawakelle," confusing, as she had when she was 2, "Dora" and "Lora." And indeed, she'd said it to the real Lora, and not her friend. Dr. Stevenson took this as quite an accomplishment, given the elapsed time between the first recognition test and this complete surprise test nearly 11 years later. It further convinced him of this case's validity. Fraud seemed to him, and seems to me, an *exceedingly* low probability explanation.

At one point, a member of our crew asked about the idea of karma, and whether or not the cases show evidence for it. As in, does what they remember doing in their previous life somehow affect their circumstances in this life? Dr. Tucker said, "Karma is a complex doctrine. In a simplified way, we don't see a lot of evidence for karma in our cases. Or certainly not evidence for karmic retribution. In the cases where the previous person was murdered, for instance, the children are sometimes born with birthmarks, or even full birth defects, that match wounds that the previous person received. But it's not that the child remembers being the murderer and then got karmic retribution with these defects, but that they remember being killed themselves, and then carrying these wounds with them to the next life."

"I feel like we buried the lead, a little bit there," I interrupted. Already knowing this information from my research into Dr. Stevenson, but knowing the crew in the room was completely unfamiliar with it, I wanted Dr. Tucker to make this astounding point very clear. "I thought I heard you say that you have kids who claim they were killed in a certain way, and then on their bodies, there are birthmarks that match?"

"That's right," he said with a slight smile, as the surprise by those in the room became evident, and it seemed to me he was enjoying (though not as much as I was) the opportunity to wedge open some minds). "Birthmarks or even full-blown birth defects. Ian Stevenson was really fascinated by these cases. He had a longstanding interest in psychosomatic medicine, the connection between mind and body, so he was really blown away by these. He spent years studying them, and he eventually published a collection of 225 such cases. It's a 2,000-page, two volume set. For instance, there is one little girl who remembered the life of a man who got his fingers chopped off as he was being murdered. She was born with markedly mangled fingers. There was a boy who remembered the life of a boy in another village who lost the fingers of his right hand in a fodder chopping machine. His left hand was perfectly normal, but he was born with just stubs for fingers on his right hand."

"Can't it be that this child sees that they have stubs for fingers, and they create a story?" I asked.

"Sure, a child could create a story to explain their missing fingers, but does the story that the child creates match someone who lived and died? That is the question. And, in many cases, they do."

"So," I continued with my questioning, "they have this birth defect, or birthmark, they are saying, 'I used to be Jerry, I lived in this place,' and in some cases we have these things documented and written down, and at some point after the fact, a person named Jerry is identified that matches those facts?"

"That's right. And not just written down, but documented, for instance, in things like autopsy reports."

For the people in the room besides Dr. Tucker and me, which consisted of four people on the crew, and a friend I'd brought with me, this information was mind-blowing. Naturally, they wanted to know more, and I asked Dr. Tucker to describe a case of his that occurred in New York City.

"There was a retired NYC policeman named John McConnell working as a security guard who happened to walk in on two men robbing an electronics store. John pulled out his pistol, and a third man from behind a counter shot him through the heart, his main pulmonary artery, and killed him. He was hit six times. Five years later, his daughter, Doreen, gave birth to a son named William. Soon after he was born, William started to pass out. Doctors diagnosed him with a condition called pulmonary valve atresia, in which the valve of the pulmonary artery has not adequately formed, and which resulted in his right ventricle being malformed. Several surgeries were needed to address the issues. Luckily, though he requires indefinite medication, he has done well. William's birth defects were very similar to the fatal wounds suffered by his grandfather. When he got old enough to talk, at about two, he spoke about having been his grandfather, giving some personal details. It started one day when his mom was trying to get some work done in her home office and he was acting up, and she finally said something like, 'Sit down, or I'm going to spank you.' And William said,

'Mom, when I was your dad and you were a little girl, you were bad a lot of times and I never spanked you!' That led to other statements about the grandfather's life, and eventually he discussed 'his' death. He told his mother that several people were shooting during the incident when he was killed. Then, one time he said to his mom, 'When you were a little girl and I was your daddy, what was my cat's name?' She responded, 'You mean Maniac?'

'No, not that one. The white one.'

'Boston?' she asked.

'Yeah. I used to call him Boss, right?'

And that was correct. The family had two cats, and only John referred to the white one as Boss."

This woman was left with no doubt that her son is the rebirth of her father. And our skeptical crew members were becoming less so by the moment.

UVA has hundreds of cases such as this, where a child, with varying degrees of evidence, claims to be the rebirth of someone who'd lived before. Over 2,500, in fact. In two-thirds of them, enough information has been given by the child to identify who the previous person was that the child is claiming to be. And having so many cases allows us to look for patterns, and in doing so, some of the most remarkable of the evidence comes to light. DOPS has picked apart and coded all of the cases, covering 200 variables, and entered them into a searchable database. To Dr. Tucker, among the most striking discoveries was this: In the general population in the United States, of the unnatural deaths (meaning death by, for instance, accident, suicide, murder, etc.) 72% are accounted for by men, and 28% by women. When it is a natural death, the statistics are approximately 50/50 between men and women. For whatever reason (which we can easily speculate on) men are more likely to die unnatural deaths than women, by a 72 to 28 percent margin. When Dr. Tucker ran a search through his database for those specific variables only, he found something remarkable: 70% of the UVA cases involve an unnatural death. Of those, 72% involve a case where the previous person was male, and 28% involve cases where the previous person was a female. Of the 30% of cases that involved natural death, 50% involved females, and 50% males. Meaning, the statistics from the more than 2,500 cases in the UVA files mirror, almost exactly, the statistics from the general population. In other words, what we see in the case numbers is what we would expect to see if they *actually are* a sampling of real, previous lives. It seemed to me that even Penn Jillette would have trouble faking that. I asked the skeptics in the room with me, after Dr. Tucker explained this, if they imagined that these 2 and 3 and 4-year-old children, the world over, were secretly getting together to figure out who needed to claim what in order to match the statistics from the general population? None of them did.

I have come to personally know some families going through this, and all I can tell you is that the *only* thing that drives the ones I am in contact with is a desire to understand, and help their children understand what it is they are experiencing. I have practically begged them to be involved in a documentary, since I wanted to follow a family in real time who was dealing with this issue, or to be in the Netflix series *Surviving Death*, and they simply would not do it for fear that it might somehow be detrimental to their children. They did not want the fact that their child recalls a past life to become a defining feature of *this* life, to somehow impede their enjoyment of now. In fact, when I told each family that children recalling memories of past lives, even ones with great emotional attachment to those memories, typically forget them by the age of six or seven and go on to have normal lives, the families were comforted, looking forward to when this emotionally difficult time would pass, and they and their children can finally be fully in the present. The parents, each time their child offered up a new bit of information would race to the computer to start Googling, desperate for answers, after the child went to sleep. They would keep me informed of these occurrences for months and into years, as they continued to try and "solve" their child's case, sometimes enlisting my help, asking me if I would feel comfortable contacting a family they'd found that matched their child's memories, because they felt awkward about it. For months and months, a mom I know agonized about whether or not she should make the call. If these people are committing fraud, they are playing the long game. And for no apparent reward. We must ask ourselves why? These are the questions Michael Shermer should be asking, rather than "Why does reincarnation, as a concept, make sense?" If this is fraud, fraud for no gain, why would so many families, thousands the world over, be going through all the trouble? And how did they get their very young children to participate so well? Are we to believe these are all Oscar-worthy performances that these 2 and 3 and 4-year-old children are giving, without ever letting the cat out of the bag, over the course, often, of years, as different investigators continue to ask questions, probing for consistency? How? Moreover, how did these children and their families get the statistics to match? Why do the stats for male/female and natural/unnatural deaths match those of the general population? Did all of these thousands of families, again, from all over the world, across the fifty-year span of these investigations, all get together to agree on who should claim what to make certain the statistics match? That, obviously, is an absurd notion. And yet, it is the only answer the critics, the ones who have actually studied the evidence at UVA, can come up with. The cases are so sound, so remarkable, that fraud, no matter how very unlikely fraud is, is literally the *only* answer they have. And it simply doesn't fit. So, if that answer, too, is out, what is left?

In all of the reading I've done, and all of the topics I've investigated, the research carried out by Dr. Stevenson, which continues to this day under the steady leadership of Dr. Jim Tucker at UVA, is perhaps the most impactful. To me, the evidence is so stark that it's a surprise it isn't an aspect of every psychology curriculum. Indeed, having spoken with Dr. Tucker in person, and beheld the rooms of tall filing cabinets, all overflowing with hundreds of thousands of pages of painstaking research pointing so strongly towards one conclusion, so convincingly depicting grounds for reincarnation, it is difficult for me to fathom why this information isn't on the nightly news. Why doesn't everyone in America know that the evidence for consciousness existing over the course of multiple lives, being processed through multiple brains, is so strong that The Journal of the American Medical Association, when reviewing Stevenson's work, wrote, "the evidence is difficult to explain on any other grounds," and that when many serious researchers take a thorough look at the voluminous research, they come to the same conclusion?

I hope you will research for yourself Drs. Stevenson and Tucker's work. Of particular interest to me is Stevenson's book, *Where Reincarnation and Biology Intersect*, which, on its own, is remarkable evidence of what we commonly call reincarnation. For more updated cases, please read Dr. Tuckers's *Return to Life* and *Life Before Life*, and Dr. James Matlock's *Signs of Reincarnation*. At the very least, the chances are high that you will come away with an expanded sense of what is possible. Writing for Scientific American, psychologist, and devout materialist scientist, Dr. Jesse Bering wrote:

> If you're anything like me, with eyes that roll over to the back of your head whenever you hear words like 'reincarnation' or 'parapsychology,' if you suffer great paroxysms of despair for human intelligence whenever you catch a glimpse of that dandelion-colored cover of *Heaven is for Real* or other such books, and become angry when hearing about an overly Botoxed charlatan telling a poor grieving mother how her daughter's spirit is standing behind her, then keep reading, because you're precisely the type of person who should be aware of the late Professor Ian Stevenson's research on children's memories of previous lives.

He later concludes the article with this:

'The mind is what the brain does' I wrote in *The Belief Instinct*. 'It's more a verb than it is a noun. Why do we wonder where our mind goes when the body is dead? Shouldn't it be obvious that the mind is dead too?' Perhaps it's not so obvious at all. I'm not *quite* ready to say that I've changed my mind about the afterlife. But I can say that a fair assessment and a careful reading of Stevenson's work has, rather miraculously, managed to pry it open.

When I asked Dr. Tucker at the end of our hours-long discussion what the bottom line is, how he might, in a single sentence, sum up the fifty years of research his division has been engaged in, he said quite simply these very not so simple words: "Some children have memories from previous lives."

And so, if such strong evidence exists pointing towards the idea that what we think of as "us," including our memories and our emotions and personality can survive death, can exist for some varying interval afterwards, and then connect to a new brain in a new body, is it still such a stretch to suggest that, perhaps, some brains in current bodies are able to connect with consciousness that is in an interval between bodies? Might this not be what a "medium" is doing? Of particular interest to me in this regard is the fact that in 20% of the 2,500 cases, the children report what Stevenson called "intermission memories," time from after the previous death and before the next birth. If, as in so many of these cases, the children's earthly statements turn out to be true, why not might these memories from the time in between be real as well? If they are, it clearly suggests that experiences can be had and memories can be made—without a brain. In a number of these cases, the intermission memories are confirmed as well, such as in the extraordinary case of James Leininger, mentioned earlier, that Mr. Shermer highlights. I got in touch with James' family to ask them to be part of my film. Bruce, James' dad, agreed, and Bruce and I spoke for hours on the phone. As with the other families going through this that I've come to know, it became clear to me over the course of our conversation, and following communications, that Bruce was a person of integrity—a man who was truly trying to understand what it meant that the evidence strongly suggested his son had lived before.

James, at age 3, began having vivid nightmares and then waking memories of being shot down in his fighter plane in World War II. You can read in detail about the perception-shifting incidents that followed in *Soul Survivor*, a fascinating book Bruce wrote chronicling his family's story. The relevant point here is that James, when he was about 3, told his dad that he was "glad he picked him." Bruce asked, "What do you mean?" James said, "Before I came, I found you and Mommy eating dinner on that beach in Hawaii in front of the pink hotel and I knew you would be good parents." Bruce and his wife, Andrea, in the first week after they decided to try for children and go off of birth control, took a vacation to Hawaii and stayed at The Royal Hawaiian, a pink hotel, and on the last night, they had dinner on the beach. About five weeks later, James was conceived. James had never been told any of these details, and had seen no photographs from this trip. There is no "normal" way he could have known about the dinner on the beach in front of the pink hotel.

Beyond this, over the course of two Christmases and a birthday, James had gotten 3 G.I. Joes. These became his friends and he was rarely without them. He immediately named each one, as soon as opening them. The names given were, Billy, Leon, and Walter. His parents thought the names funny for a 3 to 5-year-old to pick, specifically the names "Leon and Walter," and asked him how he chose them. James said, "Because they are who met me in heaven when I got there."

After a years-long, epic journey for answers, detailed in *Soul Survivor,* James' parents eventually found a person who had died in World War II named James Huston, Jr., who matched, in extremely specific details, the memories their James was having, including the fact that he had taken off from an aircraft carrier named "Natoma," along with his friend and fellow pilot "Jack Larsen" (who turned out to still be alive, and whom little James eventually got to meet—or, as James would have it, reconnect with). He was in the battle of Iwo Jima, where he'd been killed after his plane "got shot down by the Japanese." There were 10 men in James Huston, Jr.'s squadron on the *Natoma Bay* that died before he did (and therefore might be there to "meet him in heaven"). 3 of those 10 men were Billie Peeler, Leon Conner, and Walter Devlin. And for just a bit of icing: the three G.I. Joes each had a different hair color, brown, blonde and red. In real life, Billie Peeler had brown hair, Leon Conner had blonde hair, and Walter Devlin had red. James Leininger had named each of their G.I. Joe counterparts accordingly—long, long before anyone besides James knew who those people were, or certainly what their hair color might have been.

In the case we discussed earlier, where Doreen believes that her son, William, is indeed, as he claims, the reincarnation of her NYC policeman dad, Doreen asked William one day if he remembered anything from the time before he was born. Dr. Tucker tells us what happened next in his book, *Life Before Life*:

"William said that he died on Thursday and went to heaven. He said he saw animals there and also talked to God. He said, 'I told God I was ready to come back, and I got born on Tuesday.' Doreen was amazed that William mentioned days since he did not even know his days of the week without prompting. She tested him by saying, 'So, you were born on a Thursday and died on Tuesday?' He quickly responded, 'No, I died on Thursday at night and was born on Tuesday in the morning.' He was correct on both counts—John died on a Thursday, William was born on a Tuesday five years later."

William spoke on multiple occasions about his time between lives. During one such instance he told his mom, "When you die, you don't go right to heaven. You go to different levels," moving his hand up each time as he said, "here, then here, then here."

If so many statements from children who claim to be the rebirth of a former person turn out to be accurate, might not memories from the in-between be accurate, as well? Might one of the "heres" be a vantage point from which my dad has the ability to reach back into my world, the one he once inhabited, to let me know he continues? I must conclude it is possible, no matter how impossible.

I was reminded once more of Mr. Sawyer, and the long ago Phenomenology Club. We spent so many a Wednesday discussing things that "couldn't be"—like unidentified flying objects—a topic then scorned by most of the world and with near absoluteness by the scientific community. However, Mr. Sawyer often presented us with what felt like important evidence, testimony from intelligent people, people such as pilots, for instance, who were seeing things our current understanding of science does not allow for. In every other aspect of these witnesses lives, they might have been considered with the utmost respect. But this one experience had to be a mistake. It had to be a trick of the light or some other misinterpretation of a "normal" occurrence. And I soon learned in my own life, from my own family, even, how very quickly one becomes ridiculed for "believing" in UFOs. From my perspective, belief has nothing to do with it. Science is about what we observe. We observe an "anomaly," and then study it until we understand how it fits. Though it was surprising for Galileo to find a feather and a large rock fall at the same speed when air resistance is accounted for, and people didn't believe it, nonetheless, it proved to be true—no amount of belief, or lack thereof, altered the facts.

Of course, my 15-year-old self would one day be vindicated, and I'd take great joy in sharing with those deriding family members the *New York Times* article published in 2017 announcing the Pentagon's admission of its 22 million dollar program (and much more than that, it seems) studying UFOs, and the release of military footage from the most advanced camera systems on the planet showing objects exhibiting movement characteristics that are "impossible" (if my physics teachers and "mainstream" scientists are correct), and a following article in 2020, again from the *Times*, suggesting we have actual physical material from "off-world vehicles not made on this earth" in our possession, acquired through an official "crash retrieval" program.

I was seeing what I considered to be evidence back in 1992 when my family thought I was crazy for "believing" in UFOs. But it's not that the evidence hadn't already been there—it's simply that we are finally, slowly coming to accept it, no matter how uncomfortable it might be.

The same is true of these other "paranormal" areas of study, like children having memories that don't belong to their current life. Here, too, it has nothing to do with belief. It has to do with occurrences. Things that happen. We mustn't dismiss them simply because they do not fit with our perceptions of reality. Instead, we must alter our conception of reality in order to fit the new information. My physics teachers (and all of "mainstream science") are now going to have to reconsider and reformulate their ideas of "fundamental" aspects of our reality, like gravity, for instance, given the Pentagon's admission. These "objects" (or whatever one might be—perhaps many different "things") do not move according to the "rules." Which means we have to alter the rules. We don't say, "It can't happen because it can't happen" (something a debunking scientist literally said) once we see that it *is* happening.

But when something occurs that shifts at a foundational level, it can take a great deal of evidence, a weight of evidence beyond what is typically required as proof, in order to tip the scale to acceptance. When Galileo found the feather to fall as fast as a rock, yes, it was surprising, but it didn't upset our sense of our place in things. So, he just had to devise some experiments with ramps, and let balls of varying weights roll down them, and we saw it and said, "Okay. I guess that's the way it is. Sorry, Aristotle."

But with these "anomalies" we observe, the ones that upset things at a fundamental level and make us uncomfortable with where we sit in reality, it takes more than a few viewings of the balls rolling down the ramps. It takes an enormous weight of evidence. However, the evidence isn't suddenly there when it's accumulated to a certain level. The feather falling as fast as a rock was just as true the first time when Galileo witnessed it through math, as it was the hundredth time when people finally accepted it as true.

I'm suggesting there are things happening right now, "anomalies" that have been witnessed and recorded for years, that will one day reach the level of accumulation when the scale tips toward mainstream acceptance. But we don't have to wait for that day to see the evidence, if we are brave enough to look, and consider what it might mean. Feathers are falling as fast as rocks right now, and have been for quite some time. We just need to look in the right places to see them. And as fate would have it, I was about to look in the right place.

If you thoroughly dive into the research discussed thus far, and remain unconvinced that the preponderance of evidence points to something paranormal, something beyond the bounds of materialism, don't stop reading yet. Because we are about to go even further. What happened next was a journey I never expected, but one that changed everything for me. And changed it for good. Questions of whether or not "paranormality" of any kind was possible were about to become moot from my perspective, replaced by just one, new question: "What does it mean?"

# CHAPTER FIFTEEN

# Give Dad a Hand

After my trip to Virginia and close look at the work they've been doing there for over fifty years, combined with what I'd learned from Dr. Beischel, and of course, my own experiences thrown into the mix, I felt more sure than ever that the information Angelina and the other mediums had given me actually did come from my father. The very strong evidence suggesting we can live more than once and exist in some way between bodies, and that some people are somehow able to sense communications from those "in between," helped to make sense of what I was experiencing with these apparent attempts by my deceased father to reach us—no matter how unlikely science might say that is (because "science," as a whole, to drive the point home yet again, isn't aware of the evidence). I'd accepted the idea that enormously impactful things, things that bring to bear in profound ways on human life, might be simultaneously true, and also hidden from the majority of the world. I came to see how that had been the case many, many times over the known course of human history. Every time a veil is lifted, another has been found. And with each lifting, more seem to fall. Like the unexplained acceleration of the expansion of the universe, every answer brings mostly questions. And I'd made my peace with that.

Also, I'd run out of money.

Making documentaries with a professional crew tends towards the expensive side of things, as it turns out. I'd spared no expense in my quest to know if there was anything I could discover about my dad's current state, and the coffers were empty (the peace of mind I now had is priceless, so it was a tremendous bargain). Before I could do anything further, an influx of capital would be required. To that end, I decided to try my hand at a fundraising campaign, and I pulled together some highlights from our many hours of footage to make a teaser. Now much more certain that Angelina was doing what she claimed, I felt good about the prospect of continuing our project, so I hit the "publish" button, sharing the campaign on Facebook, and left the rest up to the universe.

So, on a rainy day, while I waited to see what sort of traction the campaign might get, content in the possibility, should the fundraiser fail, that I had gotten all the evidence I would of my dad's continued existence, happy to know so many things remained unsolved, and perhaps, unsolvable from our perspective, I went to a local Barnes and Noble to partake in a long day of coffee and line-learning at the Starbucks housed within. I had gotten an acting job at a theater, and for the first time since my dad's passing felt excited again about life, and was thrilled to have a play to do. It had been quite a while since I'd been able to act, because before I learned lines to a pretend situation, I had to come to an understanding about my real situation. I needed to know what my relationship with my dad was now. If he was truly gone, I had to accept and deal with that before I could move on. And if he wasn't . . . well I *definitely* needed to know that. And now that I'd been on this six-year quest, I'd gotten my answer. Given all that had happened, I felt as though my dad was indeed still around, and even pulling some strings. With that newfound peace in hand, culminating with my visit to UVA, it was time to keep going. Having a genuine sense that there is much more to our existence than meets the eye, and that there is a life beyond the one we know, made *this* life all the sweeter.

Sitting in the Starbucks reading the play, I found myself smiling. And not because it was a particularly funny script. I realized my cheeks were now hurting because I'd been imagining my dad again in the front row, as he had been so many times. Though I wouldn't be able to see him, I now felt that he would, indeed, be there. I let myself sit in that daydream and smile for quite a long time. What broke me out of the spell was the urgent need to pee. Having drunk too much of the coffee shop's signature beverage, I made my way to the back of the bookstore where the bathrooms are. On a shelf immediately to the right of the men's room, a book sitting at about eye-level stood out from the rest. Every once in a while along the shelves, certain books were placed with their covers facing out, making them more prominent, breaking up and jumping out from the monotonous pattern of the others placed in the typical bookshelf way with only their spines visible. The book's title was, *Surviving Death, A Journalist Investigates Evidence for an Afterlife,* and it was written by investigative journalist Leslie Kean. *Hmm,* I thought. The panging functions of my body delayed a thought beyond that for the moment, but while washing my hands in the bathroom it struck me as a fun coincidence that I'd noticed this book. Having just gone on my own journey, one that sounded, from the title, like it might be similar to the journalist's, I knew I'd not be leaving the store without it. What I didn't know was that I'd not leave the store without finishing it. I got back to my seat at Starbucks, stowed the play I'd been learning lines for, and began to read the intrepid journalist's book, imagining I'd go through a chapter or two before getting back to work on lines. But then hours passed, and I was turning over the last page. I looked up to see I was sitting alone in the once bustling store.

The book covered all of the topics I'd been researching, including NDEs, ELEs, ADCs, etc, and also children with past life memories and Dr. Tucker. And now, having spent so much time with him as he methodically made the case for reincarnation, it felt like I was reading about a friend. A friend

I trusted. The words in *Surviving Death* surrounding Dr. Tucker would have been impactful and compelling regardless, but having met the man and finding him to carry such intellectual gravitas, those words bore an extra weight that I found myself wishing everyone could feel. *What a different world it might be*, I thought, *if everyone could sit for three hours with Dr. Tucker*. Because when you do, it is next to impossible to leave that conversation without your perceptions and what you consider possible to be vastly expanded. Just ask our once skeptical documentary team.

Though I'd already researched much of the material contained in *Surviving Death* (it seems that those who seek out these answers end up in similar places—evidence itself, perhaps, that those places are pointing to truth), it was a great joy to read, nonetheless. Knowing that a respected journalist had experiences that reflected mine, and through them had come to similar conclusions, further cemented my sense that this . . . that my dad still existing without a body, was an actual part of reality. However, when I got to the back of the book, I was introduced to a topic I'd, up to that point, only had a passing awareness of—something I found rather dubious on the surface, so had nudged aside without further investigation, much like so many do with Dr. Tucker's work—called "physical mediumship."

Now, we've got to pause for a moment here. I need to state up front that things are about to get whacky. And I hope you can appreciate that I see that they are whacky. Were I not reading what I was in a book written by a New York Times journalist, a journalist whose word is her livelihood, whose honesty is paramount to her life's work, a journalist whose name I would eventually realize I knew from another vitally important investigation and subsequent book of hers on UFOs (and whose reporting is now helping to completely change the world, responsible as she is for breaking the story about the Pentagon's UAP program), I would have had had *great* trouble believing this stuff. Just as, in the very recent past, most people would have had great trouble believing the United States government has a program for the retrieval of crashed vehicles of an unidentified variety. Because, as you'll see . . . depending on your current sense of how things work, it's *really* whacky. But it's also true, it turns out, and lest we be one of the closed-minded that Dr. Stevenson warned about, we'll need to look at the evidence. So . . . here we go.

Remember those pictures from earlier in the book, where some oddballs decided to stick cotton in their mouth and pretend it was some sort of paranormal activity—the pictures that were from the book Mr. Sawyer had brought in to share with the Phenomenology Club when I was in high school, where obvious charlatans had tricked some more obvious numbskulls into believing spirits were somehow involved in making what looked like cotton spew from their every orifice? Towards the end of Leslie Kean's book, the word that had captioned those black and white photographs of days gone by when I thought people were apparently much more gullible or desperate to believe or . . . something, made an appearance. After reading the majority of her thoroughly researched book, going through chapter after chapter covering the remarkable evidence I'd come across myself in my search for answers, I was suddenly stopped in my tracks when I read, "Most of the time, physical mediums, unconscious in deep trance, exude a strange substance that [Charles] Richet called 'ectoplasm.'" And then, no punchline came. Instead, Kean proceeded to lay out the evidence that "ectoplasm," dismissed so long ago as nothing more than cheesecloth and muslin that unscrupulous people used to fake paranormal abilities, and that I was sure Harold Ramis had invented for the classic film *Ghostbusters* as the green goo Slimer left behind on walls and hanging from shelves, is an actual, for real, unexplainable, but nonetheless observable substance that sometimes, under certain conditions, issues from people when they go into a deep trance. According to some scientists, there seemed to be a progression that occurred within the process of mediumship. First, simple knocks were being heard, then tables were tipping, then people were being

251

put into trances and taken over by spirits who spoke through them, and then, there was ectoplasm—believe it or not, as Ripley might have said. And what Leslie so stunningly introduced me to in her book is the very tangible evidence ectoplasm has left behind. We do not have the space here to go into the evidence, because it is voluminous. As it was with the well-known and highly regarded scientists who'd studied trance mediumship, like that of Leonora Piper, so too did scientists of similar renown and caliber study "physical mediumship." Indeed, as referenced earlier, the Richet noted in Kean's quote, the person who coined the term "ectoplasm" in 1894, a few years later won the Nobel Prize in physiology. He didn't win the Nobel for poetry or art or something that might not qualify him to study a substance being produced by the human body—he won the Nobel Prize for his advancement of knowledge *of the human body*. And they don't just hand out Nobel Prizes—you've got to do some pretty remarkable work in your given area of expertise to be able to put one of those on your mantle. Keeping in mind the unvarnished reputation of Leslie Kean, and the reputation of the Nobel Prize committee, I read on.

Physical mediumship, I learned, occurs when the medium has reached another level of trance. A deeper level, it is said. It is supposedly an altered state of consciousness that is even further away from a normal state, where brain waves start to behave in very odd ways. We have seen already how, with Leonora Piper, her trance was so deep she could be stabbed with a pin and not react. With this depth of trance, the one involved in physical mediumship, not only can you poke and jab at some mediums without them flinching, but something else becomes possible, as well—"spirit people" can sort of detach the medium's mind from their brain (because the mind is not the brain, these spirit folks say) and then temporarily take control of the medium by somehow interfacing their mind with the medium's brain, once their mind has given way.

I stopped reading for a moment, and went to get a hot chocolate. This was quickly approaching what Dr. Tucker had called one's "boggle factor" for me—the point at which the information goes beyond what any given person can accept as reality, so dismisses it, no matter the evidence, and goes about their day as though the brush with this new information never happened. Nevertheless, I was in it now. Maybe you should take a quick break, as well. Grab a hot cocoa. Put some marshmallows in, too. We'll ease in together.

Ready? Once this "spirit control"—and I'll dispense with the quotation marks and qualifiers like "supposedly" and "allegedly" henceforth, but let it be understood I am not making definitive statements one way or the other—once the spirit control has attached his or her mind to the medium's brain, under the right conditions they are then able to withdraw this multi-state substance from the medium, which can issue forth from the mouth, nose or ears, the solar plexus, and even—from other places, too. Which we now know is why during controlled tests, mediums were examined thoroughly, including in their various private places, to be certain no cheesecloth or muslin was secreted away up there. Because apparently, the people who did fake this stuff (and many did and still do) could be *very* devoted to the illusion. Therefore, for a true test of ability, *every* conceivable hiding spot within a human body was examined directly before the "sitting" or "seance," as these gatherings hoping for physical mediumship came to be called. As the phrase "physical mediumship" implies, what was unique about this form of mediumship is that it had physical aspects—objectively concrete aspects that all involved could verify. As you sat in a dark or dimly lit room, with maybe four to eight of your friends arranged in a circle, things would start to happen. It wasn't just funny voices talking about deceased Aunty Louise coming out of the medium's mouth and sounding a lot like the medium putting on a character. It was funny voices talking about deceased Aunty Louise, (sometimes inexplicably coming from other areas of the room away from the medium) while also doing things like banging on tables, lifting objects by some invisible force and zinging them around the circle of sitters above your heads, words and sentences somehow issuing from midair, and . . . maybe take another sip of that cocoa . . . in the most advanced demonstration of what the spirit world was capable of, causing previously deceased people to physically, solidly materialize right there in the room. So, you, had you been sitting in that circle, could see them form from nothing right in front of you, have a chat with you as though they were really standing there, before you watched them dissolve slowly back into the floor, maybe giving a last "Until next time," as their face disappeared into the carpet.

Still with me?

As impossible and perhaps ridiculous as this might sound to some, as it certainly did to me at first, the controlled conditions in which this happened have, at times, made fraud impossible. Houdini, of course, unmasked many a fraudulent physical medium, mediums who were swallowing and regurgitating cheesecloth and using other means to create illusions. But the best phenomena—that *to this day* remain unexplained—Houdini simply ignored and left out of his explanations. However, it wasn't as easy to entirely dismiss for some scientists of the day . . . as you'll surely have gathered by the fact that a Nobel Prize winner coined the word "ectoplasm" after *studying it in his lab.* For an example of the sort of evidence Houdini simply excised from the record, we can take the famous case of Mina Crandon, considered today to be nothing but a huckster by the world at large due to Houdini's "unmasking" of her. During spiritualism's height, Scientific American had offered a $2,500 reward for anyone who could prove paranormal phenomenon. After much searching, only one medium, Mrs. Crandon, had the Scientific American panel baffled. Mina was the wife of a distinguished Harvard Medical School instructor and well-known surgeon in Boston, and when most on the Scientific American committee had decided they wanted to award her the prize, after they'd had sitting after sitting after sitting with her, witnessing demonstrations they simply could not explain (including an evening when Houdini himself signed an affidavit attesting to the events of the sitting that he'd witnessed, and that he did not dispute), it was Houdini who would not, perhaps *could not,* have it. He went on a tireless campaign to debunk Mina Crandon, doing stage shows and writing pamphlets where he claimed to expose how she did what she did. For the rest of his life, this is how he spent his time. However, the best bits of evidence, he simply left out. He conveniently ignored them entirely, focusing on what he could potentially explain, and skipping over, as though they'd never happened, the things he could *not.* And here, for instance, is one: the scientists devised a soundproof box, inside of which was placed a microphone. The microphone led to an amplifier that was set up in another room. The only way to get sound to come out of that amplifier was to speak into the microphone, which had been locked inside the box which was placed in the middle of the circle. Mina's spirit control was her brother, Walter, who had passed in a tragic accident a few years before. When they asked Walter if he could find a way to place his voice inside the box (as passing through physical matter seemed no object to Walter), he said from within the room, "Let us see what we can do, hmm?" And the next moment, from the next room, came Walter's booming voice from the amplifier, while the room they were in remained quiet. Somehow, to the utter astonishment of the Scientific American panel, Walter had spoken into the microphone locked away inside the soundproof box. It was because of incidents like this, among others, occurring under the tightest controls (multiple times), that the Scientific American panel—all besides Houdini— planned to vote to award Mina Crandon the prize money, and yet this incident is entirely stricken from the record by Houdini, instead "debunk-ing" only that for which he could have a possible normal explanation (if young Mina Crandon happened to be as great a magician and illusionist as the incomparable Houdini).

Though the evidence Leslie Kean highlights in the book is compelling, almost all of it comes from times long ago. It felt like a phenomenon stuck in the impossible to penetrate past, where for whatever reason, scientists (some of the brightest), for a time, observed something they could not explain. But whatever it was had passed from the face of the earth, it seemed, leaving only hundreds of pages of detailed reports, and these strange photos—many taken under controlled circumstances where only experimenters were in the room with the medium, meaning no accomplice could assist in any fraud, and the camera apparatus was controlled only by the team of scientists:

**ABOVE:** Photos from *Life After Death: Living Proof*, by Tom Harrison, courtesy of Ann Harrison and Saturday Night Press Publications (right-hand photo shows a fully materialized Aunt Agg)

These two photographs come from a man named Tom Harrison, whose mother, Minnie Harrison, was a physical medium. For many years, his mom, dad, wife, and three friends sat in a room in the home of one of the friends and had seances on Saturday nights. Another of the friends, by the way, was a man named William Britain Jones, who was a respected senior surgeon and the superintendent of Middlesborough General Hospital in England. So, yet another intelligent and skilled person in the long line of scientists involved in the ectoplasmic story. For absolutely no financial gain and no conceivable reason to commit fraud among the seven extremely close family members and friends, every week together they sat. They sought out no publicity of any kind. It was a simple family affair, a weekly Saturday night gathering where, for an hour or so, they sat together in a room and hoped to contact those they'd loved who had "shuffled off this mortal coil." To the astonishment of Tom and the others in the room, one night his mom seemed to fall asleep. Soon after, with her eyes still closed and her head slumped forward, she began to speak. But she did not sound to Tom at all like his mom. It turned out to be the voice, the voice claimed, of his deceased aunt Agg.

For many months they continued to gather in this way, just the seven of them, as the things that happened in the room became more and more pronounced, until physical phenomenon began to occur. Ultimately, Minnie Harrison began to produce ectoplasm, and with it, deceased loved-ones, right in the middle of the circle in the lit room (Minnie's circle was one of the very few that always worked in light), began to materialize. Here, from his book *Life After Death: Living Proof*, is the description in Tom's words of what happened that first time:

On this particular evening we sat in the red light with my mother in full view of everyone in the room, sitting on her usual dining chair. I always sat immediately opposite her at the other end of the semi-circle and could clearly see anything that happened. We sat for at least half an hour and nothing happened—which was most unusual. We were beginning to think there would be no phenomena that evening, when we saw this white disc, about two feet in diameter, on the floor between my mother and myself.

Because of the smallness of the room I was never more than five feet from my mother and could clearly see this white disc, which was linked to my mother, who was now in deep trance control and knew nothing about what was happening. We had never seen such a large quantity of ectoplasm. We were all very excited of course and as we chatted we saw this disc begin to build into a vertical white column, which grew to about five feet of solid ectoplasm! "Amazing" we said!

We then expected the column to simply gradually diminish and let the ectoplasm return to my mother—but that did not happen. The column remained still for a few minutes whilst we all stared at it, getting more and more excited. Then, as I was watching it, the top of it twisted towards me and I could just see there was the semblance of a face in it, but I could not have recognized who it was.

From the body of the column there then appeared two hands and arms covered by the ectoplasmic 'robes' of the person who was standing in front of me. As the hands approached me, I instinctively stretched out my arms and hands towards them—not in any way frightened as it all seemed so natural, but still a little apprehensive I suppose, about meeting a materialized Spirit person so close for the first time. [. . .]

My two hands were firmly clasped by the warm ectoplasmic hands in front of me. I then heard, quietly but clearly, from the face above me, the words, "For you, for you" (at which point Tom found he was being handed four ectoplasmic carnations). The hands and arms went back into the 'column' of ectoplasm and it then shrunk, slowly towards the floor, as the ectoplasm returned to my mother and we were all left exceedingly breathless after such a unique experience.

*Give Dad a Hand*

Tom summed up the appearance of the first materialized form like this:

> Here in this everyday friendly sitting room adjacent to Sydney and Gladys' shop, with the door and windows locked, we opened and closed our sitting that evening with seven of us round the fireplace, yet, for a few precious minutes during that sitting there were eight of us, all clearly visible to each other in the red light which illuminated the room during the whole sitting of some 45 minutes. The eighth person who joined us for that brief time was none other than Aunt Agg, who had been in the Spirit World for almost four years.

Poor guy. If you're anything like me you might be thinking right now, *poor guy done lost his mind. He thinks he saw a two-foot disc of white stuff sitting on the floor start to grow into a column of white stuff, and then turn into his dead aunt, who handed him carnations before she sank into the floor and disappeared. Poor guy.* And Leslie Kean was quite dubious about all of this before she began her research, as well. All of these photographs looked so very *fake.* Some are truly absurd in their appearance. Looking at them, it's impossible to understand how supposedly great minds of the past had been credulous enough to believe such nonsense. And, like me, Kean felt we'd never get an answer to that, thinking these occurrences relegated to a lost age, put forever out of reach by the march of time. So, she was very surprised when she came across a book called *An Extraordinary Journey: The Memoirs of a Physical Medium*—a book about a physical medium, written by a *living* physical medium. Kean found the book to be true to its name, describing extraordinary events that have supposedly taken place within the circle of a small group of friends for over fifty years. The medium's name is Stewart Alexander, and Kean was quite taken by what he wrote. To her, the author came across as a man of honesty and integrity. On top of that, many, many people over the years have

259

attested to the astounding events they'd witnessed first-hand in Stewart's sittings. And, he'd never used his mediumship as a means to financially profit, feeling strange about mixing something he saw as spiritual in nature with money. He even had to be convinced over many years by his friends, who believed the story was too precious a thing to keep for themselves, to write his book. Stewart worried incessantly, Kean learned from those who know him, that to pen a memoir might be seen as egotistical. Being the private, very humble man he is, his friends said, getting him to publish the book was a real struggle. Using her honed investigative skills, Leslie determined that this man seemed to be the "real deal." Over the course of many emails and much persuasion, Leslie eventually got invited to sit with Stewart in his seance circle in northern England. No matter how convincingly kind, sincere, intelligent and, mostly, honest a picture had been painted of Stewart from his book, and those who have known and sat with him, she needed to see it for herself. The experience that unfolded for her, altering entirely her sense of what is possible, is expertly conveyed in *Surviving Death*, a book that, we will see, entirely changed my life.

Leaving most of the story for Leslie Kean to tell in her own pages, I'll highlight the experience I found most compelling and nearly impossible to believe, no matter how surely I respected Kean's journalistic integrity. After inspecting the small room where the sitting was to take place, closely examining the furniture and walls and floor, being sure no secret trap door, for instance, might exist, from where an accomplice might enter to help the medium create the illusion of paranormal phenomenon, Kean felt confident no tricks were being pulled, and the small group of sitters—just five people—entered the room. While Kean watched very closely, Stewart was strapped into a simple armed wooden chair, thick cable ties tightly securing his wrists and ankles to the chair. Stewart had begun doing this years ago any time a "guest sitter" came for a seance, someone who didn't know him and had no reason to trust his honesty, so they could feel sure he had never moved from his chair. To that end, he also put glow-in-the-dark tape on his knees that remains visible throughout the sitting, so his position in the room is always known. Given the very small number of people in the little space, Kean writes, "Anyone getting up would have been noticed." She is therefore certain that whatever it was she experienced that evening did not originate from anyone in the room, as she knew exactly where the others were. Beyond the luminous tabs on his knees and cable ties securing him to the chair, Stewart's circle, unlike with other mediums who work in complete, pitch black darkness for the entirety of their sittings, has a red light that is often turned on any time a spirit person instructs them to do so. Many times throughout the hour-long sitting, the light was on, allowing Kean to see that Stewart was still strapped to his chair, and everyone in the room remained where they had been. Red light is used, by the way, if any light at all, because it is the lowest energy visible wavelength. According to the spirit folks, ectoplasm is very sensitive to light, and frequencies faster than that, that our eyes see as red can damage it, and if light is unexpectedly introduced—like, if you wanted to try and unmask a fraud and suddenly flip on the flashlight you'd secreted inside—it not only damages the ectoplasm, but can very seriously injure the medium, as well, as it quickly retreats back into his body. "Of course!" you should be thinking. "Of course, a fake medium would say that at all costs it must remain dark, or you might even kill someone!" I know how *very* suspicious that sounds. I scoffed mightily the first time I heard it. *In pitch black darkness*, I thought, *I could make some amazing things happen, too.* However, as modern researcher David Fontana—who has witnessed the formation of this strange material exuded from the body many times—including from Stewart, writes, "The fact is that darkness is usually required because light inhibits phenomena. This is not as surprising or as suspicious as critics would have us believe. Many natural phenomena, such as the germination of seeds, gestation in the womb, and the development of images on photographic plates, take place in the absence of light or in the presence only of dim red light." Okay, Mr. Fontana. I suppose that's a point—I was still suspicious, though. But in Stewart's sittings, the light is often on, lessening greatly the chances of successful fraud.

As the hour went on for Leslie Kean, many of the phenomena witnessed by renowned scientists of days gone by happened before her eyes. Objects levitated and flew around the room, voices issued from midair, from right in front of her where no one stood, and Walter, supposedly the same spirit control that once worked through his sister Mina Crandon, and with whom Houdini did battle, now boomed into the room inviting Leslie to move her chair right up to the small table placed in the middle of the circle. And then, to her astonishment, a substance came up over the top of the table (which was lit with a red light making the table top visible). It was just an amorphous blob at first, which then formed fingers, and soon a solid hand, which lifted hers, and shook it. Leslie felt the bones in the hand. She felt the warmth of the skin. She felt its larger than average size (much larger than Alexander's who she could see sitting in front of her, hands still strapped to the chair). It felt in every way like a normal human hand. And then it let go, and before her eyes, it melted away again to a blob, and the blob slipped from the table top, and was gone. She was "seeing the impossible happening, despite its own impossibility." Suddenly, all the research she had done was now bathed in the light of her own experience. She writes, "I held that materialized hand in mine. It felt completely normal and human, with joints, bones, and fingernails, but much warmer than my hand and larger, with sort of stubby fingers and very soft skin. [. . .] Stewart, his arms still locked to his chair, was too far from the center of the table to reach it. In any case, this hand was larger and fleshier than Stewart's; I could tell the difference, especially having held on to Stewart's more delicate, thinner hand [during an earlier demonstration described in her book]. Regardless,

I saw this hand form in front of me from a cloud, from nothing, into a full hand; it could not possibly have belonged to anyone in the room."

I closed the book, finished my fourth hot chocolate, and leaned back in my chair. I was flabbergasted by what I'd just read. Given who Leslie Kean is, her standing within the world of journalism, her impeccable credentials and trust of The New York Times, I had to try and accept what she had written. Could there be any way she was fooled, as critics of investigations of the past and current science insist *must* be the case? From her description, it was very, very difficult to conceive of how. After ingesting the information for a while, I concluded that, over the many years of research into this phenomenon, and Leslie Kean's personal experience, it could not be dismissed. *How I wish I could see that for myself,* I thought—knowing, the way my brain tends to work, that I'd not be able to ever fully accept it without doing so. That, of course, was not to be. Stewart Alexander, as I've said, is a very private man. It took Leslie's credentials, it seemed to me, to be let in to that very small and private world. Nonetheless, I was thrilled to have happened upon the book that day. None of my lines got learned, but my father's reality further solidified in my mind with each passing chapter of *Surviving Death.*

When I got home, I placed the book on the nightstand by my bed, intent on looking again at the illustrations depicting the formation of the hand Leslie had watched materialize right in front of her, and then I went to my computer to check on the response to the fundraising video. In a moment that I think will remain a shock whenever I summon it, I opened Facebook to find I had a message from a friend who'd seen the trailer I had posted earlier in the day. The message said, "Are you still filming? You should speak with Leslie Kean . . . New York Times best-selling author. She just wrote a book called *Surviving Death.* She wrote a quote for my book. I can get you in touch with her if you have any interest."

This, my friends, was a moment of a type I've described earlier in this book, where the sense of something "mystical," for lack of a more precise word, is attached. And of all of those moments I'd recently been the percipient of, this one might have taken the cake. I read the words over and over again. "I can get you in touch with her if you have any interest." In yet another odds-defying occurrence, I struggled to comprehend how unusual, how unlikely this was. Was it? Was I giving too much significance to these events? All I knew for sure was this: I'd gone to the nearest Starbucks by my home, which happens to be in a bookstore. On my way to the bathroom, I noticed just one book, because it happened to be right by the door to the men's room, and its cover was the only one on the eye-level shelf to be facing out. I brought the book back to my table intending to read a chapter or two, but instead devoured it and bought it. I placed it on my nightstand in order to read the last chapters again, so fascinated by them had I been, then, turned on my computer and found a message from a friend offering to put me in touch with the author of the book I'd just put down and been so transfixed by (having, by the way, *no idea* my friend had any connection whatsoever with Leslie Kean).

Quickly responding to my friend with a photo of the book sitting on my nightstand I wrote, "Yes, please put me in touch!" Though I didn't know if enough funding was going to be generated to continue filming for the documentary and to interview her on camera, the chance to speak directly to the woman who wrote about her experience shaking a spirit hand had me giddy. Whether or not she would agree to participate in the film was an afterthought—I now needed to hear directly from her. That would be as close as I would get to having the experience myself, and that, I felt, was close enough. One week later, Leslie Kean and I met for dinner at a New York City restaurant where, in exquisite detail, she recounted her entire experience with Stewart Alexander. Though we sat in the bustle of Times Square, every sound fell away as she detailed what had happened. No matter how fantastic the tale, it was brought down to earth and into reality because of who I gathered this woman to be. She was brilliant and astute and with a keen eye for details, as one must be to excel at journalism—especially her level of journalism. Everything about her resonated within me as honest. I could detect nothing but a woman of high integrity who'd had an experience very few ever will, and wanted to share it with people. "It's too important," she said, "what goes on in that room, to not be shared. To not be available for people to know, should they want to know it." And I certainly agreed. Because it's not just voices and flying objects and hands forming out of nothing—it is also mediumship in the sense I had come to know it. It is apparent people who once lived in a body, and now exist without one, trying to let those they left behind know that they are okay, that they are there, and that death does not extinguish love.

When Stewart is in trance, and another of his spirit controls takes over, a woman named Freda, who was once a teacher while alive on earth, she delivers messages to those sitting in the circle from their departed loved ones, saying things like, "I have your mother here, dear," and then she gives the same sort of mediumistic messages Angelina gives in an attempt to prove that it actually is the person's mother. And sometimes, Freda will step aside, and that person's mom will try to speak for themselves in her own words. "This can be difficult," Leslie tells me as we chat over spaghetti, and I wonder if those at the table beside us think we're totally nuts, "because it seemingly takes spirits a long time to perfect the mechanics of how it's done. When an apparent person in spirit first comes through—and I've heard many, many recordings of this happening—they often struggle to get just a few words out." But many times, it seems enough words get out to prove to the sitter that it actually is their dearly departed. The thought of hearing my dad again speak in his own words . . . well, I didn't mind the idea that I'd never have the chance to meet Stewart Alexander in person, because I doubted I'd be able to handle that anyway. I should think hearing my dad speaking to me, somehow piercing whatever the border is between what we perceive of as "reality" and wherever he is so thoroughly, much more so than directing butterfly flight paths and DJ playlists, might be entirely too much for me to process.

Leslie and I talked for a very long time, and by the end of it she'd agreed to be interviewed for my documentary. Over the following months, we communicated often, until one day she said, "I told Stewart about you." Leslie had gotten quite close with Stewart and the members of his small circle after she'd had her sitting where she somehow shook a hand that a moment before hadn't been there. Soon, they invited her to be an honorary member of the circle—an honor she could not have seen coming when she began the research for her book. Because she lives in New York and the circle sits in England, she started to sit remotely via a video call on an iPad. Though it was typically too dark to see anything, she could at least hear the voices of the people who had now become her friends, both in and out of bodies. Every week, Walter and Freda and a few others would speak from beyond the grave as Leslie listened in and dialogued with them over FaceTime. Even given the distance, and the lack of physical phenomenon she could see (which is often the highlight of these gatherings), the Monday sittings with those across the water, and across something else, became the highlight of her week. And at one of these sittings she'd said to Walter, "Walter, I have a friend named Mike, and I wondered if I might invite him to sit with me here in New York." An audio recording is made of each sitting, so I was able to hear Walter's response when Leslie later played it for me: "We know that he is pure of heart. Pure of heart and mind. And we would welcome his presence." I was stunned and thrilled at this unlikely turn of events, and I hoped I could live up to the expectations of the deep and booming voice.

The first time I walked into Leslie's apartment and saw a copy of her book on her shelf . . . the book I'd happened upon just a few short months before, I couldn't quite believe it. And when we sat in her darkened room and connected through video call with the small group of people in England, it was positively surreal. Though I completely trusted Leslie's conclusion that Stewart Alexander was "the real deal," having seen, as she had, what happens in that small room across the ocean for herself, I still needed to get my own sense of who these folks were. As the iPad got passed around from person to person, and I was introduced to the circle members, I was struck first by their apparent "normalcy." Most of them had known and sat with Stewart once a week for decades. Every Monday, with no fanfare of any kind, this small group of folks for over thirty years have gathered to have tea and biscuits—right after they talked to their deceased loved ones, and ectoplasmic hands were formed. *Who were these people? What were they like? Do they have any reasons to have deluded themselves into believing what they say is happening?* These were the questions running through my mind as I met them. There was much joking and laughter as introductions were made. A distinct light-heartedness pervaded the gathering, which surprised me somewhat. I thought, perhaps, that a gathering to contact the dead might be a somber affair, one approached with a seriousness and maybe even reverence. But it was nothing at all like that with this chatty and joking and close party of pals. *What a fun group*, I thought. It occurred to me that I might like to spend an hour each week with them regardless of whether or not ectoplasm was involved. After ten minutes or so of banter, the lights were shut off and some music was played, which Leslie informed me helps Stewart go into trance. Then, within minutes, a voice that had not been in the room before, issued from Leslie's laptop speakers. This was supposedly a Native American chief named White Feather, who opened the proceedings and specifically welcomed me. It was an awkward few seconds, as I realized I had no idea what you say to a deceased Native American chief who is

267

speaking to you from the beyond over a FaceTime call. Soon, yet another new voice spoke. This one was powerful, thundering "Good Evening folks!" It was Walter, the spirit control of Stewart's that I'd heard so much about. The quality of this voice, in particular, was extraordinary. If Stewart was faking it, it sounded to me as though he'd studied vocal production. I know quite a few actors who'd be made quite jealous by the fullness of this voice, the freeness of it, the effortless room-filling projection. Throughout the hour-long sitting, five distinct personalities with five distinct voices spoke through Stewart, including a six-year-old boy and a middle-aged woman. If this was all a show Stewart was putting on, and one he'd been putting on for some unknown reason for this small group of family and friends for over thirty years, his acting was quite good, and he'd entirely invested in each of his characters. Each supposed spirit person who spoke felt like a completely formed human being, with individual characteristics . . . none of which matched the man I'd met before he'd gone into trance.

Leaving Leslie's apartment with plans to come back each Monday, I understood why she gave the time she did to the investigation of Stewart. Having met them just for that short time, imagining that this band of friends would be perpetrating an enormous and complicated fraud was very difficult. One thing was disappointing, however. If Stewart really was a medium, and these personalities really were people who'd once lived before and are now supposedly wherever my dad is, why was there no mention made of my father? After all the trouble it felt like my dad had gone through to get the message to his family that he still existed, you'd think this would have been an opportunity he'd not let pass. If this was all real, I would have thought my dad would have been there that night, and Walter would have looked over in his "world" to see this new man standing there and asked, "Can I help you sir?" And my dad would have said, "Yes, I'm Robert, Mike's dad. Please tell him it really is me that's been trying to reach him . . . it's me who helped him notice that book . . . it's me who gently pushed him in ways that would lead to finding you, Walter, and Stewart." But none of that happened. For the next two months I sat every Monday with Leslie in New York, and no mention was ever made by or about my dad, even as I heard other supposed deceased loved-ones speak haltingly through Stewart when a family member of theirs had come to sit as a guest for the first time. But, nothing from my dad. *Hmm*, I thought.

I'd not wanted to say anything about my father, determined that whatever was going to happen, if anything, unfolded organically. With each passing week, though, it got more difficult to understand why, if this group was actually doing what they believed they were (and I now had no doubt that they at least *believed* they were doing what they said they were), my dad had not visited, or even been spoken of. Nonetheless, I was thoroughly enjoying these meetings and continued to sit each Monday. I eventually told my family about it. It took me a while, because . . . well, you know why. As I've said, I am fully aware of how all of this might sound. I was worried that if I tried to explain physical mediumship to my family, and told them that I'd been sitting in the dark in a small room each week listening to spirits talk over an iPad, they'd think, "Oh, Mike. How heartbreaking. Losing his dad completely broke his brain." And they'd start making phone calls to see exactly what kind of medical institution deals with that sort of thing. However (though I do suspect there was some of that—maybe a Google or two of "hearing voices and what to do about it"), my family listened and gave me the benefit of the doubt. Then, one week in July, Leslie was going to be at her family's home in Massachusetts for the Monday sitting. She invited me to meet her there instead of at her apartment in New York, and also kindly asked if my mom and sister would like to come. In order to participate in the circle, permission must first be given by the "spirit team," and since we'd not asked about my mom and sister joining, they wouldn't be able to sit with us. However, it was a gorgeous day, so my mom and sister came along anyway to enjoy the beautiful grounds around Leslie's home (and maybe to see who exactly this woman was that had been leading their son and brother further into mental distortions). When it came time for us to call England and have the sitting, my mom and sister sat outside on beach chairs in the backyard, enjoying the view of the ocean.

The sitting began in the usual way, after a few minutes of catching up with the circle members, during which Leslie and I said nothing about my mom and sister being outside on the lawn. Stewart went into trance (which, by the way, doesn't always happen—sometimes there are "blank" sittings, where he simply doesn't go into trance, for whatever reason, and nothing happens other than some laughs) and White Feather and Walter and all the rest spoke. Then the sitting was ended and, as he does every week, White Feather offered a farewell and a closing prayer. And then something quite unexpected happened, even for people who are used to things levitating around the room: a voice, quiet at first, began to come from Stewart again. Usually, after the circle is closed by White Feather, Stewart wakes back up. But on this day, that didn't happen. Instead, another voice was apparently trying to make itself known. The circle members heard it, and surprised, began to encourage it saying, "Come on, friend, you can do it, come on." And then the voice said, "Robert."

Carol, a member of the circle sitting closest to Stewart repeated, "Robert? Did you say Robert?"

And the voice said, in a strained and guttural way, "Robert! Yes. I'm here. I'm here. I'm here. I'm here."

Carol announced to the circle, "It's someone named Robert."

As I've said, I hadn't mentioned my father to the group, and certainly not his name. So, Carol was doing what she typically does when a name is given—she repeats it and asks if anyone knows who that name might belong to.

"My dad's name is Robert," I said into the laptop.

"Oh . . . okay, ah hah," I heard the group say in various ways.

"Dad, is that you?" I asked, feeling rather strange about doing so. It didn't sound like my dad's voice. According to the circle members, when a spirit person tries to speak through a medium in this way, it takes enormous effort and practice. When Walter and Freda and the rest of the regular spirit team speak, they do so fluently and in complete sentences with loud, full voices. The supposed spirits of deceased loved ones coming to visit for the first time try to simply get a few words out that might be evidential in some way. In this case, it was the name "Robert."

"Is that you, Dad?"

"Yes! Mike!"

"Hi Dad!"

Then there was a struggle, it sounded like, as Carol said, "Stay calm, Robert. You can do it."

After more incomprehensible sounds came the words, loudly and clearly, "I'm alive!"

The sitting was closed, as the man claiming to be my father lost control after telling me that he was alive, and we said goodbye. For those in the circle, it was like any other sitting, so used to this, were they. For me, though, my mind had a new thing to grapple with. *What was that? Was that really my dad?* The name "Robert" certainly was evidential. But what, to me, was the most powerful piece of evidence was the timing of my supposed father's first visit: recall I'd been sitting for over two months at that point without a single mention of my dad. Then, on the day that my mom and sister happen to be there, he apparently breaks through, and does so in a most unusual way, after the sitting had already been closed. Leslie, too, found the "coincidence" remarkable. When Stewart came out of trance, something happened that I'd not heard before, and neither had Leslie: he sounded almost like he was crying. "Are you alright, Stewart?" Ray asked.

"What happened?" Stewart quietly asked. "Wow. I can feel someone has been. Lord. I don't know what's happened, but I'm quite emotional. Wow.

It's only because when, you know, when somebody's been so . . . so intent on communicating . . . I'm sorry." And Stewart's strained voice trailed off as he got choked up again, and Ray said, "That's all right, Stewart, you just relax."

I certainly can't say with any certainty that this actually was my dad, but if it was, he was about to tie things together in a most extraordinary way.

Leslie and I left the room and went to the backyard, excited to tell my mom and sister what had happened. With an enormous smile we approached them, and as I opened my mouth to speak, my sister said, "Oh, you just missed this amazing Monarch butterfly that was hanging out with us for a while."

Oh my gosh. Leslie, who I had since discussed the butterfly occurrences with, and especially the one appearing over Penn Jillette's head during his "debunking" of mediumship, looked at me with great surprise. Then Jen said, "Oh, there it is!" pointing off to her left. "Where?" Leslie asked. "I don't see it." Leslie wanted confirmation with her own eyes. Jen pointed again, and from out of the tall grass it rose, flying in our direction, and then right past us. "Wow," Leslie said. "Wow," I repeated. And then I told my mom and sister that they first saw that butterfly around the same time a man claiming to be our father said to me, "I'm alive!"

We went for a walk down the quiet country road in front of Leslie's house, and as we discussed with my mom and sister what had just happened, another large butterfly appeared. Then another. And another. I know how hard this might be to believe, but I can only report what occurred. Leslie Kean, a journalist who counts on the trust in her word, as well as my mom and sister, were all there, and we all experienced this. On this walk, right after a voice claiming it was "Robert" and still "alive," an enormous number of Monarch butterflies suddenly overtook the area. They were sitting in trees, crossing constantly our path, and filling the sky. Not knowing about the migratory patterns of butterflies, we assumed this must be a "flock" of some kind. It was unlike anything any of us had ever seen, however. I'm not talking about ten butterflies. I'm talking about a hundred or more—it's really impossible to say. But they were just everywhere. To add to the mystique, Leslie said that she had not seen a single butterfly yet that year on that property. Assuming (as we must) that this was simply a natural flocking of butterflies that had swarmed this particular area at that particular time, still . . . well wow. And to put an exquisite bow on this set of events, adding more fully to the sense of amazement surrounding them, Carol, the circle member who had spoken to my dad, wrote to me the next day to say she had been "feeling my dad around her" ever since the sitting—and that something quite unusual had happened that morning that she intuitively sensed was connected to my father, and of which she therefore wanted to inform me: an Admiral Butterfly had gotten into her house. It was *inside* her house. In England. And, for some reason, she felt it had to do with my dad.

Dear reader, I realize I take a risk in reporting all of this to you. I very seriously considered ending the book after my trip to speak with Dr. Tucker. After much internal debate, I realized that if I left it out, I'd not be telling the whole truth. And, as hard as it might or might not be to believe, this is the truth. And it is because of what happened next that I have the confidence I do, it is because of what happened next that I ultimately decided to tell this part of the story.

To my enormous surprise, on a grey day in October of 2018, I sat on a plane beside Leslie, waiting to take off for the UK. Knowing I was going to be meeting with some mediums when we arrived, I decided to come up with another code word. Out of the window, I saw a plane ahead and perpendicular to us taxiing to the runway with the Boston Red Sox logo, two red socks, pictured on the tail. Since my dad and I were fans (and, again, he was buried in a Red Sox shirt), I liked to think this was a sign from him that the flight would go well—I am somewhat afraid to fly, and it was a nice thought that my dad might have sent the plane of our favorite baseball team to quell my anxieties. Whether or not that was true, in that moment I chose "socks" as my code word for the trip. In my mind (and only in my mind, said out loud to no one—not even Leslie) I thought, *Okay Dad. Our word this time is "socks." Not "sox" as in "Red Sox," just the word "socks." If a medium brings up socks in some way with me, I'll know it's you.* The plane's engines began to rumble, and I gripped tightly around the armrests. By "somewhat afraid to fly," what I mean is, I am a terrible, awful, ridiculously nervous flyer, and it takes something extraordinary to get me on a plane. Leslie Kean inviting me to meet, in person, Stewart Alexander is one of those things.

"We're here!" she said, when we finally came to a stop at the terminal of a small English airport. Not only is Leslie vibrantly intelligent and tirelessly curious, she is also remarkably kind, and knowing how hard the trip had been for me, she was constantly checking in as to my well-being, and so relieved for me that we'd arrived. Aware of how desperately I needed to understand what we were dealing with for myself, Leslie put in great effort to help that happen. For reasons she can't quite explain, she felt our paths had crossed for a reason, and she had gone out of her way to get me invited not only to meet Stewart, but to sit, in person, with his circle.

For four days, I stayed with Stewart and his family and friends. I met dear friends of Tom Harrison's, the man whose photographs of his mom appear earlier. I met the small group of people who had mostly been voices to me, sitting across the ocean in a small English town. I ate with them, I drank with them, I spoke late into the nights with them. Because I still had to know, for myself, who these people, claiming this extraordinary thing, were as human beings. I had to look them in their eyes. If they were going

274

to lie to me, I needed them to do it from a foot away, and right to my face. But as I ate with them and drank with them and spoke with them, I saw no lies. No deceit was apparent. No attempt to fleece me was there (as no money is ever asked for by these people, and would certainly not be accepted if you tried—I bought dinner one night for the small group, hoping to show my appreciation for allowing me to visit with them and take me into their homes, get to know them and sit in a seance with them. Toward the end of the meal, I surreptitiously found our waiter and gave him my credit card to pay for the table. When Ray, one of the circle members, found out, I sensed he was actually upset. "That's not how we do things, here," he said).

The weekend before the Monday night sitting in northern England, I attended a sort of conference where those interested in mediumship gather. The group was made up of maybe one hundred people, and among them, Leslie and I may have been the only two who did not claim mediumistic abilities. The group meets twice a year to attend lectures and give demonstrations, and they are very close knit. I spoke with everyone I could, hearing story after story of personal experiences people had at sittings with Stewart and other physical mediums. Suddenly, those stories told by experimenters from a century ago were coming alive. I was talking with living people telling me first-hand stories that I could not wrap my mind around, no matter how in detail the stories were told. I met Anthony Harris, whose grandfather, Alec Harris, was one of the most extraordinary physical mediums of this century. Anthony told me about the countless occasions he saw a full-form human being, in a dimly lit room, rise up from a circular mist on the ground. He talked about the hundreds and hundreds of people who'd met their deceased loved-ones in this way, who'd spoken with and held their hands, only to watch them dissolve before them. The man I was speaking to is now an accomplished business person and advanced Buddhist practitioner. If he is crazy, that crazy hasn't impacted his material success.

On Saturday, following the first day of the seminar, I sat with Leslie in a beautiful common area set up around a fireplace. The building that has been converted to a hotel is an old Victorian structure, and this gathering room, in particular, felt as though it sprang from the pages of a Harry Potter book. As we chatted about the day's events, a woman sitting across from me interrupted us. She and I had never met, but I later learned she was from Belgium. "I'm sorry," she said looking at me, "but I've got to tell you something."

"Sure," I said.

"I'm a medium."

"It seems like almost everyone here is," I responded with a smile. And then she said something that I will never forget.

"Your dad is standing behind you. He looks like you."

"Oh, okay. We do look similar, yes." And that, of course, was not at all compelling, as you might expect a father and son to look similar, given how DNA works and all. However, it was interesting that she said it was my dad. I had never spoken with this woman, and I had no idea how she could have known my dad had passed (let alone that he was the reason I now found myself in a Harry Potter book in England). But it was what she said next that floored me:

"He wants to talk about your hair. Did you do something with your hair, or something? Are you styling it differently or something? He wants to talk about your hair for some reason."

There is simply no way this woman could have known that a message from a medium regarding my hair is what had sent me on this quest six years earlier. She said many other specific and accurate things as well— including, "Your dad says you have to get your car fixed. There is something wrong with the drive belt." I knew nothing about drive belts (including whether or not cars have one), and doubted anything was wrong with mine. However, the car needed to be serviced the week following my return home

276

when the brakes began to make a rubbing noise. And in the most wonderful time I've ever had while finding out from a mechanic that something needed to be fixed that I hadn't taken the car in for, the man said, "You've gotta replace the drive belt. It's barely hanging on." But "He wants to talk about your hair," very nearly exactly what Angelina had said that night in my mom's living room after "hair" had been my code, nearly knocked me out. I'm thankful to have had a witness the likes of Leslie Kean there to hear that. I silently began to wonder if there was any way over the course of the day I could have let that slip. Could I have told the story to someone while this woman secretly listened? I went over my entire visit to that point, and could not recall ever mentioning it. But that was about to become moot, anyway. Because the next thing she said was, "Your Grandma is here, too. Mom's mom, And mom's dad. They are here, too." You may recall that this was one of the patterns. It was never my dad's dad who showed up with him, who was also deceased, but rather it was my mother's parents. And then she said, "Your grandmother is pointing to your socks. Do you have holey socks? Do you need new socks or something?" By the third time she said "socks," the code word I'd picked while back on the runway in New York, I was convinced that at least some of these folks, including the one I was talking to, really are mediums. I went to my room and quickly recorded a video on my phone so I'd have a record of the event. And then, when I returned home, and a few months later got a cat, I named him Socks for good measure.

On Sunday, I spent time with Stewart and his wife at their house, scrutinizing his every word. He and his wife, Sue, have been together since they were teenagers. I pressed Sue to give me details of how they met and what their life had been like. If they had deluded themselves, I wanted to know where and when things might have begun to go off the rails. She shared photos with me, going back to the days when their love was blossoming, long before either had ever heard of Spiritualism or seances or ectoplasm.

Stewart told me the story that I'd already read in his book about how this unusual part of his life began when he was almost thirty and had already been married to Sue for years. His brother gave him a book about physical mediumship and said, "Read this! It's fascinating. We should try it!" And so they did. I asked Sue if she found it all strange back then. She said that it all happened gradually and organically. What stood out most about Stewart and Sue as we had dinner that night at their house was how utterly "normal" they are. After we ate the delicious food Sue had made, we stood in the kitchen, Leslie and I sipping wine while Sue washed dishes and Stewart dried them. On the refrigerator beside him, I noticed photos of their children and grandchildren and drawings the youngest had made. It looked just like the refrigerator door you might find in any doting grand-parent's house. Nothing at all about the refrigerator door (or any other part of the home) would have said to you, "In this house is a nut who believes his body exudes ectoplasm that spirits use to dip their etheric bodies in."

When I got to talk alone with Stewart a bit, I thanked him for allowing me to sit with them the following night. I told him what his long, patient work over fifty years to develop this apparent ability had meant to my family. I asked him what it feels like to know he has eased the grief of so many people. And his eyes got pink. The man I was speaking to, if he was a fake, was an emotional one whose heart swelled and eyes leaked when the thought of his life having been of use was brought to his attention. He quickly tried to divert the praise saying, "It isn't me. It's *them*. The shining ones," as he calls the spirit team. Over the course of those four days, I came to know a kind, genuine, gentle man. I came to know a person who is loved deeply by his wife of so many years, since they "were kids," and his grand-children and friends. And it's not just Stewart: everyone that sits in the small circle felt to me to be exceedingly . . . good. Just salt-of-the-earth, good people, happy to be able to chat once a week with those they've lost. And the light-heartedness I'd picked up on in that very first sitting over

FaceTime was constantly evident. These were just good-natured, good people. It was as simple as that, I concluded. If they were faking this, it was because they'd faked themselves.

The day of the sitting arrived, and I was having trouble grasping the events that had led me to where I now stood, in a hotel room in a small town in England. *Less than a year* after happening upon Leslie's book, and thinking, *how I wish I could experience this for myself,* but certain I never would, I was about to. In a matter of hours, I was going to be in that same little room where Leslie describes her witnessing of "the impossible, despite its own impossibility." It was difficult to not wonder if my dad had somehow been involved in the sequence of events that guided me to this situation—one in which I was about to experience what so very few on the planet ever have.

Evening finally arrived, and before the sitting we all had dinner together at a nearby restaurant. I happened to end up in Stewart's car afterwards on the way to the home of Carol, whose house holds the small sitting room in which they meet every week, and who told me about the Admiral Butterfly that had made its way into her house the morning after my supposed father first spoke. Stewart and his wife sat in the front seat, chit chatting and chuckling about something involving one of their granddaughters, as though this were any other day, while I sat in the back freaking out. I mean, completely *freaking out.* I just could not believe what I was about to do. And if any of the things I'd heard people claim happened, actually happened, I didn't know if I could handle it. And so the sweat came. I began to profusely sweat with the thought of the supernatural that I might now be just minutes away from—while Stewart and Sue joked in the front seat about something their grandkid said.

When we arrived at Carol's, I was shown the sitting room. I asked if I could take a look, and she said, "Of course!" Leslie and I inspected every inch of the place, including the now famous-to-me table upon which so many have watched a human hand form. Though intentional deceit by these people now felt unlikely to me to an extreme degree, I knew I had to satisfy my every doubt. So, I looked under chairs and bounced on the floor and tapped on the walls. The room is very small, and I soon realized that what Leslie had written in her book was accurate: any attempt by anyone in the room to move from their seat would be easily recognized. Once I was satisfied with my inspection, the group filed in and took seats. Stewart was strapped into the chair using cable ties on his wrists and ankles, and I was asked to check them to my satisfaction. Indeed, they were tightly on his wrists—so much so that I thought it must be uncomfortable. I sat beside Leslie as the lights were switched off, making it pitch dark, other than the luminous tabs visible on Stewart's knees. Ray said, "Everybody ready?" and in the silent moment before he turned on the music Stewart uses to induce the trance, I worried that people might be able to hear my heart beating inside my chest. Then, within a minute, a voice began to speak. Ray turned off the music, and soon the voice I'd heard so many times in New York was right there in the room with me, so easily filling the entire space. "Okay, okay. Good evening, folks!"

And thus commenced the most astounding hour of my life.

Objects indeed flew about the room, not only flew, but danced, with no one holding them. The objects had the same type of glow-in-the dark tabs affixed to them that Stewart wore on his pants, so their trajectories around the room, including often coming right up to your face, even gently caressing your cheeks, was clearly visible. From directly in front of me, a voice spoke, though no one stood there. Then, the moment I'd been waiting for arrived. The red light was switched on and Leslie was invited to sit in front of the small table between her and Stewart. Walter's deep but playful voice asked, "Leslie, would you like to shake the hand of a man who has been dead to your world for a hundred years?" I need not tell you what her answer was. Leslie asked Walter if I could stand up to watch over her shoulder, and Walter gave the okay. To give me the closest vantage point possible (and throw a potential wrench into the demonstration were any trickery involved), I asked if I could instead kneel down by the table. Walter immediately said, "Yes, that is fine, that is fine." So, I did. I knelt down right beside the table. From this position, I was between Leslie and Stewart. I could see Stewart seated in the chair in the dim red light to my right. Whatever was about to happen, fraudulently produced or genuine, I was going to catch it. Leslie was asked to place her hand on the table. The table has a glass top, and it is lit from below with a red light, so everything that happens on the table top is clearly visible—especially when your face is a foot or less from it, as mine was. Suddenly, a substance came up over the end of the table that was closest to Stewart. I quickly looked to be absolutely certain Stewart was still in his place, and he was. And he was definitely too far, anyway, to reach the center of the table with his hand. But it wasn't a hand. It was an amorphous, fluid blob, undulating on the table top. At first, it was fairly flat, and spread out across most of Stewart's end of the table. It probably took up about a foot at its widest point. It slowly moved closer to Leslie's hand and became less spread out as it did so. What is impossible for me to explain here is the quality with which this mass moved. There was a fluidity to it that I could see no way to fake. It moved the way a blob of water might move in zero gravity if it were perturbed, or smoke billowing in a breeze. Just impossibly fluid in the way it transformed from an amorphous and spread out, mostly two-dimensional mass into a more defined and three-dimensional shape. And then, with that same transfixing, otherworldly fluidity, a digit began to form from the main mass, and then another. And soon, five fingers were forming in front of my eyes. And when I say "in front of my eyes," I mean it—once I was certain Stewart's hands were not involved in any way in what I was seeing, I leaned down over the top of the table so that my face was five inches from this undulating, fluidly alive, smoke-like mass. From five inches, I watched all of the substance absorb together into fingers. At one point, it spread the fingers out wide, showing a hand that was enormous, much larger than anyone's in the room, for certain, and simply much larger than any typical human hand. The substance then coalesced to form a normal looking, three-dimensional human hand that lifted off the surface, made a fist, and banged three times on the table, so everyone in the room could know it was solid. So, now I was seeing a hand floating freely in the air—it was up above the table top connected to nothing and extending off the edge of the table at the wrist end. Then, it grabbed Leslie's hand and shook it. She could again feel its warmth and joints and even its fingernails, as she expressed out loud while it was happening. It then let go of her hand, and again from inches away, I watched a hand that had just been solid enough to bang on the table and shake the hand of someone else, dissolve before me into a blob, which again spread out across the table top, receded again in a fluidly smoky way off of the table, and disappeared. I watched this happen with two more sitters. Each time, I looked closer. Each time, I saw what I saw. I saw a hand emerge from a flat smoky mass, become solid, and then dissolve away. The Amazing Randi and Penn Jillette and Michael Shermer flashed in my mind, as my brain somehow still had the space to wonder how, if they had been huddled over this table with me, if they had seen the numinous from this distance, it might have changed some of their certainties. I have seen David Blaine, perhaps the best "up close" magician currently alive, and I've seen him up close, when he put on a magic show just for a friend and me. In fact, we saw him from as near as this hand now was. And as mesmerizingly splendid as his tricks were, they did not approach what I was seeing now. This existed in an entirely different realm.

Finally, I was asked by a spirit person to sit by Stewart. I exchanged seats with June, Ray's wife, and then Freda, the spirit now supposedly in control, told me that my father was there and wanted to try something. One of the other phenomenon that sometimes takes place at Stewart's sittings is known as "transfiguration." It is said that the spirit wishing to communicate can use the same substance that Walter uses to form his hand, a substance I now know as the very real ectoplasm, to create the appearance of their face over Stewart's. And my dad, apparently, wanted to try. So, with the red light focused on Stewart's face, I intently examined his visage for any changes. Suddenly, something started to happen. I blinked my eyes quickly to be sure nothing was in them, because I was certain I was seeing Stewart's face changing. His face was just a foot or so away, but even at that close distance, I couldn't believe what was happening. An audio recording was made of the sitting, and in it you can hear my great surprise:

"Stewart's face is changing! I see it! His face is changing!"

At that point, others in the circle said they were seeing this too, helping me feel that I hadn't completely lost my mind. "I'm right here, Dad! I see you! Dad! I see you! I can see your face!"

I was utterly in shock at that point, because upon Stewart's lightly bearded face, my dad's fuller beard filled in, in the same fluid way the hand had. And then he spoke.

"Mike."

"Dad! I see you! I can see your face!"

"Hi!" the face of my father said.

"Hi, I love you!" I responded . . . and I knew right then why that is so often the message a medium wants to give from the people they are sensing, no matter how un-evidential it is. For me, I now realize, when you might have just a limited time to speak, speaking of your love is what reflexively comes out.

"I've waited so long for this," he said.

"I know you have, Dad. I see you!" I repeated, still unable to comprehend that fact.

He then said, "I . . . just . . . want to say . . . how sorry I am." But here are the words that shifted my universe: "Me. Me. Down. Down on . . . down on the office floor."

This was an overwhelming and stunning thing to hear. When the halt-ing words, "Down on the office floor" hit my ears, for the first time I actu-ally believed this was my father. As you might imagine, it is a thing nearly impossible to fully process that your dead father might have survived his death and then found a way to tell you that. Many people "believe" in life after death. Religions the world over feature an afterlife as a major reason for why you shouldn't kick puppies or hurt people. But this idea remains almost entirely abstract, no matter how concretely we think we believe it. When my father, though, said these words, "Me. Down on the office floor," the reality of his survival, the concrete truth that I was talking to him, albeit in a different form, washed over me with a mighty force. Because this was a detail we had told no one. It had been a private detail we did not share, that we found my dad on the floor of his home office. It had not been spoken outside of my immediate family that it was on the floor of his home office that I laid, for a long time, days in a row, in the place he was found, trying to imagine his last moments. Trying to see what he last saw. It was that spot that so horrendously and tortuously hijacked our attention for months after his passing, as we tried over and over again to learn some-thing from the position of his body on that office floor. From his position-ing, we searched for any clues we could glean that might somehow give us comfort that he did not suffer. It was on that office floor that my mom and sister sat with him for hours and held is hand, not wanting the paramedics to remove him, fighting the cold, disgusting, intolerable reality that the hand was no longer his, that he was no longer he. The thought of him on that office floor, and how he came to land there, consumed us. We eventu-ally became certain this was the reason each of the mediums we saw harped on how quick his passing was, on how desperately, they said, my dad wanted us to know that it was painless, how passionately he desired we should let the thought of him on that office floor go. When he said those words through Stewart, words that seemed to take great effort, I could hear a relief you might feel upon seeing your destination after a years-long, grueling journey. It seemed to me now that the entire path I'd traveled since my dad's death had been set in motion by him. I had suspected it, but with these words, and with his face now floating in front of Stewart's, I felt the truth of it. He had done all of this. He had contacted that first medium who we did not know, and nudged her until her message was delivered to us. He *had* heard me ask him to mention my hair, and he'd done it. It *was* him. For the first time, I now realized, I let myself fully accept that. My dad had survived the breakdown of the body he was in, and so great is his love for us, he had not rested until we knew it. Truly *knew* it. Hearing his words now, issuing from his bearded face, alive again in front of me, was overwhelming. The last time I'd seen his face, it wasn't his. It was that strange face in the coffin placed in a room marked by a placard that read, "Robert Anthony," but it wasn't him. *This* was him. This face that now spoke to me was him. My dad was back. Actually, truly, really back. Apologizing for the shattering shock of "the office floor."

"If I could have chosen some other way," he now said, "I would have done that. I just want you to know I love you now as much as I ever did. And Jen. Give Jen my love. I wish I could . . . ."

And then he lost control, and the beard dissolved away and Stewart's face again looked as his own. When he stopped speaking, Leslie, seeing the same thing I had just seen, asked, "Did he have a beard?" "He did," I said. "Yes, he did."

The reason I have spent so much time on the skeptics is this: what I just described *happened*. No matter how erudite and studied the skeptics' explanations might be for why my dad is gone, no matter how certain their training and expertise, no matter the conviction with which they declaim what they know to be certain . . . they are wrong. They are wrong, friends. I cannot convince you with my words, obviously. I can only say I've endeavored to honestly relate to you what I have experienced. Paranormal things happen. They. Do. Happen. I'm sorry, Mr. Jillette. As in the right place as your heart might be, it is following a brain that simply does not have all of the information. Some mediums *do* get information they shouldn't be able to know. Some children *do* have memories that are from other lives. Hands *do* sometimes form from a substance we don't yet understand that some human bodies seem to create. And my dad did die, then come back to let us know he didn't. I know it might sound nuts. I know that. But, it's the truth. It's just the truth.

A few minutes after my dad's beard dissolved from Stewart's face, left etched instead on my heart, the sitting ended, and I walked out of the room forever changed. Afterwards, we sat around Carol's living room talking and laughing about normal life things. Plumbing that needs to be fixed, what was going on at Carol's husband's job, whether his football team would win this year. In a room beside a room where some veil had dissolved between this place and some other, and through which *something* had poked itself, defying all the laws of physics we've so soundly established, crumbling the rules upon which our theories all sit, entirely changing what we think the universe is and how it operates, her husband, Mike, and I sat and talked about the chances Manchester United had that season. And it suddenly wasn't so hard to see why so much of the world did not know about this, and the scientific world, especially: once you have come to see this truth for yourself, and your personal universe expands, it is no longer so important to you that everyone else sees it. Sitting in that room afterwards, assimilating the new perspective I had, and overlaying onto the old one, I saw that not much had changed. These people were the same people, this house was the same house, it still mattered to Mike whether or not Manchester United won. Because it all mattered. Even though Mike lived in a house where direct evidence of something more than the reality we daily see exists, the daily reality we see, where we live our lives and love our loves and do what we can to be happy, is real. It's not complete, but it's real.

And if most of the world, and almost all of science does not know that there is more to the real, for these people I now drank tea with, it didn't matter. *We* knew. The others will at some point. In this life or after. For the people who I sat with now in this cozy living room, we knew, and that is all that mattered. And my tea, which was the same I'd had earlier in the day, somehow tasted sweeter.

Steve Job's sister famously penned an obituary for her beloved brother. She wrote about his last conscious moments in his bed as he slipped from this life surrounded by those he loved. After looking deliberately into each of their faces, saying goodbye one by one and showing with his eyes how deep his love ran, she says he seemed to see something beyond them. He stared at an upper corner of the room as those eyes grew wide, and then said his last words: "Oh wow. Oh wow. OH WOW." I feel I have a sense, now, of what might have been happening in that moment, as Steve's brain let down the blinders, and more of "what is" suddenly entered his awareness. The wonder that Jobs expressed in his last syllables is available to us here, too. You just need to look in the right places.

I hope you will.

Because your tea can taste sweeter. And everything else can, too.

# Afterward

"Have patience, good things will come."

Hearing those words coming from my father's smiling face on the large screen television in my living room produced a feeling in me that was entirely ineffable. It was the conclusion to a story I could not have foreseen, back when we sat in chairs staring at a coffin, holding what was not my dad, perched over an awful hole in the earth. On that day, I wondered if happiness would ever come my way again. My father, I now believe, found that an untenable situation—and set out to change it. But I wonder if even he, given his newfound superpowers, could have peered around the corners to see himself, alive again on my screen, on millions of screens, on screens all over the wide world, suggesting patience—and good things ahead. Given his humble nature, that's certainly not something he would have ever, ever expected. But given the depth and breadth of his love, he should have known that its light would shine so bright, that its power would be of such wattage, that only millions of screens could hope to contain even a bit of it.

So remarkable were the events that transpired during my journey with my dad, as described in these pages, that in 2019 Leslie Kean invited me to be part of a documentary series based on her book which was under production by Break Thru Films in New York. Surviving Death premieres on Netflix tomorrow, Jan. 6, 2021. Because of this amazing turn of events, parts of my father's story were granted a platform well beyond the reach I could have achieved with my own documentary. I may yet complete that project, but for now I am content to watch my dad out in the world on Netflix, spreading the word - the word that death is no obstacle to love.

I'd like to acknowledge something to my readers: what happened with my family is atypical. The abundance of evidence we received was unusually high. I've worried, somewhat, that by sharing these events, others might have similar expectations and be saddened if the same kinds of things don't happen for them. It's my current theory that my dad just happens to be remarkably good at communicating in the ways he did, and still does, and that the power of our bond when he was here motivated him, and us, and made it all possible. But it is not at all my theory that just because we may not sense loved ones, or notice signs from them, that they are not there, or trying to communicate. Who knows how all of this works. It does seem to me that there are things we can do, though, to meet them halfway, so to speak. If you are grieving a loss, first of all, I'm sorry. No amount of surety that death is not the end of us, or of love, does much to ease the jolt and trauma of the physical loss. I'd hug ya if I could. Secondly, if you are interested in perhaps utilizing mediumship yourself, do some research first. There are many, many people who claim the ability, and it's possible not all are practicing at an equal level, or practicing at all. Along the way, I came across a wonderful organization that might be of help to you in this regard. Called the Forever Family Foundation, this all volunteer organization has put in the work testing and certifying mediums for many years. After losing their teenage daughter in a car accident, Phran and Bob Ginsberg found comfort in a mediumistic reading in which they felt they received proof of her continued existence. This sent them down a path which led to them founding this non-profit organization. On its website, foreverfamilyfoundation.org, a list of certified mediums can be found. For a medium to be "certified" by Forever Family, it means they have been rigorously tested under controlled conditions, and that they have achieved a certain level of accuracy, assuring Forever Family that they are the "real deal." It was a wonderful full-circle moment for me when I realized, long after meeting Phran and Bob (having asked them to participate in my film), and years after my initial readings, that Angelina Diana was one of the first mediums the Forever Family Foundation ever certified.

Finally, this book is not meant to be a scholarly overview of research, but rather an account of one person's experience of discovering it. My hope is that my story might inspire you to look into the research into consciousness (of which there is much) for yourself. And in the end, though some of the evidence for the independence of consciousness from the brain is strong indeed, experiencing evidence for oneself is what truly changes perception. I thought I had been sure that "paranormal" events occur based on the studies carried out by brilliant people for over a century, but that surety stood as but a pale wisp of what certainty would come when I personally witnessed an event that the vast majority of the world considers to be fantasy. Being sure that something can happen is a quantum leap from *knowing* it can. And once you know just one "impossible" thing is possible, like the Queen in the looking glass, the mind wedges open to what else might be. Nothing I've offered here can give you the knowing. For that, you must seek it out for yourself. And I sincerely hope you do. Because my life is the richer for probing more of nature's facets, and I imagine yours might be, too.

Love,

Mike

Angelina Diana → CT
860-729-9641
angeliadiana@angeliadiana.com

# Acknowledgments

O ne day, as I left the theater, a car screeched to a halt right in the middle of 46th street, as drivers beeped in acute NYC impatience and exasperation from behind. The passenger door flew open and, to my extreme surprise, a woman came over to me and said, "Mike! I know you from Facebook!" And we hugged and very quickly chatted and she got back into the car, to her husband's enormous relief, and away they drove, residual honking scoring their departure.

*Well, that was nice!* I thought, as I continued down the sidewalk, imagining that would be the last I'd see of the sweet woman who took the time to say hello.

It wasn't until two years later that I would come to learn this woman happens to be a New York Times best-selling author.

R. Stephanie Good asked to bring some of my stories to her agent in the form of a book proposal.

She did so out of the simple kindness of her heart.

It is Stephanie's selfless, unending assistance that made my first book, *Life At Hamilton*, a reality. And we've since discovered there's a deeper, sort of cosmic connection, perhaps, between us too, that pertains to the subject of *this* book.

One morning, while I was struggling to write *Life At Hamilton*, unsure I had anything to say that was worthy of a book, my mom was in her kitchen, unbeknownst to me, talking out loud to my deceased dad. "Robert, you have got to give your son a sign. You've got to let him know, somehow, that he has to write. He has to finish his book."

Meanwhile, I was calling Stephanie after suddenly remembering she had asked me to a week before, and that I had yet to get back to her. The prior week was my birthday, and when Stephanie saw on Facebook that I was born on January 25th, she sent me a private message asking what year it was. When I told her it was 1977, she immediately wrote back, "Can you call me, please?" And I said that of course I would. However, it completely slipped my mind until the morning my mom was begging my dad to give me a nudge to go through with the writing of the book.

While she urgently requested his ethereal assistance, I sat in a coffee shop a few towns away, as it dawned on me that Stephanie had wanted to talk. I pulled my phone out on the heels of that realization and immediately dialed her number. After a brief catch up, she told me the reason she'd wanted to speak is because my birthday, January 25th, 1977, has a great deal of meaning for her. She and her husband had a son who was born with a body that wasn't working well, and, after just two weeks on planet earth, he passed. On January 25th, 1977. As he was leaving his body, I was entering mine (two weeks late, I might add). Stephanie found this coincidence extraordinary. I called my mom as soon as I hung up with Stephanie, and said, "Well, mom, you might be right, maybe I should go through with publishing this book. Because I think I just got a pretty amazing sign." And my mom instantly began to cry. I hadn't even told her what had happened, just my saying that I received "a sign" opened the floodgates. When she pulled herself together enough to speak, she told me that she'd begged Dad to send me a message about finishing the book that very morning. And when I told her what the sign was . . . well, it was a good long while before she could say anything further.

Can I be sure all of this—the way I met Stephanie when I just happened to exit the theater at the moment she was passing by on a busy New York City street, her drive to help me get a book published, and the subsequent discovery of the connection she had to my birthday—is actually meaning-ful, and not just random happenings of the universe that I am assigning meaning to? Of course, I cannot. But it sure feels that way.

So, it should now go without saying, an enormous thank you goes to R. Stephanie Good for all she has done. She not only edited my first book, *Life at Hamilton* out of nothing but wanting to help a fellow human, she did the same for *Love, Dad.* Her guidance has been invaluable, and her kindness overwhelming. If my dad did somehow direct our paths to cross, it is no mystery to me why he chose her.

Thank you to Leslie Kean. Without Leslie, the most astounding portion of my experience would not have been. She went well out of her way so that I might connect more closely with my dad. For that, I will be forever grate-ful. Leslie has enriched my life, not just by introducing me to a new world, but also with her friendship. And for that I am grateful beyond words. Leslie is changing the world in ways I wonder if she can be fully aware of. Given her humble nature, I do not sense that she is. I, though, will not let her forget what she means to humans everywhere, and to this one, espe-cially. Thank you, Leslie, from the very bottom of my heart.

An enormous thanks must go to Stewart Alexander. Given how physical mediums have been treated by history, it takes more than a little courage to share it with the world, should the discovery be made that you have this ability. Stewart has done so, for decades now, out of nothing but the desire to help people know they have not forever lost those they love. He has put his reputation on the line solely that he might ease peoples' suffering. Not only has he braved the skeptical storm, but he put in years of dedication in order to get where he is. All of it for no financial gain. All of it, for us.

Stewart, you changed and expanded my life, and my perceptions. The adventures I've been able to have with some other realm have been fantastic indeed, but the experience of your kindness has been as impactful.

Thank you to Andy Phelan. Your guidance and insight were invaluable, as is your friendship. I'm so glad to have had you on this ride. Likewise, Skyler Gallun, Jamie Guite, Amy Foss Brassard, and Bill Youmans, thank you for being early readers of the book and providing such thoughtful and enormously helpful feedback. And a special thanks to Seth Keal, whose encouragement set this book into motion.

Thanks to Nick Marcotti, Jesse Gebryel, Paul Rondeau, Karleah Del Moral, Rebeccah Milburn, Brian Wengrofsky, Robert Ellenberg, Caitlin Davis, and Chris Raddatz for lending your talents to the filming of the documentary. It's been a genuine joy having all of you on board. And to the documentary participants, thanks also to you: Edwin Bates, Amanda Phillips, Michelle Handley, Mary Atala Lessard, Rebeccah Milburn, Heather Dilly, Anne Dilly, Richard Kimball, Ray West, Jackie Gonzalez, Amie Warren Guarraia, Sara Warren, Melissa Febbroriello, Dawn McAndrews, Dr. Jim Tucker, Dr. Julie Beischel, Dr. Amit Goswami, Peter Smith, Paul Aurand, Sophia Kramer, Marie Toruño, Cathi Guy, and Lisa and Joe O'Connor.

Thank you, Chris Cox, for making that uncomfortable phone call. It changed our lives. And thank you to Christina Treger Cox (who is now married to Chris), for having been open enough to hear my dad's initial call. The path you helped to send us down has been one of comfort, joy, and eternal love. How to ever thank you enough for that?

My gratitude to Angelina Diana. Your willingness to allow me to continue to probe your work gave me the certainty I needed to believe what I was seeing. I can only guess how difficult it might be to do what you do in a world that is skeptical, and sometimes cynical. To put yourself out there in the way you have done along this journey must have taken immense courage. I asked you to work in ways you hadn't before, and you never flinched, willing always to try. You have blessed my life and the lives of my family. I'm glad you were the person my dad found.

As always, thanks to my family. To Mom and Jen and Stef and Gordon and Victoria and Jake and Olivia and Sage and Toma and Reco and Donna and Anthony and everyone else, I love you. As I wrote to my sister, "Thank you for being my tribe and taking this (these) crazy trip (trips) with me, and making it (them) so much fun. It's no wonder to me that I keep coming back, so long as you do, too."

To Jen D'Amato especially, the amount of work you put in to make this book a reality goes far above the duties of sisterhood. If we do pick our siblings out, as some of the research seems to suggest, given you and Stefanie, I seem to be particularly good at it. I love you both with all I have. Thank you, thank you, thank you.

Mom, you make life beautiful. I look at the world the way I do, with the hope I do, because you are my mom. Thank you for bringing me here. I love you much more than I will ever be able to say in words.

Finally, to Dad. I write these words believing, now, that you can actually read them or feel them or however it works. Because of your literally undying love, I, indeed, "believe." You "told Jen" after all. Your life while in a body was exemplary in every way. Your love was so big, your joy so true, that it spilled out everywhere. Simply put, you were an amazing human. It should have come as no surprise to find you're an amazing post-human, too. You can "take it easy," now. Message received, loud and clear. We love you, Dad. See you when we get there (but don't wait up . . . we know you want us to "drive safe" and not rush:)

# Appendix I

Overall, Angelina made 27 statements that could be validated or demonstrated as false, *and* that I considered to be not of a general enough nature to be too widely applicable (so if the statement could be widely applicable, such as, "He is good with the English language," I did not include it in the calculation for accuracy). 17 of those items were correct, and 10 were incorrect, for an accuracy rate of 62.9%. Of the 17 items that were correct, I considered 14 to be specific enough to make the Forer effect an unlikely contributor to the medium achieving a "yes" response.

Below is a list of everything Angelina said that could be checked for accuracy (so any statements that could not be checked, such as, for instance, statements regarding how Stewart is feeling now or what he is doing "there," etc., have been left out). The items I counted in the overall accuracy percentage are denoted by a percent sign (%) after them. You'll notice that if a statement was repeated or said in a similar way, I only counted its first utterance. Also, if a statement was incorrect, and then a following statement about the same item was correct, I only counted the incorrect statement in the tally. For instance, Angelina asked, "Did he work with a metronome?" and the answer was "No" so, I counted only the "no" in that tally, and not the "yes," to the following, related question, "Did he walk to the beat of his own drum?" In this way, multiple guesses about the same topic only harm Angelina's score. I've marked statements that I personally consider to be of greater-than-average specificity with an asterisk (*). I've also made all questions, such as "Was he a non-fiction writer?" into declarative statements like "He was a non-fiction writer." The list provided is complete and in chronological order so that readers can make their own judgments as to how significant or not the overall evidence is. Again, we must keep in mind that there is no identifiable "normal" way that Angelina could have known anything about these two people or the "spirit" they were hoping to contact, so these statements are all made against that blank canvas:

- There is a male coming through
- He has a very funny personality
  (they described him as "very funny" in the int).                      Yes%*
- (To Heather) There is a father figure passed for you
  (This is specifically who she wanted to hear from)                    Yes%*
- His energy feels smart and skeptical                                  Yes
- He is very good with the English language.                           Yes
- Not mean/very relatable man
  ("kind" was their one-word sum up of him)                            Yes%*
- He was a teacher (described as the major passion of his life)         Yes%*
- He could speak about a topic until
  people were bored, in depth                                          Yes
- Very sensitive. Very kind. Very concerned about
  people around him                                                    Yes
- Very engaging when he wants to talk with
  someone, brings them in                                              Yes
- Wants you (Anne) to relax about having to do
  more with his body of work                                           Yes%*
- He was a non-fiction writer                                          No%

- I see non-fictional work someone is writing
  connected to him (Anne's book)     Yes*
- Everything is a classroom, that's his energy     Yes
- There is a younger male there who had
  a drug-related issues     Yes%*
- "C" or "K" name connected to young male
  (Kay is his mom's name)     Yes%*
- The young male played golf     No%
- The young male had a fascination with sports     No%
- There was a separation between you (Anne)
  and younger male     Yes%
- Younger male was a big dog lover     Yes%*
- This dog is with him (passed)     Yes%
- It took you (Anne) a while to love this dog     Yes%
- There's a certain outdoor place that you
  (Anne) walk. A trail with flowers.     Yes
- You (Anne) are having trouble relaxing in your life     Yes
- Young male worked with a metronome     No%
- He walked to the beat of a different drum     Yes
- You (Heather) wrote letters to the younger male     No%
- There are words you (Heather) wrote for
  him that took a lot out of you     Yes*
- You (Anne) are selling your house     No%
- You (Anne) are thinking about moving     Yes
- You (Anne) handled the domestic things (
  finances, etc) when older male was here     Yes
- There was a flow between you (Anne and
  older male), great trust     Yes
- You (Anne) were hard on younger male sometimes     Yes

- There is an ocean community where you
  (Anne and Heather) go                                     Yes%*
- There is shifting in your (Heather's)
  relationships since dad's passing                         Yes
- You've (Heather) gotten out of a relationship
  that wasn't good for you                                  Yes%*
- Something about older male's work fell
  apart after his passing                                   Yes%*
- He's showing me pieces and squares moving
  away from each other                                      Yes
- The way older male passed made him feel
  mummied-in (Alzheimer's)                                  Yes%*
- His brain got weaker, but he was still inside             Yes
- He played chess                                           No%
- There is a boat reference for him                         No%
- There a dog breeder in a family                           No%
- Older male had a humidor                                  No%
- Older male had a hobby where he had to
  keep things at a certain temperature                      Yes%*
- You (Heather) like to entertain. (Heather is an actress)  Yes%*

# Appendix II

## WINDBRIDGE RESEARCH CENTER STUDY

Involved in the experiment are 6 people: two sitters, a medium, and three experimenters (and, perhaps, 2 "discarnates"). The center has a database of over 1,000 people from all over the country who have volunteered to be sitters for their experiments. To do so, they complete an online form which gathers information on each sitter, such as their name, age, and the discarnate they most want to hear from. To begin an experiment, Experimenter 1 randomly selects sitter 1 from the database. Software then selects sitter 2. Experimenter 2 randomly selects one of the 20 research mediums, and schedules 2 readings at different times. Experimenter 1 emails the first names of the discarnates that sitters 1 and 2 want to hear from. So, Experimenter 1 is blinded to who the medium will be, and Experimenter 2 is blinded to who the sitters are, having only the randomly generated first names of two deceased people. Experimenter 1 informs the 2 sitters to "talk to" their discarnate, and request them to show up at a certain time and find the correct research medium. Obviously, Dr. Beischel has no idea how that works from "the other side." At the appointed time, Experimenter 2 calls the randomly selected medium (who is often in a different city or state— hopefully the other side works on a similar time zone set up) at the appointed time, and gives her the first name of the discarnate she is supposed to now gather information about—and that is the only piece of information she gets: one first name. So, the medium and the experimenter both have only the first name of a deceased person, and know absolutely nothing else about them, or the living person wanting to connect with them. This means, first of all, that there is no normal way for the medium to gather information about the deceased. If she is given the first name Mark, and she tries to google the name Mark (provided by a sitter who can be anywhere in the country, or world, for that matter), the effort would, obviously, be futile. Likewise, the experimenter who is sitting in as a proxy for the living person hoping to hear from Mark, knows nothing about either the sitter or Mark, so she has no bias, and cannot inadvertently provide auditory cues to the medium, since she has no idea whether anything the medium is saying makes sense for Mark or not. Experimenter 2, once the medium has had time to connect to Mark, begins to ask the medium these questions:

1. What did the discarnate look like in his/her life?
2. Describe the personality of the discarnate.
3. What were the discarnate's hobbies or activities? How did she/he spend her/his time?
4. What was the discarnate's cause of death?
5. Does the discarnate have any comments, questions, requests, or messages for the sitter?
6. Is there anything else you can tell me about this person?

Then, at another time (usually a week later) Experimenter 2 repeats the process at the next appointed time, this time giving the medium the other discarnate's name, let's say Mick (the names to the 2 discarnates are selected by the software to be "gender matched," so both discarnates are either male or female). After each reading, a transcript is made of what the medium said. Removed from the transcript are any references to the discarnate's name, and it is distilled down to definitive statements, such as, "he liked going to the zoo," "he passed from an issue with his heart," "he mentions a green bike," etc. Experimenter 2 emails both transcripts— again, as unmarked lists of statements without the discarnate's name appearing anywhere—to the third experimenter, Experimenter 3. Experimenter 3 is given the email addresses of the 2 sitters, and emails BOTH transcripts to each sitter (so experimenter 1, who was responsible for randomly selecting the sitters and contacting them with their sitting time, never sees the transcripts—is "blinded" to them, and Experimenter 3 is blinded to which medium did the readings and to any information about the discarnates). The 2 sitters are asked to score BOTH transcripts, having absolutely no idea which one is intended to be theirs. They've simply received 2 sets of statements that a medium made, and are asked to grade each item in each list for accuracy with regard to the deceased person they had wanted to hear from. So, the sitters are blinded to who the medium is that provided the readings, and (most importantly) to which reading is theirs. They mark each statement as either being correct or incorrect, thereby generating an accuracy percentage for each reading. They then give each reading a global score on a scale from 1–6, based on how accurate, overall, each reading was. This number takes into account "dazzle shots," particularly specific and evidential statements. For instance, its possible overall accuracy of a rating might not be particularly high, however, because of 1 or more highly evidential statements, a sitter is certain that reading was meant for them, and that may affect the global score they give. Finally, each sitter chooses which reading they believe was intended for them. The Windbridge Research Center carried out this experiment a total of 58 times (so 116 readings).

# About the Author

Mike Anthony is a sometime professional actor, majority time bartender at *Hamilton* on Broadway. After a personal experience completely shifted his understanding of how the universe works, Mike turned to science for answers. Now spending his time investigating and writing about various lines of evidence suggesting we are much more than the bodies we temporarily occupy, a portion of Mike's story is featured in the 2021 Netflix series, *Surviving Death*. Mike is also the author of *Life At Hamilton*, a collection of stories chronicling his time bartending at the Broadway phenomenon, *Hamilton: An American Musical*.

Made in the USA
Middletown, DE
22 January 2021